British Social
Policy since 1945

Howard Glennerster

BLACKWELL
Publishers

Making Contemporary Britain Series

General Editor: Anthony Seldon
Consultant Editor: Peter Hennessy

Forthcoming

British Industry since 1945
Margaret Ackrill

British Foreign Policy since 1945
Anthony Adamthwaite

The Conservative Party since 1945
John Barnes

Education in Britain since 1945
David Crook

Sport in Britain since 1945
Richard Holt and Tony Mason

Class and Inequality in Britain
since 1945
Paul Keating

Parliament since 1945
Philip Norton

British Youth Cultures since 1945
William Osgerby

Terrorism since 1945
Paul Wilkinson

Local Government since 1945
Ken Young and Nirmala Rao

* Indicates title now out of print.

The series *Making Contemporary Britain* is essential reading for students, as well as providing masterly overviews for the general reader. Each book in the series puts the central themes and problems of the specific topic into clear focus. The studies are written by leading authorities in their field, who integrate the latest research into the text but at the same time present the material in a clear, ordered fashion which can be read with value by those with no prior knowledge of the subject.

THE INSTITUTE OF CONTEMPORARY
BRITISH HISTORY

*Senate House
Malet Street
London WC1H 7HU*

Managing Editor: Paul Nicholson

The right of Howard Glennerster to be identified as author of this work has been asserted in accordance with the Copyright, Designs and Patents Act 1988.

First published 1995

Reprinted 1996 (twice)

Blackwell Publishers Ltd
108 Cowley Road
Oxford OX4 1JF, UK

Blackwell Publishers Inc.
238 Main Street
Cambridge, Massachusetts 02142, USA

British Library Cataloguing in Publication Data
A CIP catalogue record for this book is available from the British Library

Library of Congress Cataloging in Publication Data
Glennerster, Howard
British social policy since 1945/Howard Glennerster
p. cm. — (Making contemporary Britain)
Includes bibliographical references and index.
ISBN 0–631–18961–0 (acid-free paper) — ISBN 0–631–18962–9 (pbk:acid-free paper)
1. Great Britain—Social policy. 2. Great Britain—Social conditions—1945–
I. Title. II. Series.
HN385.5.G54   1995   95–5489
361.6'1'0941—dc20   CIP

Typeset in 10 on 12pt Ehrhardt
by Graphicraft Typesetters Limited, Hong Kong
Printed and bound in Great Britain by Hartnolls Ltd, Bodmin, Cornwall

Contents

Figures and Tables

Figures

Tables

General Editor's Preface

The Institute of Contemporary British History's series *Making Contemporary Britain* is aimed directly at students and at others interested in learning more about topics in post-war British history. In the series, authors are less attempting to break new ground than presenting clear and balanced overviews of the state of knowledge on each of the topics.

The ICBH was founded in October 1986 with the objective of promoting the study of British history since 1945 at every level. To that end, it publishes books and a quarterly journal, *Contemporary Record*; it organizes seminars and conferences for school students, undergraduates, researchers and teachers of post-war history; and it runs a number of research programmes and other activities.

A central theme of the ICBH's work is that post-war history is too often neglected in British schools, institutes of higher education and beyond. The ICBH acknowledges the validity of the arguments against the study of recent history, notably the problems of bias, of overly subjective teaching and writing and the difficulties of perspective. But it believes that the values of studying post-war history outweigh the drawbacks, and that the health and future of a liberal democracy require that its citizens know more about the most recent past of their country than the limited knowledge possessed by British citizens, young and old, today. Indeed, the ICBH believes that the dangers of political indoctrination are higher where the young are *not* informed of the recent past.

The *Making Contemporary Britain* series to date has tended to neglect social policy topics. Yet the Institute has always endeavoured to cover all aspects of history, elite and non-elite, and social and economic subjects as much as political and diplomatic.

The gap in the series has now been brilliantly filled by Howard

Glennerster. In doing so he provides the best and most challenging single-volume account of social policy since the war to have been published.

A brief survey of some of the main features of the book illustrates the author's approach, and shows that he has written a volume, at times controversial, which advances academic debate while at the same time providing an excellent overview for those new to the subject.

Chapter 1 examines the origins of the Welfare State and focuses on the historical context of the 1930s and 1940s. The principles of the 1940s Welfare State (full employment, a national minimum, free and equal access to education and health, a crucial role for the centre, state provision and continuity) are all outlined and discussed. He concludes with an examination of seven 'myths', some of the left, some of the right, the attachment to which have dogged a clear understanding of the origins and development of the Welfare State. In doing so he takes issue with several authorities, including Ralph Miliband, Correlli Barnett and Rodney Lowe.

Chapter 2 reappraises and scales down the importance of William Beveridge's contribution to the development of the National Health Service and the post-war system of social security. The next four chapters offer a chronological account of the development of social policy from 1945 to 1976. Chapter 3 examines the work of the post-war Labour government of Clement Attlee (1945–51), and focuses in particular on the development of its health and education reforms. The complex history of the social policy debates from 1940 to 1951 are discussed in a way that illuminates clearly the key features.

Chapter 4, on the Conservative governments from 1951 to 1964, dismisses the charge that, at least for social policy, these were thirteen wasted years. Spending on welfare in fact increased during this period. The Conservatives in opposition had attempted during 1947–50 to devise their own less universalist model of a Welfare State, but attempts to change and cut back services ran into problems and opposition, and were largely abandoned. Glennerster in these chapters puts forward important arguments which challenge the existence of a 'post-war consensus' as argued by Dennis Kavanagh and Peter Morris in a companion volume to this.

Chapters 5 and 6 examine the high point of the post-war Welfare State, under the Labour government of Harold Wilson (1964–70), the Conservative government of Edward Heath (1970–4) and Labour (1974–6, again under Wilson) until the economic crisis of 1976, which ushered in an era of less universalist policy. Glennerster sees the legislative agenda of the 1960s in important ways as advancing and completing the collectivist targets of the 1940s. But in other ways the concerns of social policy in this latter period were different, preoccupied with equality *per se* rather than equal access to state services, and embracing a whole set of new issues unknown to, or unimportant in, the 1940s, including personal freedoms, immigration and race relations.

Glennerster argues that the power of the central state was not reduced by Mrs Thatcher in the 1980s, as she and her supporters wanted, but in the 1960s, in terms of intervention in personal lives, the power of the state *was* rolled back. Homosexuality, abortion, divorce, lone parents and domestic violence are all considered in this context.

In terms of social policy provision, the change of government from Labour to Conservative in 1979 was not a major turning point. Social policy in these years of reduced state largesse is considered in Chapter 8. The next chapter considers the extent to which 1988–95 has seen an altogether new direction in social policy. The point of departure was the 1987 Conservative election manifesto, and the years that follow saw important changes in education, in health and community care, and in a range of other social provision. He shows that though some radical right-wing ideas were rejected, such as education vouchers, there were nevertheless important departures, including delegation of spending control to schools, hospitals and housing estates, with the tone and future direction set far more in Mrs Thatcher's last years than under John Major after November 1990.

The final chapter returns to examine how far the principles and ideals of the founders of the Welfare State have been achieved over the last fifty years. It also considers possible future directions, and the problems that will face policy-makers in the later 1990s and early twenty-first century.

Howard Glennerster's book is published at a time of major debate over social policy. Indeed, Hugo Young complained in the *Guardian* (5 January 1995) that party disagreement had become about little more than social policy. There can be few more important or timely books of contemporary history to be read.

Anthony Seldon

Acknowledgements

This book would not have been possible without many people's help. It was Anthony Seldon's idea and his gentle pressure and advice have been there throughout. My colleagues in STICERD (Suntory-Toyota International Centre for Economics and Related Disciplines) at the LSE have provided much of the material and the insights. Martin Evans did much of the work for Chapter 2, which draws heavily on LSE Welfare State Discussion Paper WSP/86. John Hills and the Joseph Rowntree Foundation are to be thanked for allowing me to reproduce figures that were published first in John Hills's *The Future of Welfare*. Sophie Sarre was an enormous help in filling the gaps in my knowledge, especially of issues in Chapter 7 and elsewhere. She made it possible for me to finish in an otherwise impossible time scale. José Harris and Jane Lewis, as proper historians, have sustained my interest and sharpened my wits. I am grateful to the librarians at the LSE Library, i.e. the British Library of Political Science (BP in the references), and the Public Record Office (PRO). Jane Dickson sorted out the typing in her usual cheerful and efficient way.

I am very grateful to the Michio and Yoko Morishima Fund for its support and to them both personally.

I had my first lesson in social policy from my father in July 1948. He took me to the last meeting of his sick club. Here was a group of men agreeing to close their organization. It had apparently looked after the family when we were ill and I was puzzled why they seemed to be celebrating the event. My father explained that though it had looked after us, everything was going to be better now. Something bigger and better was going to take over and we would all be safer. This memory came back to me, hidden for years, as I wrote. So this book is for him.

Finally, Ann not only helped me with the drafts and research but gave up a summer for me to get it done. We first met writing a Fabian pamphlet together. We have shared much of the period covered in this book and it is for her too.

1 The Welfare State: Origins and Myths

Nearly half a century after the end of the Second World War, in February 1993, the then Chief Secretary to the Treasury, Mr Michael Portillo, announced a long-term review of public spending. It would 'question the basic principles of the Welfare State'. Though he passed on to other things the quest remained and the new leader of the Labour Party declared that the Welfare State needed to be modernized. If these principles are to be questioned it is worth trying to understand both their origins and their robustness.

Origins

The very term 'Welfare State' has an uncertain paternity.

It was probably not even English! The term *Wohlfahrsstaat* was used by right-wing critics to describe the German social democratic Weimar Republic in the 1920s (Flora and Heidenheimer, 1981). It was a term of abuse. It meant a soft society over-concerned with social benefits, not with Germany's pride in itself and its military power.

Just how the term came to be translated into English and given a positive image is not entirely clear but Hennessy (1992: 121) attributes the original translation to Professor Zimmern of Oxford University, and to an economist Sir George Schuster, whom Hennessy quotes as saying, 'The best way for what I term "welfare" states to undermine the influence of dictators in "power" states is to show that they themselves produce welfare for their people.'

It was this central idea that the Archbishop of Canterbury, Archbishop Temple, picked up and popularized in his book *Citizen and Churchman*, written in 1941. It captures the feeling of the time in which whole state systems were in competition for their very survival, not just through military contest but in winning the allegiance of their peoples. The competing systems, of course, included that of the Soviet Union, not just Hitler's Germany. Russian communism was appealing to many bright young people at university and members of an older generation too, such as Sydney and Beatrice Webb, Fabian socialists and founders of the London School of Economics. The massive unemployment of the thirties caused many to question the principles on which British capitalist society was based.

In the 1930s the central government was forced to take on responsibility for the relief of the long-term unemployed and in the early years of the war the elderly poor too. The task had grown too big for local poor relief committees.

There was nothing new about the state, local and national, being involved in the relief of poverty or in financing and providing education and health care. The Tudor state had taken a close interest in containing and regulating the treatment of the poor. The limited and localist basis of state activity in Victorian Britain had been gradually transformed into a growing central state by the outbreak of the Second World War and was to be given a great boost by its end. Thus 1945 marks merely a staging post, not a new departure in social policy (Harris, 1992).

A coherent legacy

Nevertheless, the social legislation passed in the five years 1944 to 1948 does constitute one of the most coherent and long-lasting institutional legacies in modern British history. It was passed in such a short period that it sharply reflects its time. It embodies a distinctive set of political values and assumptions about the role of the state that were well understood by contemporaries, as were the compromises made between the powerful interest groups of the day. These welfare institutions had common design features, just as do the different architectural styles of Bath, Hampstead Garden Suburb, or the sixties in Britain. This was not the case in many other countries. The Second World War had more unsettling consequences in occupied Europe and in Germany itself. New welfare institutions were slower to emerge in France and Germany, for example (Ashford, 1986).

The 1944 to 1948 social reforms had eloquent advocates, like Sir William Beveridge, whose ideal blueprint was never fully implemented, but sustained the imagination of later generations. His report was also influential in many other countries (Hills, Ditch and Glennerster, 1994).

They also had academic interpreters, the Whig historians of their age, such as Tom Marshall, Professor of Social Institutions at the London School of Economics. His writings on social policy and citizenship were to be influential all over the world (Baldwin, 1994). Richard Titmuss, also at the LSE, the official historian of social policy during the Second World War (Titmuss, 1950) reached guru status. They stamped these institutions with a moral authority and a historical legitimacy. Any attempt to reform them or attack them has produced a kind of moral outrage akin to that provoked by attacks on the monarchy.

Although many adaptations *were* made to this design in the next forty years, it was not really until the late 1980s that a similar concentration of social legislation was to occur that had a similar coherence. This time it derived from a very different kind of politics, that of Mrs Thatcher.

A desire for change

The inspiration for the 1940s legislation was generated in a period of remarkable social change and danger. Common risks were widely experienced. Bombs were no respecters of class or property. Class attitudes and conflicts remained, as did fierce political disagreement during the war (Morgan, 1990). But there was an unusual readiness to contemplate fundamental institutional change. Proposals that had been bogged down in interest group squabbles for much of the previous two decades suddenly became feasible politics (Gosden, 1976; Harris, 1977).

A successful state

The emphasis on the role of the central government in these social institutions reflects the context of the time. The central state apparatus, whatever its largely obscured inefficiencies (Barnett, 1986), was *seen* as having won the war with the support of the people. Above all it had done so while securing a basic food supply, clothing, emergency medical care and jobs for the whole population in a period of extreme shortages and danger. It might have made mistakes and been crucially supported by the United States, but, in comparison with the other war machines against whom it was pitted it had done rather well. It had, after all, emerged victorious. A popular recurrent theme of the time was 'We have won the war, now we can win the peace.'

If the agency of victory had been the state, the means had been central planning and resource allocation. Competition, even between local milkmen, had been abolished. Furniture and clothes were designed to 'utility' standards, the best designers set to produce designs that used the minimum raw material. 'Rational' planning and central state power probably reached their pinnacle in these years and with popular support.

These assumptions about the virtues of centralized state power were necessarily to colour the social policy institutions that emerged at such an unusual time. There were critics of this view, of course, notably another professor at the London School of Economics and a refugee from Hitler's totalitarian state, Professor Hayek. In a brilliant attack, *The Road to Serfdom*, he forecast disaster if Britain set off down the road to planning and social provision in peacetime. He was read by a youthful Margaret – later Thatcher – at Somerville College, Oxford (Thatcher, 1993).

The world of 1945 was very different from the end of the twentieth century. The memories of the 1930s as well as the experience of total war were strong in people's memories. The mass of the paid working population was employed in factories and manual work, mining and construction. Work in factories included women, who had been drawn into work on a much larger scale. Vast unions threw up powerful leaders. Britain was a world power. In many ways the Britain of 1945 looked like a fully employed 1930s. But it had changed. The war had changed attitudes and its economy was weak and with a massive debt, which had been raised to pay for the war. Its economy had been in relative decline for decades. America had taken over world leadership. People were impatient of old ways and ready for a change.

The Basic Principles of the 1940s Welfare State

The social policies of those extraordinary years contained six central principles.

Full employment   The guarantee of a job for all those genuinely seeking work. The idea that the national budget should be used for macro-economic purposes and not merely to balance the budget had been accepted by the Chancellor of the Exchequer for the first time in his budget of 1941, but in 1944 the Coalition Government formally accepted that post-war governments too should seek to achieve the goal of 'a high and stable level of employment'. The document itself is a dry and technical one. Nevertheless, it embodied the great shift in economic thinking that found its clearest expression in John Maynard Keynes's book, *The General Theory of Employment, Interest and Money*, published in 1936. This was arguably the most important of all the planks in post-war social policy. Sir William Beveridge had included full employment as one of the fundamental assumptions that underlay his social insurance scheme. The fact that full employment was largely achieved over the next thirty years probably did more than any other element in the 'post-war contract' to change the lives of ordinary people. But, in a caveat that was to have growing significance, the White Paper noted that if prices could not be held reasonably stable, the policy would fail (Cmd 6527, 1944, para. 49). So it was to be.

A national minimum   The second central element in post-war social policy was the provision of a common safety net that central government would place under all members of society, to protect them when afflicted by one of life's accidents: the loss of earnings through sickness or long-term disability, unemployment or old age, through losing income with the death of one's spouse or other exceptional reasons. There had always been ways in which individuals in extreme poverty could seek help, not only from charities but from public agencies. The old Poor Law had been such an agency. But it was local and varied in its generosity as well as being deliberately demeaning. What the provisions of the 1945 to 1948 legislation aimed to do was to remove the stigma from this experience. Linked to this goal was the intention to give reality to an idea originally advanced in the 1890s by the Webbs, the idea of a national minimum (Webbs, 1897). They saw it as the logical culmination of trade unionists' attempts to fight for a living wage. Individual trade unions would never be able to do this they argued. The state must take on the responsibility to set a national minimum wage, hours of leisure and a standard of living for those not able to work. The labour colonies they advocated to achieve this last goal fortunately did not find support, but the idea that the state had some overall responsibility to put a floor under the living standards of its population did. As we shall see in the next chapter this was not to be achieved in the way advocated by the main architect of the changes, Sir William Beveridge, but implemented it was, largely through the agency of the National Assistance Board. The idea of setting a national minimum was not particularly revolutionary nor egalitarian. Indeed, as we shall see, Beveridge was at pains to emphasize that fact in his famous report, but it did mark Britain out from many European welfare states, which introduced quite generous pension and sickness schemes for workers but did not put in place a clear national responsibility for sustaining a basic minimum for families and non-insured workers.

Equal and free access to health and education   The third plank in these post-war reforms was the removal of the price barrier in access to two services deemed to be a basic right of citizenship: health and education. Prior to this period elementary education had been free in state schools but not secondary schooling. Access to the doctor was free to workers on lower pay but not necessarily to their families or to many other workers or the middle class. Hospitals charged for their services, though these might be remitted on a means test. Free access to health care for everyone was introduced in 1948, a principle that, interestingly, Mrs Thatcher's own reforming White Paper forty years later was to declare inviolate. Her personal foreword to the document stated, 'The National Health Service will continue to be available to all, regardless of income, and to be financed largely out of taxation' (Cm. 555, 1989). Aneuran Bevan would have recognized the language, if not the reality.

A crucial role for the centre   To make these goals a reality the central state took on clear responsibilities for the key areas of social policy: social security, health, education, and housing to a lesser extent. Local authorities in these respects became agents of a central government while retaining initiative and independence over detail.

State provision   Not only was central government given a large role in financing social services but the services themselves were to be placed in the hands of state agencies who delivered services to the voters who elected them. This was a striking change from the pre-war structure and differed sharply from the systems that were emerging in continental Europe. The 1911 national insurance legislation had built on the approved societies: trade union and occupational groups, which already existed as self-help organizations and were regulated by state rules and contributions but were self-governing. These were replaced by the central single National Insurance scheme, as we shall see in the next chapter. Much the same story held for the hospitals, very many of which were run, before the war, by voluntary self-governing trusts. These were nationalized in 1948. It is this which marks the United Kingdom out from the central European tradition in social policy. This did not happen in France, for example, where the old *mutuels* (like our approved societies), and private and voluntary hospitals continued to exist as they had before the war. Local authorities working to strict government design standards and subsidized by central government became the main providers of new rented housing. Again this was not the pattern followed on the continent of Europe, where housing associations and other social housing agencies shared the task. Voluntary agencies, despite the intentions of Beveridge and the warnings of Archbishop Temple, were driven to the margins of social policy, tarnished with a Victorian authoritarianism and a lady bountiful image that took decades to wear off.

Continuity Despite the clear common principles and design features of the new institutions, they were all built very firmly on previous foundations – by no means always for the good. The new secondary modern schools looked remarkably like the old senior elementary schools. The local authority old people's 'homes' *were* the old poor law buildings. The Health Service retained the clear separation between GPs and hospitals and the local authority health services of pre-war years.

These new services were all initiated on the 5 July 1948, 'vesting day', just three years to the day from the election of the Labour government. This was itself a deliberately symbolic statement.

The Myths

Like any major social institution the Welfare State has produced mythologies: hostile, legitimating and just plain odd.

The classic Welfare State

This was, perhaps, the earliest myth of all. It retains its power. The Welfare State, it was believed, reached its perfect form in 1948. Like some Greek temple it had logical, intellectually satisfying proportions. It embodied a classic compromise between the duty to work and to contribute to the community. This is reflected in the link between contributions and benefits embodied in the National Insurance scheme. It balanced the personal duty to contribute in work with the duty of the state to provide the reasonable chance of a job. Certain basic requirements of life, like health and education, were to be free and equally available in all parts of the country, hence the strong central planning powers exercised by the central government over school and hospital building and over the spread of skilled people in different parts of the country; teachers and doctors were the main examples.

Rights and obligations, central and local power, state minimum support and market production were all in balance. The whole was in harmony like the Parthenon itself. The passion and the belief that a new world was being built comes through in the second reading speeches of the ministers who introduced these bills to Parliament and justified them to Labour Party Conferences. James Griffiths and Aneurin Bevan were men capable of bringing vast crowds to their feet and making grown men cry. The National Assistance Act of 1948 begins with the phrase 'The existing Poor Law shall cease to have effect.' A 350-year-old law was destroyed at a stroke of the legislator's pen. Alas, it was not to be so simple.

Historians such as Morgan (1990) represent the 1944–8 structures as near perfect. But no social institution stands still and none is perfect even at the time of its creation. As we shall see, equality of access was not achieved merely by abolishing the price barrier and making services free at the point of use. Poverty persisted. Benefits never reached a definition of adequacy. Critiques of the structure and its results began to be voiced by those on the left and by social scientists of the post-war generation, as well as by Conservatives who had never been happy with the changes made. The aspect of the Welfare State that was most in tune with its time, the centrally planned, national monopoly element, was least perfect and has aged the most.

Economists in the 1930s on the left were fascinated by central planning that they thought was working so well in Soviet Russia. Even the young revisionist economists of the New Fabian Research Bureau in the 1930s produced outline programmes that gave a lot of weight to central planning. Yet not all those young economists agreed that this entailed centralized and nationalized industries. One in particular, Evan Durbin, and his friend Hugh Gaitskell, were convinced that this would be disastrous. Public monopoly organizations not open to competition would fall into the hands of the workers in those industries who would exploit the consumers. What was necessary, Durbin argued, was central strategic planning with smaller competing public enterprises (Durbin, 1949; 1985). Durbin was to die tragically in a bathing accident in 1948. He was not explicitly concerned with the social services but it could be argued that his diagnosis fitted exactly what was to happen to the National Health Service. It was a theme returned to in the 1980s when some later young economists on the left picked up the ideas of market socialism and competition again (Le Grand and Estrin, 1989).

A consensus?

It is often argued that the period from 1945 to 1979, when Mrs Thatcher was elected, represented some era of consensus about the Welfare State. It was universally supported by both political parties. The Labour Party may have invented the Welfare State, but the Conservatives came to terms with it and extended it. Only in the age of the Iron Lady did things change.

This consensus view of the early post-war period is now under considerable attack (Harris, 1986; Pimlott, 1989). Others have suggested that if there was a consensus it only lasted for a short period. Lowe (1990) has urged that we do not abandon the idea that there was something special about the war and the post-war years. They were different from the 1930s in temper and degree of agreement and public support for social policy. At the same time there was never an absence of conflict or party battles or interest-group resistance to change. This will become evident in later chapters.

The social policy legislation of the 1940s was introduced amidst much controversy. The Conservative Party did not come to terms with it, at least in the form that it took. That party was from the outset opposed to a universalistic system of services supported out of taxation. It developed a very coherent alternative right at the beginning, in 1947–50. In many ways what Mrs Thatcher did was to implement that agenda when the economic and social structure made it opportune.

A betrayal of the working class

This myth was really a reaction to the first. The advocates of the Welfare State were claiming too much. Those on the left of politics increasingly made the case that the changes had been only superficial. The evils of a capitalist economy remained and with them the inequalities of income and power that were a necessary part of such an economy.

The most thoroughgoing expression of this view (Miliband, 1961) was that the pursuit of change and amelioration through social policy had diverted the Labour movement from its true mission: the revolutionary overthrow of the entire system. The leaders of the Labour movement had sold out, been absorbed by the trappings of power which had gained the working class nothing. No welfare state could achieve fundamental improvements in the lot of ordinary people because the state was a capitalist state:

> the state in these class societies is primarily and inevitably the guardian and protector of the economic interests which are dominant in them. Its 'real' purpose and mission is to ensure their continued predominance, not to prevent it. (Miliband, 1969: 265–6)

Other Marxists were later to challenge this view of the state as a monolithic entity and view the Welfare State more favourably (Gough, 1979) but, in the sixties and seventies, this counter to the orthodoxy of the forties was very influential amongst socially concerned young people and academics. The left began to do an effective demolition job on the Welfare State long before Mrs Thatcher began.

Yet it, too, was exaggerating and hitting at the wrong targets. It was not just Labour parliamentarians who supported the reforms of the postwar period. It is very clear from the evidence given to the Beveridge Committee by all sections of the Labour movement, trade unions, socialist societies and the women's movement that there was a wide degree of consensus about what they wanted after the war. Differences in detail there were, certainly, but on the importance of social legislation and its broad form there was really little popular dissent. The same can be seen from analysing the evidence from Mass Observation and the comments of working people to G.D.H. Cole's survey conducted for the Beveridge Committee. Unless one takes the view that the British working class were merely stupid or duped by the system, it is difficult to sustain the argument that the post-war welfare institutions did not have the widespread and very positive support of the working people of the 1940s.

The second part of the myth is also difficult to sustain: the Welfare State made no difference. It is a claim the working people of the period would have found incomprehensible. As we shall see in later chapters, slowly and gradually over the period from 1940 to 1975 there was a significant and continuous equalization in incomes and access to basic services, as well as improvements in life expectancy, health and educational attainments. In the 1980s these egalitarian trends were to be reversed again, especially in incomes and benefits. Yet this only went to show the importance of the institutions of the 1940s. It was only when they were removed or reduced in effectiveness that people began to realize just how important they had been.

Social policy had played a part in achieving these egalitarian changes but the main driving force was economic. It was the faltering of the economy in the 1970s and the changing nature of the economy in the 1980s that was to make society increasingly resemble the divisions of the 1930s. The critique of the left was unfair to the classic Welfare State but it was not entirely wrong either. What is clear is that without the institutions put in place in the 1940s the necessary economic adjustments of the 1980s would have been excruciating for large parts of the population, bad as life was in many cases.

A post-war settlement?

A more favourable interpretation of the events after the Second World War, often advanced by left-leaning historians of the period, is to see the 1944–8 legislation as a kind of temporary tacit agreement between the classes: a post-war settlement. Labour had become so powerful and had so well played its part in winning the war, that it was able to wrest concessions from Capital. In a classic compromise the ruling class was prepared to give the Labour movement significant social rights, to be embodied in the post-war Welfare State, while in return the Labour movement put off pressing for revolutionary change.

The problem with this interpretation of this period is that the working class had gained most from earlier social legislation. The main gainers from the 1944–8 legislation were the middle classes. The point was made by Brian Abel-Smith in a collection of essays by young radicals in 1958:

> Before the war, there were fairly well-developed social services, and from most of them the working classes were the main beneficiaries. With some exceptions, people with incomes under £5 per week were in the State social security system. In unemployment a single man got 20s a week, in sickness 18s a week and in old age 10s a week. Now all employed persons rich and poor can get 50s. Prices have multiplied by about two and three quarters, the earnings of the average worker have multiplied by about four. So the single working man in sickness and unemployment had a better deal pre-war than he does today. The working classes could also get free education and health services before the war. The contributor to National Health Insurance had the services of a panel doctor and anyone who was poor could go to a voluntary or local authority hospital without any payment. Secondary education was available subject to a means test . . . Middle class people who bought their own social services often paid more than the cost (to subsidise the cost of free care to the poor). The main effect of the post war development of the social services, the 'creation of the welfare state' has been to provide free social services to the middle classes. They are now entitled to use the free health services, to send their children to grammar schools without charge, to get the same state pension as everyone else . . . Thus the major beneficiaries of the post war changes in the social services have been the middle classes. (Abel-Smith, 1958)

This argumentative, and broadly correct, view does play down the extent to which the Labour movement objected to the stigmatic kind of provision made by the pre-war system and the extent to which working-class women gained from the National Health Service, for example.

There is a perfectly simple interpretation of the events of the 1940s and indeed subsequent decades. It is that the institutions of the Welfare State were genuinely popular with the mass of the electorate of all classes for most of our period and it was this which both brought it into being and sustained it.

The bankrupting New Jerusalem

The Thatcher decade of the 1980s produced its own attempt to reinterpret history in tune with the dominant ideology of the day. All new political elites need to expunge the old myths and create their own. The Thatcher period was no exception. It returned to the view that had been expressed the Conservative Party in the 1940s. The most lucid exponent was Corelli Barnett in a book published in 1986, *The Audit of War*. Barnett lays the blame for Britain's relative economic decline at the door of the Welfare State. It was an attempt, as he sees it, to build a Utopia which Britain did not have the resources to achieve. This disastrous attempt was the combined work of naïve churchmen, closet socialists in high places, philanthropists and believers in a new post-war order. They were able to persuade a gullible people, and the troops who were brainwashed through political education that was in the hands of socialists, while the nation's true leaders were engaged in winning the war. The central villain in this respect was Sir William Beveridge.

> It was the Beveridge Report that provided the battlefield on which the decisive struggle to win a national commitment to New Jerusalem was waged and won. (Barnett: 26)

It was the 'cunning Beveridge' who 'manoeuvred' the Cabinet into accepting the report and, as a skilful and single-minded publicist, he drove his report through and campaigned for it. He was assisted by socialists in high places who used his report to conduct propaganda with the armed forces who then went on to vote Labour in 1945.

> So it came to pass that a romantic vision a century and a half in the making had at last found incarnation in the committed programme of a British government with a crushing majority in Parliament. Yet the cost of realising this programme was to fall not on the richest country in the world, not on that Victorian and Edwardian Britain in which that vision first had gleamed and which had made the New Jerusalemers what they were, but a country with a ruined export trade, heavily in debt to its bankers (the Sterling Area Commonwealth and the United States), and with huge and inescapable continuing burdens with regard to the war with Japan. Yet the wartime promoters of New Jerusalem had pursued their vision in the face of economic realities perfectly well known to them – on the best romantic principle that sense must bend to feeling, and facts to faith. (p. 37)

There are numerous problems with this account. Like its Marxist counterpart, it turns, in part, on the stupid gullibility of the British people, who were taken in by the New Jerusalemers. It also gives the impression that Beveridge was able to ride roughshod over His Majesty's Treasury. As we shall see, this was far from being the case. It sees the social planners as the originators of the demands for a better life after the war. The evidence from the documents of the time suggests that the government and the Treasury were very aware that there was a strong head of steam growing behind calls to improve existing benefits (Evans and Glennerster, 1993). One interpretation of the setting up of the Beveridge Committee is that it was created to head off such demands. If the people could be offered jam tomorrow in a New Jerusalem they might accept less today. Political pressures stopped the Treasury getting away with this. They insisted on higher pensions now, not in forty years' time. The problem, from the Treasury's point of view, was that all the people now had the vote, not that they were manipulated by William Beveridge.

The second problem with this kind of interpretation of history is that it assumes that the demands placed on the British economy were excessive and greater than those placed on the economies of Britain's industrial competitors (Harris, 1990). Although Britain's competitors in Europe were to out pace it economically, it was not because the Welfare State was taking more resources than theirs; it took fewer, and grew more slowly. The Health Service was the main early butt of criticism for its extravagance. Yet the total resources devoted to the new National Health Service in the 1950s fell and was modest compared to what had been the case in the 1930s (Guillebaud Committee, 1956). If the argument was that economic resources taken for health care were not available for investment in industry then the NHS did its bit by *reducing* the share of capital spending taken by health. Whether that was good for the NHS is another matter. The centralization of financial responsibility for services lead to the Treasury having more, not less, say in controlling social spending. The very diversity of the welfare systems that grew up on the continent of Europe after the Second World War have made it very difficult for them to contain their welfare spending as the British government successfully did in the 1980s.

In the companion volume to this one, *The British Economy since 1945*, Alec Cairncross says,

The 'New Jerusalem' thesis is badly out of focus. In the context of the early post-war years the increase in the expenditure on the social services, though substantial, was not the main burden on the Exchequer. Expenditure on the social services, including education, health, housing, pensions, and unemployment benefit amounted in pre-war years to about £400–£500 million, or about £1,000 million in terms of post-war prices, and had risen to about £1,500 million by 1950. Expenditure on defence, which did not exceed £200 million until 1938 was never less than about £750 million after 1945, and rose again to over £1,400 million in 1952–3. The food subsidies cost more than any of the social services, reaching nearly £500 million in 1949. Neither of these is mentioned in Corelli Barnett's attack on the 'illusions' of the post-war years . . . If instead of the early post-war years the argument relates to the whole period since the war, then it is difficult to see why so much weight should be attached to expenditure on social welfare as a factor in industrial decline when such expenditure is known to fall short of the level in most other industrial countries. (1992: 5–6)

Where Barnett is on stronger ground is in saying that the Beveridge Report did not really add up either intellectually or financially, a subject we discuss in Chapter 2.

Citizenship rights established

One of the most popular academic interpretations of the origins of the post-war social policy settlement was that advanced by Professor Marshall in the 1950s (Marshall, 1950; 1963). The marks of being a British citizen were the legal rights embodied in the Magna Carta, the Toleration Acts and others, won during the Middle Ages and up to the early nineteenth century. They guaranteed the negative freedoms, as philosophers call them, freedom from arbitrary state power to arrest and keep in gaol without trial, the right to free speech and worship. It was these freedoms that had been prized by the American and French revolutionaries. To these freedoms and rights had been added the right to vote, which had been won in stages during the nineteenth and early twentieth centuries. Women's right to vote had only recently been won in full. All citizens of the United Kingdom shared these rights and with them the correspond-ing duties to abide by the law and to exercise the vote and serve the community. These were political rights and responsibilities. Marshall argued that to these civil and political rights had been added social rights. The state undertook to maintain full employment and secure a basic standard of living in the way we have described above but in return for contributions to the society through work. This added positive freedoms to the negative civic and political freedoms that citizens had in the past. The freedom of speech was not of much value to a starving person. The guarantee of a minimum standard of life and a job rounded off the march to a fully free society. Marshall claimed that Britain, and indeed Western Europe more generally, had evolved an answer to Marxism: equality of citizenship before the law. This meant that the slide into communism that was happening all over Europe in the 1940s was not inevitable. Here was an interpretation of history designed to challenge Marxism on its own ground of historical inevitability.

Laudable as his motive might have been it was not particularly good history. Nor was it a good description of what the legislation of the 1940s actually achieved. It was true that all citizens, as of right of being a citizen, or indeed a resident in the country, could receive free health care. In that sense the National Health Service came closest to Marshall's ideal type. It was much less clear for National Insurance. People were not to receive benefits as a result of being a citizen. Such a proposal had been advanced during the Second World War by Lady Rees Williams but no one had paid it much serious attention, least of all Beveridge. Pensioners, the unemployed and the sick could only receive insurance benefits if they had contributed to the National Insurance scheme for a minimum period. They must have been full-time workers. If they were married women they did not receive a benefit as a right but only on the basis of their husbands' contributions. We discuss this more in the next chapter, but whatever the rights to benefit, they cannot be said to have attached to being a citizen alone.

José Harris (1994) has argued that the appeal to citizenship as an ideal at this time had other and more complex roots than those described by Marshall. The debates of the 1940s, she points out, laid much stress on the rights to benefit that the new insurance system gave in contrast with the means-tested benefits of the Poor Law. However, the Webbs' view of 'universality' had been of *locally* financed services, imposed on the poor.

It was the Poor Law that had for many centuries given members of the local community, as citizens, relief in times of distress. The Poor Law

Commissioners and central government had indeed tried to limit those citizens' rights in the nineteenth and early twentieth centuries, not always successfully. Yet those rights to relief were grounded in citizenship, not contributions paid by male breadwinners for a defined period to a central state. The real hope of ordinary people in the 1940s was that the new system would avoid the intrusive means testing of the 1930s.

People feared the intrusiveness of the tax-financed systems of relief they had experienced in the 1930s, whether based on theoretical citizenship rights to relief or not. Harris concludes,

> Contributory insurance became the financial keystone of the post-war welfare state, not because as Beveridge claimed, interruption of earnings was the major cause of poverty, but because insurance fitted in with current evaluations of fiscal reality and with current evaluations of virtue, gender, citizenship, personal freedom and the nature of the state. It was a package that was to prove extraordinarily tenacious. (Harris, 1994: 19)

The state rolled back

Perhaps the most recent myth is that, after forty years of growing state intrusion into social affairs, Mrs Thatcher was able to reverse the tide and push back the boundaries of state power. This, too, is myth, though it suits both left and right in British politics to foster it.

Mrs Thatcher and her governments did not succeed in reducing the share of national income going to finance the Welfare State. Central state power grew very substantially in the 1980s. Power passed from local government to central government and from accountable central departments to hived-off appointed agencies of various kinds. The central state was deemed to be the proper agency to foster particular ways of living together and a return to 'traditional' family values. In contrast, the 1960s can be seen as a period when the role of the state in these respects was challenged. Its intrusion into partners' capacity to break a marriage contract was relaxed. Its right to make sexual acts between consenting adults a criminal offence was challenged. Its right to prevent a woman from terminating an unwanted pregnancy was decreased. In many ways it was the 1960s that rolled back the state's power to intervene in personal lives. It produced what, in retrospect, we can see as the real period of freedom, the first true revival of individualism. But it was short lived and limited.

A Re-evaluation

In what follows I seek to tell a story not driven by any of these myths. Yet it will be, inevitably, an account of its time like any other. Its author has lived through all of the period. I failed the eleven-plus examination like four-fifths of my contemporaries. I worked in the Labour Party Research Department in the early 1960s on the programme that was implemented by the Wilson government of 1964 to 1970. Inevitably any such account reflects the values of the author and the prejudices of the age. It is as balanced as I am capable of within those limits.

2 Beveridge: Founding Father?

All over the world Beveridge's name is associated with British social policy. Television programmes on the latest new government statement or challenge to the Welfare State usually begin with a clip from one of the wartime newsreels showing Beveridge addressing the nation in his rather prissy 1940s style. He is often credited with founding the National Health Service, which he definitely did not do. He is more plausibly credited with founding the post-war system of social security, the subject of his great report (Cmd 6404, 1942). Yet in many ways that is also a mistake. The report undoubtedly had an enormous impact at the time. It sold in its hundreds of thousands and summaries of it were parachuted into occupied Europe and distributed to British troops. After the war the Labour government promised it would implement the report, reversing the Labour Party's pre-war hostility to insurance, rather than tax-based schemes. At the 1950 general election the party claimed that its major achievement had been to implement the report.

Yet the report, on closer study, is far less coherent than its superficial unity and grand claims suggest. Nor were some of its fundamental precepts ever implemented. Those that were, notably the flat rate or poll-tax-like system of contributions, were to damn social insurance in the long term. Unlike other European and the United States social insurance schemes, its flat rate and minimalist character meant that social insurance in Britain never won the support of the vital middle class. They never identified with it or saw it as crucial to their security in old age. If they wanted a decent pension they soon learnt they had better join their own private occupational pension scheme. That was not to be true in Europe or in the United States. Thus the failure of this crucial part of the Welfare State can be traced back to Beveridge.

Who was this man who has cast such a shadow over British social policy? Why was he so influential? What did his report say? What actually happened after it was published?

Beveridge: the Man

Beveridge was born in India, the son of one of the many Anglo-Indian civil servants who went to India with high ideals. His father became a district sessions judge in Bengal. His mother was a much more lively and ambitious person, who gave William his drive and self-confidence. The most authoritative and beautifully written account of his life and work is that by Harris (1977). His social conscience and interest in social issues were aroused at Oxford and, again like many similar young men of his generation, he went to Toynbee Hall in the East End of London. Founded in 1884, to enable young men with social concerns to find out about poverty at first hand, Toynbee Hall also gave them the opportunity do something about it in practical ways. Beveridge was no social worker, however. He wrote furiously on social issues from then on and became what we would today call a policy analyst!

He was given a fellowship at University College Oxford in 1903 and wrote for the *Morning Post* on social issues. This journalistic experience was to stand him in good stead when he came to write his report and campaign for it.

This early encounter with the poverty of the East End sparked his lifelong interest in both solving the unemployment problem and giving some form of income support to workers who were unable to earn an income either through lack of a job or old age. For Beveridge, 'One of the major objectives of social policy should be to ensure that everyone shared both an adequate amount of leisure and a necessary minimum of work' (Harris, 1977: 98).

Beveridge's first major contribution to social policy, indeed, was his advocacy of labour exchanges. He had written an article on the subject for the *Economic Journal* in 1907 which gained a lot of notice and he was asked to give evidence to the Poor Law Commission, which was considering the whole issue of poverty and its causes. It was to be influential evidence. He believed that unemployment was the result of poor information about the availability of jobs. Workers must be put in touch with the right jobs. Labour exchanges would do this. He had seen them at work in Germany and became something of an expert on the subject. He called them, at this stage, 'the final solution' to the unemployment problem.

This did not prove to be the case, of course, and over the inter-war period Beveridge struggled to understand why. He collected mountains of statistics on regional and local unemployment, believing they would reveal the answer. When Keynes's *General Theory* was published in 1936 he was shattered. Keynes had, it seemed, solved the problem in an elegant theoretical way, making Beveridge's own work redundant. Nevertheless, he became a convert. It is no surprise then that government responsibility to achieve full employment was to feature as one of the key explicit assumptions in his 1942 report. He went on to produce a popular and passionately argued book which advocated that government take responsibility for ensuring a full and stable level of employment, *Full Employment in a Free Society* (Beveridge, 1944). 'Without full employment', he wrote, 'all else is futile'. Free political institutions depended on it, as did his social insurance plans.

Social insurance was his other life interest. He objected to the original plans for universal tax-financed old age pensions advanced by Booth and others in the late nineteenth and early twentieth centuries. They would discourage thrift and be very expensive. A visit to Germany convinced him of the virtues of the contributory principle. Workers must pay for their pensions through work. He remained steadfastly of that view. He played an important part in helping to devise the unemployment insurance legislation in 1911. He wrote a pamphlet in 1924 called *Insurance for All and Everything*, which contained most of the basic ideas that were to find their way into his 1942 report.

It is not surprising then that Beveridge saw the chance to write his report as the culmination of a lifetime's effort. Yet his appointment and the report itself was something of an accident, and certainly not what the wartime Coalition Government originally had in mind.

The Ambition: a New Britain

Beveridge was 60 at the outbreak of war. His experience of academic study and of social reform gave him the conviction that he had the vision, experience and application better to advise the war effort, and he made himself available.

His thinking, often changeable, had altered in the late 1930s under the impact of unemployment, and then the advent of war. Once convinced of *laisser-faire*, Beveridge now believed that, 'the so-called free market had irretrievably broken down' (Harris, 1977: 472 and 324–33).

The radicalism of the late 1930s and 1940s sat awkwardly with some of his other views on economics and social welfare. When reading Beveridge one is struck by the contradictions which occur, not only between writings, which are long periods apart, but also by the number of contradictory influences which he tried to combine in his own intellectual vision. The suggestion that he represents a coherent philosophy of 'liberal collectivism' (Cutler *et al.*, 1986), is questionable. One of Beveridge's difficulties was that he never fully married his old ideas, for example on the insurance principle, with his new enthusiasms for a national minimum and some appreciation of the feminist case. He was, as Harris (1975) argues, not so much an originator as a fuser of disparate ideas that were in the air. Yet his ambitions were high.

Beveridge's saw himself as a crusading reformer. He could put over ideas clearly and understandably to the general reader, and had a track record as a broadcaster and newspaper columnist. Social reform was written as a rhetorical pilgrimage, in which, Bunyon-like, 'five giants on the road' – 'Want, Ignorance, Disease, Squalor and Idleness' – had first to be defeated. Days after the publication of the report Beveridge led his national campaign for New Britain, based on planning, reconstruction and a new commonwealth based on service to the community and a new altruism (BP IXa 29, Notes for a speech in Oxford, December 1942 and a letter to Tawney, 16 November 1942).

Beveridge's crusade was emphasized by his view of the war as a 'revolutionary moment in history'. The opportunity was there for a new Britain, and neither the vested interests of capital, nor the trade unions, should thwart his plans (BP IXb 28, Notes for a speech 12 October 1942). There is no doubt that Beveridge saw himself as a man with a mission; he was encouraged by Janet, whom he was to marry two weeks after its publication, to take on the chairmanship and writing of the report as a millennial task (Harris, 1977: 387).

A climate for change

External proposals for post-war planning were gaining momentum. Articles appeared in the press; *ad hoc* discussion groups formed. PEP

(Political and Economic Planning) had been founded in 1931 to prepare a National Plan to rescue Britain from the depression (Pinder, 1981). Supported by the Elmhursts, it produced a series of well-researched middle ground proposals for reform. Both François Lafitte and the young Michael Young joined the staff. More to the political point the trade unions expected change. Nevertheless, within government there was both support for and considerable resistance to change (Lowe, 1990).

The Reconstruction Secretariat had already been in contact with various groups planning social reconstruction. Five months before the Beveridge committee was announced in June 1941, PEP's research into the social services was viewed by the Reconstruction Secretariat as supporting radical change:

> a clean sweep of existing legislation, but it should be possible if sufficient courage is forthcoming. At any rate further nibbling is a waste of time. (PRO CAB117/177, Davidge to Sir George Christal 27 February 1941)

Expectations were high. There were demands for increased pensions, better health insurance cover and other service improvements. A plan which emphasized the longer-term nature of reform could dampen current demands.

> There will be very strong pressure – to introduce the millennium at once. (BP VIII, 27; Hale to Chester 22 June 1942)

And, as the British Employers' Federation put it,

> We did not start this war with Germany in order to improve our social services. (PRO CAB 87/77 SIC42, 17th meeting)

Diverting pressure for change

Setting up a committee was seen as a way to meet these demands half way and contain more radical reform. The Treasury was worried.

> The present situation is more dangerous. On the one hand, it will be claimed that our obligations are greater, on the other, the kind of proposals that are in the wind (see for example, the PEP memorandum) are much more hair raising. (BP VIII, 29 December 1941)

The committee, at the outset therefore, can be seen as an attempt to side-track social reform, not to advance it. Yet, in the eyes of the public, it spoke increasingly in the government's name. Those who had, reluctantly, agreed to be seen to be doing something about reconstruction were on a slippery slope to planning it.

The sixteen months between the committee's formation and the publication of the report were a period in which progressive and conservative elements vied to expand or restrain the impetus for reconstruction. The committee, under Beveridge's chairmanship, was of fundamental importance, not in the development of radical ideas on social security (there were many of those already (Harris, 1975 and 1977)) but because the plans that were being made by Beveridge's committee were in the government's name. The status of the committee was a typical Whitehall battleground of little interest to outsiders but of considerable importance to insiders and to the outcome. Both the terms of reference and the interpretation of them were the subject of dispute. The establishment of the Interdepartmental Committee on Social Insurance and Allied Services was largely a response to actual and perceived trade union pressure, both for improved work-related benefits in general and to overcome the hiatus in the Royal Commission on Workmen's Compensation brought about by the employers' refusal to continue to appear during wartime. In the original discussion on the setting up of an enquiry, Greenwood, prompted by Bevin, had envisaged a small committee which would look at health insurance and workers' compensation (PRO PIN 8/85, Greenwood to Ernest Brown 10 April 1941). Once departmental representatives gathered to discuss the suggestion it became obvious that any survey of existing schemes would 'involve questions of major policy' (PRO PIN 8/85, Notes of conclusions reached at a conference 24 April 1941). The Ministry of Labour was determined not to have family allowances included; the Treasury only wanted an administrative review. Death benefits, originally included in the draft terms of reference, were excluded. The finally agreed terms of reference were: to undertake, with special reference to the inter-relation of schemes, a survey of the existing national schemes of social insurance and allied services, including workmen's compensation and to make recommendations. They could be seen as wide enough to enable radical reform or narrow enough to limit study to administrative reform only. The membership and its terms of reference were a compromise between departmental interests. It was a committee designed by committee.

Keeping a radical agenda

A civil servant or Tory backbencher as chair would have probably ensured a conservative outcome. Indeed, Sir Hector Hetherington was the
civil servants' nominee. The appointment of Beveridge, kicked sideways
by Bevin from any further involvement in wartime labour planning, was
thus resented by conservative forces and appreciated by the radicals. Two
further influences helped ensure that a radical paradigm would predomin-
ate. In Parliament, the status of the committee grew as more questions
of policy were deferred because of it. The government, fending off demands for better national health insurance rates, and later family allowances, helped to increase expectations of Beveridge. In addition, the press
responded to the appointment in terms which supported a radical review.
Several papers had exactly the same words: 'The widest and most comprehensive investigation into social conditions has begun . . . with the
object of establishing economic and social security for every one on an
equitable basis' (PRO AST 7/551). These are not the words to describe
a 'tidying up exercise' and the use of common copy between national and
local papers points to a common briefing to that effect. Evidence also
points to a covert campaign to raise the importance of the review from
within government, both for propaganda purposes, but also as a mechanism by which radicals within government could maximize its opportunities. Secret instructions had gone out to 'build up Beveridge' in America.
Norman Chester pressed the propaganda value of Beveridge within the
War Cabinet and was later to be a strong advocate for full implementation
(PRO T172/2093).

Once the committee sat, Beveridge's own ambitions were encouraged
by Mary Hamilton, the Reconstruction Secretariat's representative:

> Any provision whether by the State, by local authorities or by voluntary
> effort designed to afford greater security might, at some date, be the
> concern of the committee. (PRO CAB 87/76, Minutes 1st meeting)

In this way the wide-ranging and radical nature of the committee was
kept open from the first, and other members sympathetic to such an
approach were happy as long as they were not unduly compromised. The
civil servant membership of the committee were all middle-ranking officials and most of them were social insurance specialists.

Members of the committee were not all in favour of a radical interpretation of its terms of reference. Later on instructions were given to members to react to a radical agenda by playing a straight bat, merely emphasizing points of administrative difficulty. However, those departmental representatives who were in favour of radical changes, even if cautiously so, joined in the debate with Beveridge, usually through telephone or private correspondence.

Beveridge as chairman played the decisive role in ensuring a radical review. He suggested that a wide-ranging and fundamental change was on the agenda when the committee first met in July 1941, and the first task he set the civil servants was a comprehensive review of existing provisions by each department together with its proposals for reform. Then, in late November and early December 1941, Beveridge himself drew together his long-term desire for a comprehensive insurance scheme with his new-found belief in state planning and a national subsistence minimum, to produce his own vision of post-war social security. Most of his preparation of this vision was undertaken in Oxford over a couple of weekends.

The resultant memorandum, 'Problems of Social Security and Heads of a Scheme', SIC(41)20 was presented to the surprised officials on the 17 December 1941. In Beveridge's words it

> contained all the essentials of the Beveridge Report as published . . . Once this memorandum had been circulated, the Committee had their objective settled for them and discussion was reduced to consideration of means of attaining that objective. (Beveridge, 1953: 298)

Putting the genie back in the bottle

The timing of the memorandum showed forethought on Beveridge's part. It was handed out as the last item at the last meeting before Christmas 1941. To add insult to injury Beveridge also then asked Hale, the Treasury representative, to cost the family allowance assumption of the memorandum. This ensured that family allowances became part of Beveridge's remit, a position opposed by both Treasury and the Ministry of Labour, and flushed out Hale's own work for the Treasury on family allowances – a subject which the Chancellor had kept close to his chest.

Once the nature of Beveridge's intentions was clear a campaign of containment was mounted, particularly by the Treasury, for whom a commitment to such wide ranging, and as yet uncostable, reforms was untenable. The Chancellor insisted that Greenwood altered the status of the committee to one where the civil servants who attended were only advisers. They could not be seen as party to radical reform, and would compromise government and their departmental positions on such reforms if they continued as equal partners.

Beveridge became the sole signatory of the report and the government thought that it had the opportunity to lessen its importance and retain an element of distance from the final contents. In fact, the change of status made little difference to the work of the committee; during January 1942 and throughout the year until October it continued to meet, to hear evidence and to discuss Beveridge's scheme and the problems of implementation. Later, after Beveridge had produced his first draft of the report, in the early summer of 1942, the Treasury called together all the departmental representatives and told them not to discuss points of principle with Beveridge but merely to accentuate the administrative quagmire he faced. The Treasury tried to curtail publication of the report, and when that failed, to have radical evidence, such as the proposals by the National Federation of Old Age Pensions Associations, taken from the companion volume of evidence given to the committee.

The Report: Radical, but did it add up?

Despite its single authorship the report was a compromise between Beveridge's own conflicting ideals and between his ideals and financial reality.

The contributory principle and citizenship

At the heart of Beveridge's thinking was a contradictory struggle between his deep desire to cover everything and everyone and his choice of method, contributory insurance through employment. He wished to give security to all but to base this security, apart from family allowances, on participation in the labour market, not on citizenship status. Why did Beveridge not choose a citizenship basis for benefits? Denmark had already introduced a citizenship element into social security. PEP was advocating

Figure 2.1   The making of the Beveridge Report

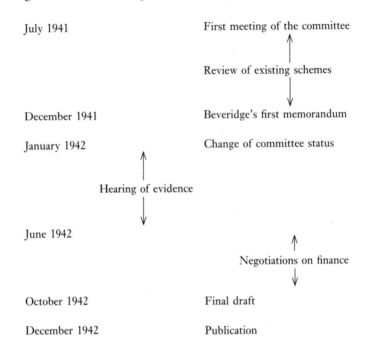

finance through a universal progressive tax system, so was the left. Meade and Keynes, as we shall see, favoured a unified tax system though they came to accept insurance contributions as a temporary expedient.

Beveridge's long-standing commitment to the contributory insurance principle has already been noted. He accepted the compromise between employers, workers and the state on a contributory principle as being immutable. To have gone back on it would have lost the support of the trade unions that would be necessary if the conservatives in government were to be defeated. The historical advantage of the contributory principle was that it had given recipients moral worth through contribution. There is some evidence that the passing of the 1934 Unemployment Act, which separated the administration of insurance benefits from means-tested ones, had increased the acceptability of the contributory principle amongst working people (Harris, 1990). An extension of the contributory principle to cover all eventualities meant that 'We are all, so to speak, made "deserving" by Act of Parliament' (Wootton, 1943: 361).

But, as the International Labour Organization pointed out in its evidence, when it came to women and other groups not in the labour force, the contribution principle would not work (PRO CAB/79; SIC(42)39). Contributors and citizens in need were not the same thing. As the discussions advanced some groups at risk lost status either by being dropped from consideration at all or by being left to be provided for by the National Assistance scheme, because they would not fit the contributory principle. Moreover, his contributory logic lead him steadily to downgrade the generosity and acceptability of means-tested assistance. In his original heads of a scheme he makes this clear:

> An assistance scheme which does not in some way leave the person with an effective motive to avoid the need for assistance, undermines the Security scheme . . . an assistance scheme which makes those assisted unamendable to economic rewards or punishments while treating them as free citizens is inconsistent with the principles of a free community. (PRO CAB37/76; SIC(41)20)

At the first meeting Beveridge had set up a subcommittee to discuss assistance. The groups it was to provide for were defined as

> Cripples and deformed, deaf and dumb, mentally deficient, and vagrants and moral weaklings. (PRO CAB/77; SIC(A) (42))

But also destined for assistance were those whom Beveridge was to exclude from contributing: separated or single women bringing up children and those who fell out of the scheme because of administrative difficulty or cost, that is, the unemployed, self-employed and domestic spinsters. Largest in numbers would be those who would need supplementation for their insurance benefits in the supposedly transitional period and those with 'exceptional' needs, above all those with rent above a minimum level. Despite this growing residual group Beveridge stuck to his belief that insurance could cover virtually all categories of need. He was therefore led to downgrade assistance and reinforce its stigmatic nature at just the time when the Determination of Needs Act 1941 was beginning to mitigate the harshness of the pre-war means test. The abolition of the household means test and the new Assistance Board was beginning to hold out the possibility of a more humane system of means testing. Beveridge himself recognized this but it did not change his basic insistence that the contribution principle was fundamental (BP VIII, 33 Typed note, Means Tests, undated).

What was to clinch the matter, however, had little to do with that argument.

Contributions or taxes?

Modern critics of social insurance cannot understand why the state should have two kinds of tax: National Insurance contributions, which are a tax by another name, and income tax. Why have a system of collecting revenue separate from the ordinary tax system? The Treasury and the Economic Section of the Cabinet made exactly that point in the wartime debates.

The Treasury's timeless view

> did not favour assigned revenues and felt it was objectionable to give a first charge on any source of revenue. Experience indicated that if such a fund showed a balance, there was a demand for increased benefits; but if it showed a deficit, the Treasury was asked to provide a subsidy. (PRO CAB87/76; SIC(41))

The Economic Section's view of contributions was ambivalent. In the main they considered contributions were an outdated, illogical, regressive tax. James Meade was right on target here, as in most of his comments on Beveridge's draft:

> The continuation of the principle of social security financed by compulsory *insurance* premiums is probably due to conservatism rather than to any logically more cogent reason . . . Why is it not proposed to add the costs of family allowances to the Social Insurance Fund? Surely it is just as logical to finance these by compulsory contributions as it is to finance old-age pensions by these means? Why is not part of the cost of education borne by the Social Insurance Fund, while the greater part of a national health service is to be so borne? The answer, of course, is that we all see the dangers and inequities of compulsory contributions; we are therefore unwilling to add to them, but are not yet ready to drop those which already exist – which in my view would be the sensible thing to do. (PRO T230/ 101; Note by James Meade 20 February 1942)

Keynes realized that arguing for a progressive tax basis for social security was ahead of its time. Beveridge's aims but not his methods were important to support. Keynes summed up the pragmatic approach in his response to Meade:

> I am very much in favour of something along the lines of Beveridge's proposals, as I gather you are . . . I agree in theory that employees' and employers' contributions are inferior to a charge on general taxes. On the other hand, it seems to me essential to retain them, at any rate in the first stages of the new scheme, in order that the additional charges on the Budget may not look altogether too formidable. (PRO T230/101 Keynes to Meade 8 May 1942)

Most workers did not at this point pay income tax, it should be remembered. It was not until the 1960s and 1970s that income tax took in the great majority of ordinary families. When Keynes and Meade were discussing the problem, financing social security out of income taxation would not only have hit the rich very hard but would have drawn the bulk of the working class into the income tax system for the first time.

In the end Meade and Keynes concluded that since the mechanism for collecting contributions existed and workers were used to it, while they were not used to income tax, they would go with 'contributions' as the only feasible immediate way to raise the revenue. But Keynes for one thought that after the war the two systems could be merged. For Keynes the flat rate contribution was a short-term administrative expedient. For Beveridge it was a matter of principle.

Securing a national minimum

In 1924 Beveridge had not seen a unified insurance scheme as a vehicle for achieving a national minimum. That was a new ideal and one he tried to fuse with his universal insurance scheme. He was convinced of this when he read Rowntree's new poverty study (Rowntree, 1941).

Beveridge was convinced by Rowntree's study that the causes of poverty had changed and were now amenable to solution though insurance benefits. The main reasons for economic insecurity and poverty had ceased to be low wages and were now unemployment and old age. The importance for Beveridge of this change, shown in Figure 2.2, is difficult

Figure 2.2   Causes of poverty: Rowntree's evidence, 1899 and 1936, from his Surveys of York

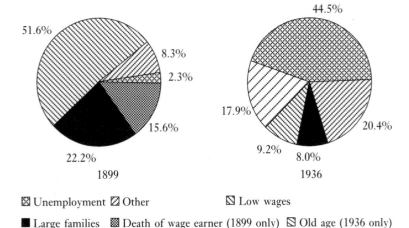

☒ Unemployment ▨ Other   ◧ Low wages
■ Large families   ▦ Death of wage earner (1899 only) ◧ Old age (1936 only)

to underestimate. His notes on Rowntree's book confirm that he took this causative model as his own and relied on it:

> the causes of poverty directly amenable to social insurance accounted for one quarter of the primary poverty in 1899 and for five sixths of the primary poverty in 1936. (BP VIII, 28; Draft, Scale of Benefit and Subsistence Scales)

This finding proved to Beveridge's satisfaction that a universal national insurance scheme could abolish poverty in the majority of cases if the benefits covered periods of non-earning and were set at the poverty line. This step in Beveridge's logic was suspect. He underestimated the numbers who would not be able to draw benefit because of a poor contribution record. The real problem lay in his definition of poverty.

Firstly, Beveridge took something close to Rowntree's statistical measure of primary poverty as the basis for setting his benefit levels. Yet Rowntree had always claimed that people's basic human needs required a higher regular income than that because no one could be expected to spend their income with perfect efficiency and to have no emergencies (Viet-Wilson, 1994). Secondly, the critical flaw in Beveridge's claim was that a single flat rate benefit for the whole country would be sufficient. Yet it could not take account of varying rent levels. Rent was an essential need which varied so greatly that it could not be brought within a flat rate subsistence definition. Either a common sum equal to the highest rent in the country had to be added to the flat rate benefit, which the Treasury would never wear, or benefits would not in practice be enough to live on.

Rowntree saw the problem only too clearly and said so in correspondence with Beveridge:

> I feel that if this principle is adopted it will go far to defeat the purpose that you have in view in recommending different rates of benefit, namely, to get rid of poverty. (BP VIII, 28; Rowntree to Beveridge, 1 July 1942)

The problem of rent proved to be the easiest to exploit of the weaknesses in Beveridge's scheme. The matter was later discussed by the government committee, the Official Committee on the Beveridge Report (PRO PIN 8/85), which was set up to consider and if possible scupper the report. The problem of rent was seized upon to undermine the case for setting benefits at subsistence level.

The problem of pensions

It was critical to Beveridge's simple appealing plan that *all* benefits should be set at the same level: enough to meet all basic costs. That would have meant raising the basic pension from the 10 shillings a week (50p) it stood at before the war to 25 shillings for a single person and £2 for a married couple. That would have cost £3 million and Beveridge knew that was impossible to get past the Treasury. His report finally proposed a pension of 14 shillings for a single person and 25 shillings for a couple, which taking into account the rising prices since the war started was barely a real increase at all. He proposed that the pension rise gradually to reach the subsistence poverty level by 1965! So much for his wild visions of an immediate New Jerusalem. The Labour government found such low pensions politically impossible to sustain and set pension levels at 26 shillings (single) and 42 shillings a week (couple). That still left about a quarter of pensioners on means-tested additions to their pensions that were necessary mainly to cover the costs of their rent.

Women in Beveridge's scheme of things

Modern feminist writers tend to portray the social security system as containing a hidden set of assumptions about the structure of the family and gender relations. There was nothing very hidden about Beveridge's views on women's role!

The role of the family is a consistent feature of much of his writings. It was the pivotal focus of human life:

> What matters vitally to every human being, is the handful of other human beings to whom he is linked by birth or marriage, not the indifferent millions with whom he shares this changing world . . . Mating and birth, the fundamental processes by which human life is arrived at, are the same for all men and women at all times. They give rise to relations of companionship between man and woman, and mutual support between parents and children and brothers and sisters and kindred – which are at all times similar. (BP XIa Notes for Changes in Family Life broadcast, 23 January 1932)

Society's ideal unit, he believed, was

> the household of man, wife and children maintained by the earnings of the first alone. The household should have at all times sufficient room and air according to its size – but how, if the income is too irregular to pay the rent? The children, till they themselves can work, should be supported by the parents – but how, unless the father has employment? Everywhere the same difficulty recurs. Reasonable security of employment for the breadwinner is the basis of all private duties and all social action. (Beveridge, 1924: 4)

The difficulty for Beveridge was to bring together his largely unchanged view of the family with the changes which had occurred in his assumptions about women's status. This meant an unhappy juxtaposition of his view of women as equals and their role within domestic arrangements which undermined and excluded such status.

His view of marriage was based on a companionship of different but equal partners. In this his views matched more modern 'progressive' ideas, 'the basis of what was considered an ideal marriage had changed profoundly from patriarchy to companionship' (Lewis, 1984: 120). In the 1930s he broadcast on family issues and expounded the view of modern marriage as one that was evolving into a partnership of equals. Thus, for

Beveridge, the question of whether married women should work was a matter of freedom of choice, but that choice was made in an idealized partnership where the realities of power and discrimination were unrecognized:

> It is true that most married women will not wish to go on working for pay because they will have plenty of work to do as housewives and mothers. But in a free society it ought to be left to the wife herself and her husband to decide on this. (BP IXa, 80; Typed draft 'Looking ahead' undated 1945)

Equality of status for Beveridge meant that man and wife were a *team*; within this team each was performing work of the same importance. The difference was one of practice:

> More than seven out of every eight married women in peace time follow no gainful occupation; provision for married women should be framed with reference to the seven rather than the one . . .
>
> [Women] acquire by marriage a new economic and social status . . . On marriage a woman acquires a legal right to maintenance by her husband, as a first line of defence against risks which fall directly on the solitary woman. (PRO CAB/76, SIC (41)20 Basic Problems with Heads of a Scheme)

Women should therefore be insured through their husbands, not in their own right.

The Report's Main Proposals

Unification

Unemployment and sickness insurance regulated by the state had existed since 1911. It covered manual workers in certain occupations. The scope had been gradually extended so that by 1940 it covered agricultural workers and less well paid non-manual work. All people employed in these occupations had to pay contributions which would give them a defined benefit if the need arose. Widows' and orphans' benefits and pensions had been added in the 1920s. About 20 million people were covered in 1938, or half the population. Unemployment benefits were administered by civil servants, officers of the Ministry of Labour. The national regulations on sickness benefit were administered by 800 approved societies: friendly societies, private insurance firms, trade unions and employers' provident funds. They had thousands of local branches, all separately administered.

Beveridge proposed to assimilate all this Byzantine system into one scheme administered by the national government.

> Change 1: Unification of social insurance . . . enabling each insured person to obtain all benefits by a single weekly contribution on a single document. (p. 20)
>
> Change 2: Unification of social insurance and assistance . . . in a Ministry of Social Security with local security offices within reach of all insured persons. (p. 22)

Pooling risks

The sickness benefit and health coverage schemes were administered by approved societies of the kind mentioned above. They collected the required contributions, the same from each worker, and paid out benefits in sickness and paid for health care. Yet some societies had members who were much more likely to be ill for longer periods – miners for example. This meant that fortunate better-off societies could give much better benefits than other workers would gain. Workers had always resented this. Hence Beveridge's insistence that everyone should pay in and receive the same benefits. Risks would be pooled across the whole of society. Health *care* should be separated from this system too and all citizens should receive treatment free on the same basis.

> Change 3: Supersession of the present system of Approved Societies giving unequal benefits for equal compulsory contributions. (p. 23)

Workers injured at work had redress from their employer under laws passed at the end of the nineteenth century and in 1906. An employer had to compensate the worker. This was again an enormously complex and cumbersome process of individuals claiming from their employers. Beveridge proposed to include industrial accidents in his scheme and remove this legally costly and time-consuming process.

> Change 4: . . . inclusion of workmen's compensation and . . . industrial accident in the unified social insurance scheme. (p. 35)

A national minimum

The remnants of the old local Poor Law remained, with local authorities administering means-tested benefits to all those who were not old or unemployed. Beveridge proposed to amalgamate all means-tested provision in one national agency, again his proposed Ministry of Social Security (Change 19).

There were many other detailed proposals but Beveridge summed up his plan thus:

> Under the scheme of social insurance, which forms the main feature of this plan, every citizen of working age will contribute in his appropriate class (self employed or employed) according to the security he needs, or as a married woman will have contributions paid by her husband. Each will be covered for all his needs by a single weekly contribution on one insurance document. All the principle cash payments – for unemployment, disability and retirement will continue so long as the need lasts, without means test, and will be paid from a Social Insurance Fund built up by contributions from the insured persons, from their employers, if any, and the state . . . benefit in return for contributions, rather than free allowances from the state, is what the people of Britain desire. (p. 11, para. 20)
>
> National Assistance is an essential subsidiary method in the whole Plan for Social Security . . . but the scope of assistance will be narrowed from the beginning and will diminish through the transition period for pensions. (p. 12, para. 23)

The flat rate principle

To base the scheme firmly in the contributory framework, everyone was to contribute the same sum and receive the same benefit. This had been the basis of British insurance schemes from the beginning but it was not the pattern followed by other countries. Better-off workers in Germany and the United States paid a percentage of their earnings into the scheme and got a pension or benefit that was a percentage of their previous earnings. For Beveridge it was crucial to keep benefits to the minimum consistent with poverty relief, to encourage people to take out voluntary and private insurance on top of the basic pension. He would probably never have got his proposals accepted by the insurance lobby if he had not made this very clear.

> The first fundamental principle of the social insurance scheme is provision of a flat rate of insurance benefit, irrespective of the amount of earnings which have been interrupted by unemployment or disability or ended by retirement . . . This principle follows from the recognition of the place and importance of voluntary insurance in social security. (p. 121, para. 304)

This was matched by the second fundamental principle of flat rate contributions.

> All insured persons, rich or poor, will pay the same contributions for the same security. (p. 121, para. 305)

The assumptions

Despite the detailed mechanics of social insurance the report may be remembered almost as much for its somewhat arrogant 'assumptions', that is, policy proposals going far beyond his remit: child allowances, cash payments to mothers for their second and subsequent children, a free national health service and full employment. As we shall see it was the principle of a free health service explicitly stated here that galvanized the Ministry of Health into action; this, together with the full employment principle, was to be central to post-war policy.

The Rejection of Beveridge?

The Labour government claimed it had implemented the plan. Hill (1990) claims that to a remarkable extent this was indeed the case. Others, such as Hennessy (1992), seem to agree. Recent authors disagree. Lowe (1994) claims that Beveridge's most important principles were rejected immediately and the rest were abandoned later. How can we explain the disagreement?

The most important structural changes *were* adopted. The old complex variety of schemes and approved societies went and were replaced by a single National Insurance scheme with local offices run by a central ministry. These elements remain to this day. The benefits and the contributions *were* flat rate. Later income–related elements were added and some abandoned again. The flat rate low floor to the scheme has also remained a persistent characteristic.

No Ministry of Social Security was created but a Ministry of National Insurance was, and a separate National Assistance Board dealing with the means-tested benefits and charged with a growing task of implementing the national minimum. But the goal of a nationally set minimum was carried through, though not in the way Beveridge intended.

Beveridge was rejected where his own scheme was a muddle or a deception. This was the case in the confusion that surrounded his claim that his benefits would be sufficient to raise everyone above the poverty line. He had never managed to define his benefit levels in a way that would have made that possible (Veit-Wilson, 1994). He rejected the idea of setting benefits exclusive of rent and having a separate housing benefit as Rowntree urged (Lowe, 1994). That was to wait another twenty-five years. The subsistence principle was to be rejected formally in the 1950s, as we shall see. He wanted benefits for the unemployed and sick to be unlimited in duration and subject to a test that the circumstances were genuine. This was rejected. He wanted pensioners to wait twenty years to draw a full subsistence pension. This was rejected because the voters would not wait. Pensioners got more than he envisaged in 1946 but were never to catch up with his implied levels of adequacy. Pensioners with only a basic pension have ever since his time been forced to apply for means-tested additions. As Beveridge's biographer puts it,

> Paradoxically, though Britain was believed to be the homeland of a Beveridge' based universal insurance system, almost the opposite was really the case. It was the European countries . . . which most wholeheartedly adopted a contributory social insurance system . . . whereas Britain . . . maintained a substantial means tested tax financed welfare system directly inherited from the Poor Law . . . In other words, contrary to what most academic commentators and popular folk-law have believed, it was not contributary insurance, but 'full' services financed out of direct taxation that was the most marked characteristic of Britain's Welfare State . . . after the Second World War. (Harris, 1990: 182–4, quoted in Lowe, 1994)

Family Allowances

The most innovative of all the cash benefits introduced at this time were family allowances. Beveridge had long favoured family allowances, introducing them for staff at the LSE in the 1920s. His biographer points out that he first became interested in them because of his concern with population questions and the steady decline in the birth-rate that was occurring especially amongst the educated middle classes and in the 'white man's world' (Harris, 1977: 341). Increasingly he became interested in the idea for reasons of labour market economics and insurance. He read Eleanor Rathbone's book, *The Disinherited Family*, in 1920 and became converted by it. Families' needs varied through a lifetime. Rathbone said that when they had several young children their needs were high but their incomes were low, driving many families below the poverty line. Yet there was no reason why employers should pay workers more money just because they had children. The worker was not worth more to an employer just because he had children to support. Rowntree's solution was to impose a statutory minimum wage sufficient to enable the average family with children to support itself above the poverty line. But, as Rathbone pointed out, this would be wildly expensive. It would force employers to pay all their employees more than the labour market required to hire them despite the fact that only some had children. The answer, Rathbone suggested, was a system of family allowances paid by the state. That would solve the problem of child poverty, a falling birth-rate and keep the labour market free. She was drawing on experience in France, Poland and Belgium.

There was another issue that was closely related and which had exercised the Unemployment Assistance Board in the 1930s and the Beveridge Committee. What should the level of benefits be? They must be below what the low paid could earn to keep incentives to work in place. But that would mean giving benefits below the poverty line for those with children. If you gave extra benefits to take account of the number of children in a family such a worker would end up getting more out of work than in it, because though benefits took account of children wages did not. As Macnicol (1980) points out in his study of the origins of family allowances, it was *this* argument that clinched the case for having them with the Treasury and the Cabinet.

An Unsound Foundation

The appeal of the report lay in its apparent simplicity and comprehensiveness as well as its Bunyanesque prose. Yet, we have argued, that simplicity was illusory. The central flaw was the attempt to achieve a national minimum through contributory social insurance. Rights to benefit did not come as a right of citizenship. They came from a contribution record in full-time paid employment that excluded most women, the disabled and many more. The flat rate benefits that were earned were not to be set at a level sufficient to meet all financial needs, notably rent.

Paradoxically what we owe most to the reforms of this period *is* the implementation of the Webbs' old idea of a national minimum: a poverty line which the central state sustained. Beveridge claimed that that was what he was advocating. Yet he did little to advance it practically. We owe that to the much despised National Assistance Board and its successors. It was a national means-tested safety net that was to mark the UK out from many of its European neighbours and from the United States. That was what has given the UK, until recently, a good record in sustaining a low but effective safety net. Beveridge, by casting assistance as a minimalist agency, of lower moral standing, the recourse of 'cripples, the deformed . . . and moral weaklings' only made that task more difficult.

This muddling of the minimum with social insurance was also to damn the future of social insurance in the UK. As a flat rate scheme it never had a hope of securing the support of the middle class, as social security has done in the US. In 1992, after a decade of serious erosion, the decline of the state pension did not even raise a murmur in the general election. Nor was anyone taken in by the term 'contribution' any more. Politicians of all kinds simply lumped it and income tax together as a combined tax rate much as Keynes and Meade foresaw.

Beveridge's reasoning, drawn from his reading of the newly published Rowntree study, was that poverty was almost entirely caused by unemployment, which could be made a short-term phenomenon, and old age. That has proven, and is increasingly proving, ill founded. The lifetime insured population of Beveridge's world is a declining group. 'Exceptional' categories of the poor are becoming the norm. The emergence of a marginalized secondary labour force has profound implications for any notion of a universal system based on a contribution record. The assumptions Beveridge made about the relative unimportance of low wages and impermanent jobs are even less sustainable now than they were in the 1940s. So, too, are his assumptions about the family team, female responsibilities and the permanence of husband and wife relations.

Beveridge was caught between the Edwardian world of social policy

3 The Right to Health, Knowledge, Food and Shelter, 1945–51

Citizenship Rights?

The post-war social security scheme began with a Utopian plan, widespread public support and a relatively smooth political passage. The National Health Service did not. The wartime Coalition Government merely edged its way cautiously towards expanding the pre-war system of national health insurance to cover most, but by no means all, of the population. Its proposals would have left the hospital system in a fragmented and financially precarious situation. The post-war Labour government wanted something much more radical. This provoked considerable controversy and the opposition of the British Medical Association. It is true that there was widespread agreement that the old system needed reform. The notion that there was some kind of broad consensus about the *kind* of health service that should be created after the war is another comfortable myth made up after the event.

In contrast the post-war social security scheme, which apparently generated such consensus, soon began to lose public support because its promises were never realized. The National Health Service soon established itself as the most popular of the institutions created at this time.

The service did, alone amongst these new agencies, embody the principles of citizenship that Marshall had claimed for the Welfare State as a whole. It sought to give equal rights of access to care, free at the point of use, to all people who needed it. Rights of access were not dependent on some contributory work record that mainly men could earn. As we shall see it would come to fall short of these citizenship goals in many instances, but it came nearer to achieving them than the schemes that had preceded it or than the other services created at this time.

'Ignorance' was another of Beveridge's giants to be slain, though it did not feature further in his report than this phrase. As in the case of health, the principle sought in education was that of equal access, a service free at the point of use, for all those capable of benefiting from it. England adopted that principle, which we now take for granted, later than any other advanced economy. The American colonies, Prussia and France had begun to provide education by the mid-nineteenth century, or before in places such as Massachusetts. So had Scotland. England dragged its reluctant feet, fearing the challenge to established authority that an educated population would bring. When public elementary education had been introduced in 1870 it was still on a fee-paying basis. Fees for elementary education had only been removed in the 1890s. They remained for secondary, that is to say academic, grammar-school education, at the beginning of the Second World War. Scholarships were available for bright poorer children to go to grammar schools free but their availability varied widely between different local authorities and different types of grammar school. The fact that some could buy their way into grammar school, while others could not, was a deep source of resentment for working families. Only very limited access to universities and other post-school education was available. Of those born between 1913 and 1922 less than 2 per cent went on to university and less than 1 per cent of children of the manual working class (Halsey *et al.*, 1980). Yet they constituted the overwhelming proportion of the population; two-thirds of all jobs in the 1940s were manual jobs.

In no sense, therefore, were health care and education universally available to the population in 1945. The right to both had been firmly on the political agenda since the First World War but progress to both had been uneven. What the mass of the public expected was that after this second great war these goals would be reached once and for all.

The system of care for the elderly and disabled was still essentially part of the Poor Law and the care of children in danger or without parents was in administrative chaos.

Top of the politicians' immediate agenda in 1945, however, was housing. Many homes had been destroyed or damaged by enemy action. Millions of servicemen would be returning home in the next year from round the world and from army barracks. Virtually no house-building had taken place during the war. Something rapid had to be done or terrible disillusion would set in as soldiers, airmen and sailors came back to find themselves living in overcrowded slums with mum and dad and a family on its way. In the same way food, the most basic of all human requirements, was in short supply and was firmly under state control, both rationed and subsidized.

A National Health Service Created

The roots of the NHS

Although the National Health Service is sometimes portrayed as if it sprang fully armed from the forehead of Aneurin Bevan, its form owed a great deal to the nature of health care before 1939. But there was nothing predetermined about the form it took. Many possible models were under discussion in the pre-war period. (The detailed history of this period has been chronicled by Harry Eckstein (1958), Frank Honnigsbaum (1979, 1989), Charles Webster (1988) and others. Klein's (1989) history of the health politics from 1945 is the best brief account.)

The story really has many strands to it. The state had played an active role in health promotion since the middle of the nineteenth century. It was better diet, the laying of sewers, the piping of clean water, the invention of the water closet and, much later, immunization campaigns that were decisive in extending the British people's expectation of life, long before the Health Service was legislated (McKeown, 1979). The local authorities and their Medical Officers of Health led this advance and in the 1920s and 1930s took control of the Poor Law hospitals for the long-term sick and began to run general hospitals too. They were also expanding maternity and health visiting services, which inspected the health of young children under school age and set out to teach working-class mothers how to look after their children (Lewis, 1980).

One possible future direction the health services could have taken was to expand the responsibilities of the local health authorities. This had been the route favoured by the Webbs and the Minority Report of the Poor Law Commission in 1909. Another way forward would have been simply to expand the coverage of the existing national health insurance system. The hundreds of approved societies based on men's places of work could have collected the insurance contributions of their members and paid for their care. This scheme had been expanded steadily in the inter-war period and could have been expanded more to cover all but the really well off. This was the route favoured by the BMA.

The voluntary hospitals were an old-established and central part of the health provision of the country. They ranged from the great old foundations of St Bartholemew's and St Thomas's in London to the small local hospital supported by flag days. Patients paid to go to these hospitals unless they could convince the hospital almoner that they were too poor to pay. Charitable donations had proved incapable of covering these hospitals' costs and they had begun charging at the end of the nineteenth century. They were in deep financial trouble by the beginning of the Second World War (Abel-Smith, 1964). The fewer were the people who could pay their fees in the recession the higher were the fees that the middle class had to pay to cross-subsidize the costs of the poor.

A possible way out lay in the expansion of voluntary hospital insurance alongside the National Insurance scheme that covered the costs of the GP. During the war, however, the finances of the voluntary hospitals had been transformed by the infusion of large sums of public money to pay them for the care of war casualties. A steady supply of public money seemed less frightening to many working in these hospitals than it had before the war.

Yet one of the main difficulties, much discussed in the 1930s, had been the confusion and rivalry between the voluntary hospitals and the local authority hospitals. It took the war to get the Ministry of Health to collect some kind of inventory of what facilities and specialities existed where.

In the ordinary way of incremental politics the gradual growth of these various health-care systems would have probably gone on side by side. The Ministry of Health, created with such optimism after the First World War, had begun with ambitious aims to create a unified health service but sectional interests had prevented anything but incremental and opportunistic growth between the wars.

At the beginning of the Second World War the Ministry of Health tried again. Like their colleagues in the Board of Education, the civil servants began to discuss what a comprehensive pattern of health services after the war might look like. They did so against the background of great dissatisfaction with the system of health care that most people experienced. Though working men in many occupations were covered for family doctor services, many of their wives and families were not. The generosity of cover, and whether your wife and children were covered, depended on whether you worked in a healthy occupation or not. If you did, your contributions went further and could pay for better benefits. Hospital care had to be separately insured against or would mean a means test. There was, therefore, a lot of dissatisfaction with the health services of the 1930s and a public opinion survey in 1941 suggested that 85 per cent of those surveyed supported a state organized medical service (Webster, 1988). The ministry and the officials started in a very tentative way to discuss how the local authority and the voluntary hospitals might work together on a regional basis, building on the War Time Emergency Hospital Service. Even this limited move to integration provoked a furious response from the Labour leader of the London County Council, who said the ministry and the voluntary hospital movement were trying to 'steal the people's hospitals' (1988: 31). Just as conservative was the response of the British Medical Association to the Beveridge Report's Assumption B, that there should be a comprehensive health service replacing the old patchwork of approved societies. This sideshow to the Beveridge Report proper had galvanized the Ministry of Health into action. It had feared it might lose control of the situation if it did not come forward with some ideas of its own, so positive had been the public response to this proposal, as the Ministry of Information reported to the Cabinet (1988: 28–9).

Yet the British Medical Association was furious. In 1939 it had proposed the extension of the old National Health Insurance scheme to cover the wives and children of the existing members but not to extend the coverage from the existing low-income limits. Its position had not moved since 1930. Now it was being asked to support a service that covered the whole population. It wanted to keep the insurance basis of the scheme, which would pay doctors' fees for half the population and allow plenty of room for private practice fees from the rest of the population. It was determined not to accept a salaried public service for doctors, which it felt might well result from Beveridge's initiative. All the sectional interests were therefore at loggerheads.

The first proposals

Early in 1943 the ministry drew up an outline of possible legislation. The service would be free at the point of use though charges for the 'hotel costs' of hospitals might be necessary. It would probably be paid for out of National Insurance with exchequer support. It preserved a place for the voluntary hospitals. The basis of organization was to be local, with the medical interest represented. The scheme owed a lot to the BMA proposals of 1939 but had moved in the direction of universality.

From then until 1945 medical interests of different kinds fought over the scheme. The BMA lead outright opposition to the scheme and opposed the official plan both in principle and in detail. A universal scheme would harm doctors' private fee income. Doctors refused to be run by local authorities. So did the voluntary hospitals. The BMA wanted the service to grow incrementally and to be administered by independent bodies that would be – not to put too fine a point on it – dominated by doctors.

As the discussions dragged on and as the ministry firmed up the proposals, the opposition grew. The ministry wanted to group GPs together in health centres wherever possible. That was opposed as a restriction on professional freedom. The Labour Party members of the Cabinet were growing increasingly concerned that the scheme did not go far enough.

When the White Paper of 1944, *A National Health Service* (Cmd 6502) was published it was deliberately non-Utopian. Any mention of the Beveridge Report 'was expunged at the late proof stage upon request of the Cabinet' (Webster, 1988: 55). To a significant extent the original headings of the scheme drafted in January 1943 remained, and the pre-war insurance system to cover GPs' fees would stay, though extended. The separate occupationally based schemes would remain. The local authority hospitals would be grouped together and run by Joint Boards of local councils, a proven recipe for disaster. The voluntary hospitals would remain separate under uncertain financial support.

Public reaction

The plan was not a public success, in contrast to the education White Paper published the same year, and especially in contrast to the Beveridge Report. The more radical reformers in the Labour Party were only mildly impressed with the compromises, while the BMA blew its top, complaining that the whole thing was going too far too fast.

The BMA was blessed with a superb communicator, Charles Hill, who was not only an officer of the BMA but was heard regularly by the mass of the population as 'the radio doctor', an avuncular-sounding purveyor of homely advice on the BBC. When he and the *Daily Express* told the public that this plan would stop people getting advice from their own doctor, the battle was joined. In the period between the publication of the White Paper and the general election the government began to backtrack and give way to the medical interests.

Bevan changes tack

When the Labour Party won the 1945 election with such a large majority the BMA feared the worse, but even so it never expected to be faced with the man who had hounded the Coalition Government from the Labour backbenches through the war for its backsliding on social issues, the *enfant terrible* of the Tory press – Aneurin Bevan.

Members of the BMA were meeting when the election results were coming through. Beveridge, who had been elected as a Liberal MP during the war at a by-election, lost his seat and a cheer went up. Little did they know that they would be faced with Bevan!

In his first discussion with his new Deputy Secretary, the civil servant in charge of health matters at the ministry, Bevan put his finger on the main problem with the Coalition Government's White Paper proposals: its failure to produce any basis for a comprehensive *hospital* service. That civil servant was later interviewed by Bevan's biographer, Michael Foot, and said,

> Of course he was right. They [the Coalition White Paper proposals] would never have worked. I came away that night with instructions to work out a new plan on the new basis he proposed. (Foot, 1975: 130)

That new basis involved the nationalization of all the country's hospitals, local authority and voluntary, small cottage hospitals run by GPs, the large ancient foundations, the London teaching hospitals – the lot. It was this feature that was the sharpest break with previous proposals for reform and was to make the UK's health service unique. It was on all fours with the other major nationalizations that were being contemplated at the same time: the nationalization of the huge mining industry, the railways and the largely local-authority-run gas and electricity works. The plan was bitterly opposed within the Cabinet by Herbert Morrison and others who wanted to keep the local authority hospitals as well as by the supporters of the powerful independent voluntary hospitals. They were supported by the Conservative Party, whose spokesman was the minister who had negotiated the previous government's White Paper: Willink.

Why did Bevan go down this controversial road? Partly, it was the sheer incompatibility of the end he passionately wanted to achieve – equal right of access to the best medical care regardless of residence or income – with the means available. A huge variety of different kinds and quality of hospital existed in 1945, dependent on different sources of finance, some weak and nearly bankrupt, others well staffed and equipped because they were in prosperous areas where private patients could pay the fees. Any visitor to the United States would recognize the pattern. Local authorities were too numerous and too poorly financed to cope with the responsibility of running the nation's hospitals. A national service required national administration, he concluded.

Other possible ways out did exist, of course. The Swedes adopted a local authority model for their health service and the education reforms did the same in the UK, but Bevan could not wait for the reform of British local government.

As important as rationalizing the hospital situation was the need Bevan had to win over key members of the medical profession; without them the plan would never have flown. Perhaps more than anything the hospital consultants feared being employed by local authorities. They were not to lose much sleep knowing that their incomes would be secured by the national government. It freed them from the necessity to drum up business from GPs and rich clients to pay for their basic income. If private fees came as *extras*, that would give consultants both security and a bonus. That was the basis of the deal Bevan struck with the consultants.

Lord Moran, one of the leaders of the Royal Colleges who represented the consultant interests saw the point very early on. Bevan also gave the teaching hospitals separate Boards of Governors to administer them. The governors would have considerable independence and direct access to the minister. Regional Hospital Boards would run the other hospitals, with local management committees looking after each hospital. Both would have medical representation. Regional Hospital Boards would hold consultants' contracts. Consultants would work for the NHS and for a part of their time could take private patients if they wished.

The nationalized hospital service was, therefore, a vehicle for giving the consultants what they wanted as well as what Bevan wanted. Moreover, it was not altogether revolutionary because the wartime Emergency Hospital Service had shared many of these characteristics. These doctors knew from firsthand experience that working in such a scheme did not make them part of a Hitler state, as the BMA and Conservative Members of Parliament were to argue.

While Bevan moved to solve the hospital problem with an apparent sharp shift to the left, he responded to the GPs by giving up what had been a central plank of Labour Policy: a salaried service for family doctors, much favoured by the Socialist Medical Association. Bevan favoured patients having choice of doctor. People could go elsewhere if they were not getting treated properly. Restricted choice of GP had been one of the complaints about the old 'panel' scheme. Choice was difficult to marry with a salaried service, as he argued during the committee stage of the bill. If you were a bad doctor and lost all your patients should you go on receiving a salary? The simplest thing to do was to pay doctors a basic sum to run their practice and then pay them for each patient they took on: the basis of the old pre-war scheme, in fact.

The idea that each doctor would have responsibility for a given list of patients gave the NHS another unique feature that other countries were to look upon enviously in later decades.

In paying hospitals centrally a given budget and paying doctors a fixed capitation sum for each patient each year, Bevan unwittingly built into the NHS a powerful mechanism by which the Treasury could control the costs of health care far more effectively than in any other western country. Yet it was for exactly the opposite failing that he was to be criticized by his opponents, i.e. the profligacy of the scheme.

The battle for the NHS

Early in 1946 the BMA was informed of Bevan's outline plans and then they were announced. He had succeeded in his prime task, which was to split the profession in its opposition. Some on the BMA were amazed he had offered them so much. Others were determined to fight this upstart all the way. The furious opposition from the BMA and Tory press actually helped Bevan to get the Labour Party to swallow some unpleasant medicine: the end of a salaried service for GPs and the existence of private practice for consultants.

Bevan introduced the bill to the House of Commons with a speech lasting an hour and a quarter without consulting any notes and received a tumultuous ovation from the Labour benches (Foot, 1975). It was attacked by the Conservatives for breaking the consensus there had been over the 1944 White Paper. As the bill passed through the Commons the Opposition grew more critical and took up the claims of a more and more strident BMA. Nevertheless it passed the Commons with a large majority and the Lords did not dare to reject it. The BMA, however, decided to wreck the scheme. It had tried to do the same with the 1911 legislation and was to try again with the 1990 Act. It refused to negotiate or collaborate. The chairmen of the Royal Colleges stepped in and went to see the minister to get discussions under way. They were to go on for the next eighteen months (Webster, 1988).

The new service was planned to begin on 5 July 1948, like the other great Acts of the period. Early in 1948 the BMA held a national ballot of its members as to whether they would join the scheme. Altogether 41,000 voted against the NHS and 4,000 voted for it. Bevan simply pressed ahead. Arrangements were made for doctors to sign up with a service that would begin in July. The two sides were playing a rather dangerous game of chicken.

Again the leaders of the Royal Colleges stepped in and proposed that the 'fears of the profession', put there by the BMA it must be said, that the government would force a salaried service on them, could be allayed by amending legislation. It could be drafted in a way that would make such a step impossible. Bevan accepted. Fearing another 1911 débâcle, the BMA, after much agonizing and internal dissent, decided to put the idea to the vote of all its members. A small majority voted against taking part in the NHS but it was too small a margin for the BMA to risk carrying through a full boycott. The NHS would be born in July 1948 after all.

Whatever words may be used to describe this train of events, 'consensus' is not one of them. Churchill described the period as one of 'Party antagonism as bitter as anything I have seen in my long life of political conflict' (Hansard, vol. 416, col. 2534, quoted in Foot, 1975).

The New National Health Service

The new service carried with it features of the old pre-war arrangements but it was a decisive shift and created a health system unique in the western world. Other systems on the continent of Europe that did come to give free access to most of their populations more closely resembled the kind of mixed insurance scheme that the Conservatives favoured: mixed ownership and control of hospitals with doctors and hospitals charging fees, and patients recovering some or all of the costs from a social insurance scheme. In Scandinavia something more like the British NHS emerged but was run by locally elected councils. The key features of the NHS, legislated in 1946 and begun in 1948, were, thus, unique and were to last for over forty years.

The National Health Service Act 1946

The following were the main features of this milestone Act.

- The service was to be run on a national basis and paid for out of general taxation with a small token element contributed from the National Insurance fund – a relic of the pre-war system. This did not stop many people assuming that they were paying for the NHS out of 'the stamp', i.e. their National Insurance contribution.
- All citizens could register with a family doctor of their choice and receive free treatment for simple ailments and be referred on to hospitals for those conditions the GP could not treat.
- GPs remained private professional people, increasingly often grouped in a common legal entity called a partnership. They owned their own premises, aided with loans from the profession. They received an annual payment for each NHS patient who signed on at their surgery and had a duty to provide care for that person. What this care should amount to was ill defined at this point but was taken to mean normal primary care and diagnosis. They were overseen by appointed bodies called Executive Councils, which were also responsible for dentists and chemists. Nearly half the membership was nominated by the relevant professional body.
- Attendance at hospital was free. Virtually all hospitals in the country

were owned and run by the national government. They were administered at two levels. Regional Hospital Boards, covering about 5 million
people, decided how to organize the hospitals, how many there should
be, what should be built and they employed the senior doctors and
allocated them to hospitals. (In the past specialist doctors, or consultants, had gone where they thought they could generate enough custom
from fee-paying patients. This meant there were very few in poorer
regions.) At local level hospitals or groups of hospitals were run by
hospital management committees appointed by the regional boards.
The exceptions were the famous teaching hospitals that had their own
Boards of Governors, rather like the trust hospitals of the 1990s. They
received a grant direct from the central government.

• Medicines prescribed by the GP could be picked up from the chemist
  free. Eye tests and spectacles were free from the optician and visits to
  the dentist and fillings and other treatments were free too. This was to
  change.

Once established the National Health Service acquired popular support. It also attracted increasing Treasury concern. The economy was
expanding, faster than in the pre-war period, but it was sucking in imports of raw materials needed by industry. The country was burdened by
debt and in 1949 the first of many post-war sterling crises forced a
devaluation of the pound. The Treasury demanded economies not only
in housing but from the NHS. Bevan fought off these attacks but when
the Korean war required an increase in the defence budget something had
to give. Charges on spectacles and dentures were demanded and Bevan
and the young Harold Wilson resigned from the government. A new
phase in the Health Service's history was about to begin.

Education For All

Controversy

The reform of education was also controversial. It, too, had been bogged
down in sectional interest group politics for the inter-war period. The
main resistant protagonists here were not so much the professions as the
churches. From the early nineteenth century on the religious issue had
dominated education debate. As late as 1861 a major Royal Commission
on Popular Education was arguing that the state had no role in education

except facilitating the work of the churches in bringing education to the masses. For the most part 'the churches' meant the Church of England and more recently the Roman Catholic Church. To the growing Non-conformist population, especially in the new industrial towns, this was unacceptable. The radical and working-class element in the Liberal Party was to a large extent drawn from the Nonconformist chapels of the industrial towns. They were enraged at the idea that their children should be forced to go to Anglican schools and that their taxes should pay for such schools. Catholicism was gaining ground, too, and the Nonconform-ists were even more adamant that there should be no 'Rome on the rates'. Here was the stuff of conflict deeper than any party politics could achieve.

The 1918 Education Act had legislated for a higher school-leaving-age as soon as it could be achieved. It was still 14 at the outbreak of the Second World War. Some local authorities had expanded places in sec-ondary grammar schools quite rapidly between the wars. About 12 per cent of the population went to such schools by 1939, but they were required to charge pupils fees and provide scholarships for those who could not pay but could pass an examination. Some local councils chose to provide a great many scholarships, others few. Some of the best gram-mar schools were private schools that the state had been subsidizing since 1902 (Glennerster and Wilson, 1970). More varied still was provision for the bulk of the population who went to elementary schools. Elementary education was defined as instruction in reading, writing and arithmetic. Many were still what were called 'all-age' schools. They typically con-sisted of schools taking children from 5 to 14 divided into two classes of about 50 children each; the 5- to 10-year-olds would be in one class and the rest in a senior class. Leicestershire had pioneered a system of separ-ate junior and senior schools and the Haddow Committee had recom-mended the general adoption of such a scheme, but by 1939 only about a quarter of elementary schools had been reorganized in such a way.

The issues

Debate centred on:

• abolishing the all-age elementary schools;
• abolishing fees for secondary education, i.e. buying places in grammar schools;

- raising the school leaving age to 16. The significance of this may not be evident to people a half century later but the reasoning was clear in Tawney's famous bible for many reformers, *Secondary Education for All*, published in 1924. If ordinary children were to have opportunities comparable to those enjoyed by children who went to secondary grammar schools, he argued, they must have the same length of school life. Grammar school children went to school until they were 16. Other children should be able to stay for the same period and have the same level of resources devoted to them. He did not argue they should go to the same school, it should be noted. At that point only one in ten of children going to grammar schools stayed on beyond 16, so 16 would be the end of full-time schooling for nearly the whole population.

What largely stood in the way of such changes was not simply money but the fact that the churches, who still provided a large part of the nation's schools, would have to find the money to build and equip their schools up to the standards these changes would require. They could not afford to do so. Should the state provide them with the cash? Yes, said the Anglican and Catholic churches. No, said the Nonconformist churches and the left.

Thinking about reform

In the first years of the Second World War the Board of Education was mainly concerned with evacuating children from London and the south coast to get them away from air attack. They went with their teachers and were evacuated school by school. After the immediate danger faded pressure began to mount on the government to get on with thinking about the reform of education. A committee of officials came into existence in November 1940, several months before Beveridge's committee was to meet (Gosden, 1976). Unlike the social insurance committee, its education counterpart did not have an outside chairman. It was a purely internal group of senior civil servants. Indeed, it had no formal existence. It was a set of informal discussions between the five principle assistant secretaries responsible for the main areas of the Board's work. In the inter-war period the Board had drifted and lost direction under weak political leadership. Now it determined to pull its collective socks up. In an early memorandum the deputy secretary said,

> The prospect of educational reconstruction that lies ahead offers an admirable opportunity to re-establish the position of the Board as the body competent to lead and direct the educational system of the country. (Gosden, 1976: 240)

The civil servants struggled with the issues that had not been resolved in the twenties and thirties. The debates are fascinating to a modern reader who lived through the debates on education in the fifties and sixties about comprehensive education and the eleven-plus. Virtually all the issues were prefigured and hammered out in those private discussions in Bournemouth, where the Board had been evacuated. The main protagonists were the head of the secondary schools branch, responsible for the grammar schools, and the head of the elementary schools branch.

Separate systems?

Getting the churches on board was going to be the main task but the civil servants agreed that was a political problem. Where they differed was on the system they would try to sell the churches and the local authorities. The Deputy Secretary was very concerned at the early age at which scholarship exams were taking place and at the effect that preparation for these competitive exams was having on the junior schools' work. Very few of the children would after all win a scholarship but the exams were dominating the curriculum. He favoured exams at 13, which would coincide with the age at which pupils in the private sector took entrance to the 'public' schools. The head of the grammar schools branch felt this would denude these schools of their pupils and their capacity to get pupils up to standard by 16 and the school leaving certificate exams.

The head of the elementary schools branch had much more fundamental concerns. He felt that if the senior elementary schools were merely to extend their age range to 16, this would not remove the divisions between the two systems, senior elementary and secondary grammar schools. This division would prove unsustainable in the more democratic post-war era. The war was emphasizing the essential unity of the nation. All secondary schools must have the same levels of resources and age range but even so, so long as some secondary schools remained places that prepared children for careers in the professions and other schools did not they would remain distinct and resented. He concluded,

> The obvious and perhaps the only satisfactory answer is the multilateral post-primary school attended by all children over the age of eleven. (Gosden, 1976: 247)

This view did not carry support. It was decided that the age of transfer had to be 11 and that selection for the academic schools would have to take place. However, the interchange almost perfectly reflected the debates that were to occupy the politicians and the education world for nearly thirty years after the eventual Act was passed, and that are not dead today.

Getting the churches on board

Very early on the civil servants agreed that the only way to break the log jam with the churches was to offer them enough money to build and staff the new secondary schools that would be needed for the children of their congregations. In return they would have to be more directly regulated by the local authorities. Carrying this off would be a major political task.

An outline of the group's proposals was included in a confidential discussion paper that was sent to the churches, the teachers' organizations and a few other educational bodies in 1941. The 'Green Paper', as it was called, could not have been launched in a way more different from the Beveridge Report a year later. The education press naturally knew about the document and complained at the inexplicable secrecy. More to the point it did not satisfy the churches. Fortunately, at this point a master craftsman politician was drafted to take charge as the President of the Board of Education: R. A. Butler.

Butler was anxious to make progress and wrote to the Prime Minister seeking some reaction to his list of priorities. Mr Churchill was not impressed. He could do without a row with the churches and said, 'I certainly could not contemplate a new Education Bill' (Gosden, 1976: 269). Butler decided to ignore this and get on with the task his civil servants had begun, especially negotiations with the churches. In his autobiography he describes the interminable round of visits to bishops and archbishops, while his Labour deputy Chuter Ede saw the Non-conformists (Butler, 1971). Chuter Ede was a Nonconformist and an exteacher. Each made an almost perfect foil for the other.

The churchmen had something they badly wanted to achieve and would cost the government little money. In 1941 the Archbishops of Canterbury, York and Wales had issued a statement pressing the case for the Christian religion to be taught in all schools, state as well as church, for there to be religious instruction on the syllabus and for all schools to start the day with an act of worship. Over 240 MPs signed a motion supporting this. Butler, on the advice of Ede and the civil servants, tied his response to progress on the wider issues of reform: 'We will give you religion in the classroom if you support the reform of education.' In the end, part of the price that was paid for getting the churches to accept the plans for post-war education was acceptance of these measures: religious instruction and worship in state schools. They still puzzle many observers from abroad.

The details of the arrangements that Butler worked out to accommodate the churches need not detain us but anyone looking up the 1944 Education Act will be surprised to see, if not knowing this history, that the majority of the sections of the Act have to do with the relationship of various kinds of church schools with the state, the composition of their governing bodies, of their rights to teach denominational education in their schools, of the duty to teach religion in school and on the means of agreeing what to teach! Essentially the state was to pay not only to run the denominational schools but to contribute heavily towards their capital costs. The churches would continue to be able to teach their version of Christianity.

The master craftsman had, however, done his job. Before the 1944 Education Act religion had dominated education politics. Afterwards it was never to do so again. This must be one of the most lasting beneficial legacies any politician has bestowed on his successors!

The 1944 Education Act

With this log jam broken the Act was able to make provision for:

- an end to all-age schools and a building programme to create separate primary and secondary schools in every local authority;

- the abolition of fees in secondary schools, indeed in any state school at all;
- a statutory school-leaving age of 16 to be reached in two stages, first to 15 and then to 16;
- the right of young workers between leaving school and age 18 to day release from work; they would go to colleges to be taught citizenship and extend their education;
- those going to university would be able to receive scholarships to support them;
- religious instruction would be a compulsory subject unless the parent held principled objections, and there was to be a daily act of worship.

The Act said nothing about the kind of secondary education there should be, about selection, or the eleven-plus as it came to be called (rather oddly since most children took these exams at age 10). Nor did it say much about technical education, though provision was made for further education colleges. With these exceptions it was to prove a remarkably enduring piece of craftsmanship. Its main administrative features underpinned the education system for the next forty-four years.

Labour's Policy

Two schools of thought

From its very origins the Labour Party had been divided about its approach to education, especially secondary education. At one extreme was the Fabian socialist Sydney Webb, who was an active member of the London County Council Technical Education Board. 'Virtually single handed he created a scholarship ladder for the able child' (Barker, 1972: 16). The Webbs had no faith in the intelligence of the bulk of the population. For them society was hierarchical and the key to a socialist Utopia was to ensure that able people were diagnosed early and put in senior positions in the administrative machine. Secondary grammar schools and the competitive examination scholarship system did this admirably; 'the greatest capacity catching machine the world has ever seen', Sydney Webb called it (p. 17).

At the other extreme, left-wing socialists, trade unionists and the growing ranks of elementary school teachers in Labour's ranks felt suspicious or completely hostile to the idea of creaming off able working-class children, sending them to middle-class establishments and denying the bulk of the population the same access to good education. As the Labour Party gained electoral strength in urban centres and gained control of many education authorities in the 1920s and 1930s Labour councils busied themselves creating more secondary grammar schools, and scholarships to enable poor children to go to them. By the 1940s most local Labour members of these education committees actually saw the expansion of the grammar school as the way forward, especially in the north of England. They had often made their way through just such a route. This split was to emerge very clearly in the way the Labour government approached the implementation of the 1944 Act.

The realities of bricks and mortar and resource constraints were on the side of those wanting minimal change, but the political divide and the force of the civil service were to be decisive. The party's advisory committee on education had begun meeting in 1938 with a new younger generation of reformers; they were growing increasingly concerned about a system of education that was emerging with three separate streams, that for the academically able, that for the technically able, and that for the rest. It seemed to replicate the class structure and reinforce it and they looked for alternatives. The only solution that seemed available was something called a multilateral school, encompassing these three streams on a single school site.

The official report of the Spens Committee in 1939 had rejected such a solution and debate centred on whether such a model should be *one* of the models or *the* goal of future Labour policy (see Barker, 1972 for an account of the period).

In the end the committee became convinced it should be *the* long-term goal of Labour policy. The idea was still not what we today call a comprehensive school. That seeks to include all children in one school, not separate them into different buildings or streams from the outset. The multilateral idea was carried at the Labour Party Conference in 1942.

The eleven-plus

The 1944 Act, it will be recalled, said nothing about what kind of secondary schools would be created under it. Just before the general election the

Ministry of Education, as it was now called (not a mere Board), issued a document advising local authorities how to plan their schools in the post-war period: *The Nation's Schools* (Ministry of Education, 1945). It suggested there should be a tripartite system with three types of school:

- grammar schools: essentially the secondary grammar schools that existed already but with access to all the places by competitive examination;
- secondary modern schools: essentially the old senior elementary schools. Just what kind of schools these would be became a matter for much discussion amongst educationalists;
- technical schools that would take students at 13 with technical abilities and probably headed for apprenticeships.

There was no encouragement for education authorities to introduce multi-lateral schools. Those in the Labour Party who had supported the new policy were furious. They saw the document as a move by the ministry to pre-empt the policy of a future Labour government. Many of those who spoke out were to become leading figures in the party in the 1950s and 1960s – Margaret Herbison and Alice Bacon, for example.

The two Ministers of Education whom Attlee appointed first, Ellen Wilkinson and then George Tomlinson, however, did not share the younger reformers' views. Labour councils were divided; some, like London, were strongly committed to multilateral or – later – comprehensive schools; others were opposed.

What followed was a story to be repeated in later decades. Labour Party Conference attacked the Labour government for not implementing party policy and the government mostly stuck to its position. Both Wilkinson and Tomlinson were in the Webb tradition. As Ellen Wilkinson told the Labour Party Conference in 1946, 'I was born into a working class home and I had to fight my own way through to university.' She believed children had different capacities and these were linked to distinctive types of school. (See Barker, 1972: 81–97 for a discussion of this period.)

The ministry advice was reissued with barely any move to the critics' position but in a circular issued later that year (Circular 144, 1947) it did entertain the possibility of a common or comprehensive school. It favoured a large six- or seven-form-entry school that would be big enough to generate more than one academic stream and a sixth form large enough to give pupils choice of advanced study. This was the route followed by the London County Council, Coventry and – on a much smaller scale – a few other authorities.

The Ministry of Education had to approve all plans for the future organization of schools in every part of the country. It rejected several of the plans for comprehensive schools of different kinds put forward at this point, much to the anger of the councils concerned. In 1950 the Labour Party came into open conflict with the government over the issue at Conference and in 1951 published a policy document in direct opposition to government policy calling for the reorganization of secondary schools everywhere on comprehensive lines, eliminating the eleven-plus examination. Tomlinson protested that this was simply not possible with the existing stock of buildings. This conflict of views was to dominate education debate for the next twenty-five years.

The Labour Party was reaching the end of a period in its ideological life history. The revisionists in the party were beginning to turn their attention to social policy as the central core of its concerns. The left wanted to extend public ownership still further. This contest was to consume the party for much of the next decade. The challenge to the leadership on comprehensive education in the late 1940s was the first sign of this shift of emphasis.

Again, whatever word we use to describe this series of events, 'consensus' is not the most appropriate.

Children

The evacuation of children from the big cities to live with families in more favoured parts of the country had alerted many to the extent of poverty in which many of these children normally lived. Social questions raised longer-term issues about the way services were organized before a wider audience than in the 1930s. This is well illustrated in the case of child care.

Children at risk or without parents could be placed in the hands of a local authority, as they can be today. What part of what local authority was actually responsible, however, was unclear. In 1945 two brothers were to be placed with foster parents. The family that was to have taken them had accepted another child and could not help. A child attendance officer took them to the country anyway, where the wife suggested he try two other local farms. He found a couple who had some space and seemed nice enough people – they were 'clean and tidy'. The boys were left and later murdered. The Government Report of the Enquiry gives a graphic picture of a chaotic administrative process, lack of trained or even specialist staff and unclear accountability (Monckton Enquiry, 1945). A committee was set up to look at services for children at risk: the Curtis Committee. Out of it came a clear set of proposals (Curtis Report, 1946) that were legislated in the 1948 Children Act. A separate department of the county councils and of county borough councils had to be created specifically to look after the interests of such children. A chief officer, the Children's Officer, had to be appointed who would be held statutorily responsible for all such children in the authority's care. Working under this chief officer would be trained specialist children's social workers. Their training was organized under the auspices of the Home Office, who oversaw the whole service and inspected its standards, much as it did with the probation service created before the war.

A new social work profession had been created. It was to be predominantly female and the chief officer role often went to a woman too. Women had for the first time been given a route to the top in local government and in the Home Office.

Food Rationing

Much traditional social policy writing has concentrated on traditional services such as health, which have remained state services for the whole period since 1948. In fact, the most basic commodity of all, food, was also clearly part of social policy in the 1940s. During the war grain and a large part of the country's staple diet had to be imported in conditions of extreme danger through a blockade of German submarines. Food became a very scarce commodity. Left to itself there was no reason why the market should deliver enough for the whole population to live on. The few with enough money could simply have bought up the lot. The workers in the munitions factories and mines would not have been able to keep the war effort going. The government introduced a comprehensive system of food rationing very rapidly. Every member of the population was issued with a ration book. You had to register with a grocer, as you might today with a GP, and before you bought anything little bits of paper, 'coupons', had to be cut out of the book and given to the grocer; the number of coupons related to the amount of food bought. Money, except on the black market, was not the crucial means of exchange; coupons were. This ensured, not complete equality of food intake, but a minimum standard of nutrition that actually improved the health of the nation during this period. This system lasted for all the period of the post-war Labour government and was only dismantled in the 1950s.

What this history illustrates is that there is no such thing as an absolute boundary line between the market and socially provided goods and services. Where a commodity that is essential to existence becomes so scarce that its distribution by the market may destroy the society's norms and values and undermine law and order, the market will be replaced. Rationing and coupons may be unthinkable for today's trolley-pushing supermarket masses, but it was only common sense and fair play to their grandparents.

When the dire scarcity of food retreated, so did the support for rationing as an allocative mechanism. Much the same story was to unfold in the case of housing. Terrible scarcity after the war was met with a largely rationed system of provision but as housing came within the reach of more peoples' own pockets frustration with the rationing system grew.

Shelter

The first preoccupation that ministers had when the new Labour government came to office in July 1945 was to plan for the peace. Millions of servicemen and women would be returning to civilian life. Basic industries, including the construction industry, would have to be turned from war production to normal peaceful activities – swords beaten into ploughshares. The great fear was of mass unemployment. Second only to this was fear of homelessness. Not only were the troops returning and wanting to start families, the birth-rate was to rise sharply in the years 1945–8; but 200,000 houses had been destroyed and a further 250,000 badly damaged in the war and one in three damaged to some degree. The number of homes without lavatories or bathrooms seems unbelievable today. Nearly half of all households lacked the sole use of a bathroom.

Two in every five households lacked a bath at all. Nearly a quarter had no exclusive use of a lavatory.

The number of men employed in the construction industry had fallen from a million before the war to a third of that level. Yet, unlike the other policy fields we have discussed, there was no blueprint, no committee of enquiry setting out a considered plan of action or way forward for housing, though there was for wider urban planning and land ownership (Donnison, 1960).

By the 1990s planning had become an unfashionable term, associated with tower blocks and eastern European failure. It is noticeable in this period that where the wartime government had tried systematically to consider the range of issues that concerned a service – social insurance, education or child care – some relatively coherent action did follow in the 1940s. The fact that no such coherent thought was given to the future of housing was to have lasting effects. The incoherent and contradictory set of policies that was to afflict housing in the post-war period can in no small part be traced to this lack of systematic thought at this time. The government in 1945, then, struggled to put together some ground plan for housing in the post-war period and to move very rapidly. It was estimated that for every family to have a home of its own would require three-quarters of a million new homes. The only agencies that Bevan, also responsible for housing, thought could respond were local authorities (Foot, 1975). Britain did not possess a national network of housing associations or organizations providing housing for the poor. The local authorities would have to be mobilized to do this vast job and paid to do so. For every house they built they would receive a subsidy for the next sixty years, to help pay off the loan they would have to make to build the houses. This would keep their rents within the means of ordinary families. Government economic policy was keeping interest rates at 3 per cent, a figure that seems barely possible to the home owner of the late 1980s.

Building materials were in desperately short supply. Britain had little or no foreign currency reserves to pay for imports. The rest of the world was rebuilding too. Bricks and timber were in as short supply as food. The only way out, Bevan concluded, was to put the local authorities in charge of the housing drive. House building was rationed. You had to have a building licence to start to build a house and four-fifths of all licences were given to local councils for their own building in 1948.

Building materials themselves – wood of different kinds, bricks, steel – were rationed. Price controls were also in force. They only began to be relaxed in the period after 1949. Factories that were still on a war footing were given the task of making prefabricated industrialized houses – 'prefabs'. Permanent housing standards were improved, however. Standard three-bedroomed houses were enlarged from 750 to 900 square feet. The working class was to be given decent accommodation. It still shows. In later years these standards were to be reduced. Anyone who knows the history of council house subsidies and standards can walk round a council estate and date the buildings. The 1940s houses stand out as well-constructed and comfortable dwellings, in the main.

The overwhelming emphasis on building new units at all costs was to leave its legacy. Little or no thought was given to how to manage these houses once they were built, how to ensure good maintenance and oversight. This was to become worse in later periods (Power, 1988). Little attention was paid to building commercial and social facilities or creating communities. Building extra units was the prime goal.

Private renting

Most ordinary people were still tenants of private landlords, though. Desperate shortages would have led, in the short run, to landlords charging very high rents and though this might have been the logical market response it was not one that politicians could contemplate. Rent controls had been introduced at the beginning of the Second World War, as they had been in the middle of the First. Retaining them was politically popular, but it meant that the private sector saw no point in even trying to contribute to the post-war housing effort – there was no profit it. Home ownership was severely constrained to devote most of the available resources to council housing. That also fitted in with the Labour ministers' preconceptions about the evils of private landlords and distrust of owner occupation and small builders. Given the acute nature of the housing crisis of the time, ministers' instincts and public sympathy were not far apart. This prevented the Labour government giving any fundamental thought to housing policy in the longer term. Did it make any sense to starve the private landlord sector of resources when it housed most ordinary people? What would replace it as it withered away? Was owner occupation to be confined to the wealthy and the professional classes? In the 1930s, with low interest rates and cheap houses, it had spread into the working class. Could it be stopped? Should it be stopped? The Labour Party blocked its ears to such ideas and the issues had to be fought out in the 1950s and 1960s and 1970s before the party finally reconciled itself to a plurality of home ownership as the ultimate goal in the 1980s.

Public pressure on the Labour government was not to revive the private sector but to build more council houses faster still. The first economic crisis of the post-war period began to make the Treasury fearful that the production of nearly 300,000 a year reached in 1948 could be sustained. The target was cut and actual house-building cut back to about 200,000. The Conservative Party in opposition was pressing for more and gained much support by committing itself to build, not 200,000 but 300,000 houses a year if it was re-elected.

Services for Citizens?

The first and overwhelming feeling that one is left with after reading the detailed accounts of this period is simple admiration for what was achieved. Here was a society and an economy reeling from the most devastating war in its history. Government had to organize and help rebuild a neglected economic infrastructure and housing stock. People had a standard of living and incomes of about a third of the level enjoyed by households in the 1990s. Yet government was able to begin to house and educate and care for the health of all its citizens and accept that this was the state's prime duty. To say, in richer times, that education and health care for all cannot be afforded, is simply absurd. It may well be that people no longer care or want to achieve these goals but the 1940s show that if there is a collective desire for them they can be achieved.

There are some less encouraging lessons to be drawn from the early history of these 'citizenship' services. First, it was generally perceived in the 1940s that the main barrier to equal access to health and education was one of price: the charges people had to pay to enter hospital or go to the doctor or to secondary school. This was not surprising when these barriers existed and were resented. However, merely to remove them did not mean that all sections of the community would use the services or benefit from them to the same extent. In the next decade this realization began to dawn on academic analysts and on politicians. Why this was so and what, if anything, they could do about it raised practical and philosophical issues that moved to the centre of debate in the 1960s.

Second, what universal free health care and free secondary and university education had done was very largely to benefit those just above the cut-off point at which the old systems of welfare had ceased to operate (Abel-Smith, 1958).

Finally, all these services were creatures of their age, the age of belief in the virtues of central planning and monopoly provision. Markets and competition stank of the failures of the 1930s to most Labour politicians. The social services they created were in the image of the other economic institutions of the time: British Rail, the Gas Board. This made it possible to allocate resources more fairly to different parts of the country, to equalize opportunities of access. But it also built in a corrosive element that was to eat away at their effectiveness and popularity over the much longer term. The Health Service was the prime example. It was a monopoly, and its employees, especially the medical profession, were given monopoly power with little democratic accountability, in return for agreeing to join the service. What Durbin (1949) had predicted for the nationalized industries was to hold for the social services. They would gradually come to fall into the hands of the providers and not the consumers.

4 The New Conservatism and Social Policy, 1951–64

It is commonly believed that, after 1945, the Conservative Party came to terms with the Welfare State and between 1945 and 1975 there was a broad consensus between the parties on social policy. This is the view expressed in a companion volume to this, *Consensus Politics from Attlee to Thatcher* (Kavanagh and Morris, 1989). It is the view expressed in Marwick's standard Penguin social history of the period (Marwick, 1990). Deakin accepts it, for the early period at least (Deakin, 1994). It is the basis of Morgan's history of the period (Morgan, 1990: ch. 4) and follows on from Addison's argument in *The Road to 1945* (1975). Mrs Thatcher's own account of her decisive leadership reinforces the view. She claims she changed the spineless post-war consensus (Thatcher, 1993).

A less charitable view is that the Conservative Party has always taken a cynical and unprincipled view of social policy:

> Disraeli's 'one nation' rhetoric in the 1870s was a smokescreen for a social policy consisting of two essential and enduring principles; the identification of the Tories as the party of all property owners not just landlords; and the trumping of whichever social reforms . . . were judged necessary for electoral success. (*Weekend Financial Times*, 30 July 1994: 1; see also Adonis and Hames, 1994)

Neither view is sustainable in the light of the most recent work on the archives (Harris, 1986; Jones, 1992; Lowe, 1990; Pimlott, 1989; Webster, 1990). We have already seen evidence in the last two chapters that there was both a wide degree of public support for many of the post-war measures and a severe limit to that support on particular issues and from particular groups like the medical profession.

The Conservative Party never did accept the universalist principles that were key to much of the 1940s legislation and between 1947 and 1950 it did manage to forge a new social policy agenda based on principles different from those of the 1945 Labour government. It is true that political reality tempered its advocacy in the succeeding decades, but a distinctive set of ideas about targeting benefits and encouraging home ownership, for example, can be traced through the policies of all post-war Conservative governments. These ideas have their origins in the important work done by the party in opposition in the 1940s.

Back to the Drawing Board

Contested ideals

The Conservative Party has always embodied within it very different strands of thought about the appropriate role for the state on social issues. There had always been those who saw the state as an organic entity, more than the sum of its individual subjects. Social policy became the handmaiden to that vision. The state should foster a sense of national unity, of belonging and allegiance, it should support traditional forms of family life and the established Christian religion.

Education policy encapsulates this last view most clearly. We have already seen it reflected in the discussions on the 1944 Education Act. It is not surprising that this organic view of the state should have been at its strongest in Tory policy during the Second World War. Butler, who was responsible for Conservative Party home policy in this period, was initially attracted to this position. He called on Karl Mannheim, an Austrian refugee at the LSE, and others, to work on Conservative reconstruction policy (Harris, 1986). Reading the reports of their work on education, even at this distance, sends a certain shudder down the spine.

They envisaged a powerful moral order that the state, through its educational institutions, would foster. The Christian religion would be firmly at the centre of school activity. This would continue into early adult life as young workers were given compulsory day release, not to train in vocational skills, but to acquire proper attitudes to citizenship. The echoes of the Hitler Youth Movement are clear. In addition, it was argued, the public schools should be taken over by the Board of Education to reduce the class divisions in society (Harris, 1986).

When these documents were circulated more widely on a confidential basis within the party, the proposals were dismissed, with some contempt, by the rank and file (Harris, 1986: 245). Nevertheless, the view that the state education system was there to instil a proper respect for authority and the British way of life is a thread that can be traced from the discussions on the 1944 Education Act to Conservative education policies of the 1990s and in ministers' views on the content of the National Curriculum. It is also reflected in the family values theme that re-emerges in the 1980s and 1990s. In contrast to this strand of Conservative thought is the very opposite: liberal and deeply suspicious of any organic concept of the state. The state is seen as a regulator of individual action that may harm others and as the rule-maker within which free markets can work. The outstanding exponent was Professor Hayek, another Austrian *émigré* at the LSE (Hayek, 1944). He was, later, to become Mrs Thatcher's philosophical mentor, but he was influential at the end of the war too.

Less radical and more pragmatically concerned with the nuts and bolts of policy were a group of young Conservative MPs – the Tory Reform Group – who saw a role for social policy, but not the extensive one that the Mannheim group did. Then there were the foot soldiers, Conservative backbenchers and rank and file, who were deeply suspicious of the direction Beveridge was dragging the country.

Forging a new policy framework

This fundamental division of ideas about social policy, and how to react to the Beveridge bandwagon, was only made worse by the fact that the Conservative leadership was preoccupied with the war effort in the early 1940s. The Conservative Research Department did not operate during the Second World War. Little coherent work came out of the study groups Butler set up to chart a post-war Conservative approach to social policy (Jones, 1992). The party's study group on the Beveridge Report was critical: it said that it was excessively costly and did not concentrate spending on the really poor. 'The Conservatives advising Churchill objected to the Beveridge Plan on financial, moral and distributive grounds' (Jones, 1992: 79).

Yet nothing coherent could be set against Beveridge and to oppose his report in 1945 would have been political suicide. The consequence was that the Conservatives lost the 1945 social policy debate as well as the election.

For a period after the Second World War there was a policy vacuum that tended to be filled by backbenchers taking hostile stands against Labour government policy, notably on the health service. Butler and those in Conservative Central Office were deeply worried by this as they thought it would be electorally disastrous. The need for a worked-out social policy position was clear. At this point Conservative Central Office was revived by some able young people who had been newly recruited; they included Iain Macleod, Enoch Powell and Reginald Maudling, all later to become ministers.

What emerged from this rethinking was not, however, a meek acceptance of the Welfare State as it was being created by Bevan and Griffiths. The cost, the way it was being financed, and the form it was taking were all offensive to the liberal view of the state that became the basis of Conservative philosophy. There should be some welfare provision, to be sure, but it should have a Conservative face.

Housing The first opportunity to make a distinctive stand came with housing policy. Labour was insisting, as we saw, on local councils doing nearly all the building. Despite the rapid expansion in house-building that had taken place there was enormous impatience and popular desire to go faster. Small builders urged that they could do better if given their head. Freeing them to build, including for owner occupation, became the first distinctive challenge to the Labour government's social policy. The party was very worried that coming out firmly in favour of owner occupation would restrict its appeal as overly middle class. It decided it would favour owner occupation but cautiously. Above all it would seek to trump Labour by going for a higher house-building target. Henry Brooke was cautious about giving a number but a policy committee and then Conservative Party Conference bounced the party into committing itself to a target of 300,000 houses a year. This was the pre-war rate of house-building, but it was now unlikely to be reached without reducing the higher standards that had been set for building after the war and Conservative Central Office knew that (Jones, 1992).

A clearly distinct Conservative housing policy was hammered out that gave a much larger role to the private sector, to private landlords and to owner occupation. It remained the basis of Conservative policy through to Mrs Thatcher's period and increasingly came into its own as more families became able to afford to buy their own homes. The party carefully tended its policy presentation to meet the needs of electoral convenience, but to suggest that it had no distinctive policy is simply incorrect. The same is true of Social Security.

Social security   From the start the Conservative Party was unhappy with the Beveridge scheme and its promise of universal flat rate pensions that were not means tested. The work that went on within Central Office was based on a fundamentally different philosophy. Social services were becoming a way to redistribute wealth and not merely a means to relieve destitution and misfortune, it was argued. To relieve poverty was legitimate. To go further was not.

When they emerged as MPs from their backroom jobs in Central Office Macleod and Powell published a pamphlet that summed up the principles that underpinned their and the party's thinking (Macleod and Powell, 1952). High taxes meant disincentives to work while the expansion of social services had produced a decline in individual initiative and family responsibility. Social policy had moved too far from the insurance principle. The Beveridge scheme involved too great a subsidy from the taxpayer and the NHS was based on large expenditure from general taxation. The NHS should return to being financed on an insurance basis. In addition, policy had moved from charging as a basis for finance. Benefits were given regardless of need. This, they argued was a principle that should have no place in social policy.

> The question which therefore poses itself is not should a means test be applied to a social service, but why should any service be provided without a test of need. (Macleod and Powell, 1952: 5)

Conservatives, throughout the post-war period, would return to this question.

Education   In education, too, there was a distinctive line. As we saw, the Labour Party was moving steadily to a position that favoured comprehensive schools and the abolition of the eleven-plus; the Conservative Party moved firmly to support the principle of grammar school education. The 1951 Conservative Manifesto, *Britain Strong and Free* said, 'We must safeguard the independence, the high standards and the traditions of the grammar schools.'

Health   Health was more difficult. The NHS was rapidly proving to be *the* real success of the Attlee government. The party could not attack it outright but again it was deeply unhappy with the Bevan construction. It had favoured the retention of the voluntary hospitals. It wanted to see the private sector encouraged. It considered policies to charge for services, of ways of encouraging the private sector, of going back to an insurance basis. It wanted to cut grants to the regional hospital boards, which were considered extravagant, and to charge for board and lodging in hospitals (Jones, 1992). Anyone familiar with the proposals trawled in 1988 for Mrs Thatcher's review of the NHS, will find a very similar agenda.

The Conservative vision

The Conservative Party in 1951 therefore came to power with a distinctively Conservative liberal agenda on social policy. It had not accepted the 1945 Labour institutions or indeed those of the Second World War 'consensus'. It had its own coherent, and arguably far-sighted, set of policies. It was to prove difficult to implement them, however. The social and economic climate were not to prove fully compatible with these ideas for another thirty years.

Trying to Contain the Welfare State

The new Conservative government, under Churchill, came to power in 1951, when the Labour government had effectively run out of steam and was deeply divided about social expenditure. The new government was both fortunate and successful in many ways in its early years (Seldon, 1981). After the economic impact of the Korean war had receded world trade prices worked in Britain's favour. The government could dismantle the irksome restrictions and rationing that were a hangover of the war period. Income tax reductions were made in the 1952, 1953 and 1954 Budgets in line with the philosophy the party had worked on in opposition. That required a firm grip on public expenditure despite the growing economy.

Containing the Welfare State

Butler, the new Chancellor, immediately considered ways of reducing the scale of public expenditure on social policy. The previous Labour government had begun the process. It was that which had caused the resignations of Bevan and Wilson when health service charges were imposed. More radical ways of cutting the budget were considered by the new government: the reintroduction of fees in secondary schools, a reduction in the school-leaving age, changing the school meals service and the way local education authorities were financed, health service charges (Jones, 1992). At this stage all the more fundamental changes were rejected. The government only had a small majority. Even so, it made some unpopular cuts.

A circular was issued in December 1951 telling local education authorities they must reduce their estimated education spending for the coming year by 5 per cent, concentrating in particular on school transport, playgrounds and the youth service (Circular 242). At that time there was still a specific education grant. Central government met a share of local councils' education budgets that it approved. The new Conservative government was saying: we shall not match your spending unless you reduce it in given ways. In February 1952 councils were told to reduce their school building programmes substantially. No proposals would be approved that were designed to relieve overcrowding, replace unsatisfactory schools or enable the old all-age schools to be reorganized (Circular 245). These priorities were to remain in force for many years. 'Roofs over heads' to accommodate the new births of the post-war years dominated the Ministry of Education's concerns. The result of this circular was to reduce the value of school building projects approved from £53 million in 1951 to £39 million in 1952.

The government was pledged to increase the house-building rate to 300,000 houses a year. There was no prospect that this could be achieved by the private sector in the short run. This meant *more* public expenditure on council houses. Macmillan fought effectively to sustain that commitment. The effect was to reduce the expenditure on each house. Very early on the government took steps to get local authorities to reduce the standard of the houses they were building. The Labour government had already set a review in train. Macmillan made a virtue of the changes. There was to be a new 'people's house', good, cheap and plentiful. In fact, the controls and the design limits were very tight and precise. The overall floor space for a three-bedroomed house was to be 847 square feet, the staircase was to come off the living room, there was to be no separate access from hall to kitchen, no external storage (Circular 70/51). Approvals for three-bedroomed houses were also reduced sharply. Under the previous government four-fifths of all council houses built had three or more bedrooms. That figure was reduced over the 1950s to two-fifths.

In June 1952 the first prescription charge was imposed. The Labour government had created the legislative power to do so but had held back from implementing the change. It was a charge of one shilling (5p) on each prescription form.

Hospital capital expenditure was kept within tight limits despite growing concern in the Ministry of Health which pointed out that the level of new building had been higher in the days before the war when the voluntary hospitals and local authorities had been doing all the building. The Treasury returned to its demand that health service 'manpower' be reduced. In December a freeze was placed on administrative and clerical staffing numbers. The Treasury demanded a reduction of 5 per cent in non-medical and nursing staff. In December 1952 a circular was issued freezing establishments. Additions had to be approved by the administrative layer above. The aim was a reduction in staffing of 5 per cent in a year for certain categories of staff. Since senior medical staff establishments were held at regional level this meant ministerial approval for any increase (Webster, 1988: 302). The circular did not succeed in reducing staffing levels but it did secure a virtual freeze in numbers employed. No really fundamental reduction in the cost of the Welfare State had come out of these measures nor the reviews of spending that were initiated in this period. However, two committees were set up to consider the longer-term financing of pensions and the National Health Service (see below).

All in all, Butler, with the help of an able Treasury civil servant, Sir Richard (Otto) Clarke, was able to keep a fairly tight grip on social service expenditure during this period. From 1951 to 1956, the share of the GDP going on social security, health and education barely increased and was held at just over 11 per cent. Part of the reason for this success lay in the substantial improvement that took place in the world economy and in Britain's place within it. The economy enjoyed one of its temporary post-war booms and this put off the need for more fundamental ways of cutting public expenditure. But not for long.

Stop–go begins

In 1955 the first of what was to become a recurrent cycle of events began. The economy began to overheat, to suck in more imports than exports were earning. Bank rate was raised first to 3.5 per cent and then to 4.5 per cent. After the election in May 1955 other measures followed, including a credit squeeze on the banks and the capital programmes of local authorities were cut. With growth slowing down it was going to be more difficult to contain spending and prevent a rise in taxes. The Treasury needed to have another go at getting the government to think radically about social spending.

Immediately after the election the Treasury put a paper to Cabinet that reviewed the spending prospects for social services over the next five years. The sharply rising school population, the result of the post-war bulge in the birth-rate, was in its more expensive secondary phase. Pensioners would begin to earn rights to a pension under the post-war scheme. All this was coming on top of a weak economic position. The share of the GNP going on social policy would rise. The Cabinet was sufficiently worried to appoint a special Social Services Committee, chaired by Butler, to consider what to do.

Lowe gives a fascinating account of the work of this committee and the way in which the spending departments essentially defeated the Treasury and hence, in the longer run, provoked the resignation of the Chancellor of the Exchequer and a new way of controlling public expenditure.

> To the social policy historian, the contrast between this committee and both the Geddes Axe and the May Report of the inter-war period is irresistible. Neither Geddes nor May in the long term staunched the relentless . . . increase in social expenditure; but they did consolidate a widespread demand for retrenchment and enable the Treasury to make significant short term cuts . . . [however this] Committee identified no acceptable economies and social expenditure continued to rise. It was, indeed, so counter-productive that Treasury officials had to seek its early demise for fear that it would rebound against them. (Lowe, 1989: 507)

The spending departments showed themselves very well briefed about the fundamental case the Treasury was making but above all were able to gain support from the majority of those on the committee, who were spending ministers. The Treasury learned its lesson and later pressed for a fundamental change to the way public spending was controlled, to reduce the power of the natural majority spending ministers possessed in Cabinet (Heclo and Wildavsky, 1981). On this occasion the spending ministers were able to see off proposals to remove the dental service and ophthalmology from the NHS, to raise the entry age to school to 6 and reduce the leaving age to 14, and other measures.

The spending departments began to counter-attack, suggesting that areas of social spending were advantageous economically and had been neglected for too long. The publication of the Guillebaud Committee Report arguing this in relation to health was a help (see below). The Treasury wound up the committee. It is wrong to suggest that the spending departments' victory was complete, however.

Various measures were taken to reduce net government expenditure, net after discounting the income from charges. The doubling of the prescription charge was rejected but the 5p originally applied to each prescription form now applied to each item on it. Outside the work of this committee housing subsidies to local councils were substantially reduced. Subsidies on bread and milk were abolished and local government finance was reformed.

Ever since the 1920s the Treasury had objected to the way local authorities were financed, especially the way local education was paid for (Glennerster, 1992). Local councils received a matching grant for this purpose; a percentage grant, it was called. The local authorities proposed to spend so much and, if the ministry approved, the government paid out an equivalent amount. This was a very good way to encourage an expanding education service but did not encourage economy. The Treasury had returned to its old objections several times in the early 1950s and this time got its way. The government agreed to move to a new system of local government finance under which local councils would get a block grant based on their population and other factors, which would subsidize all their activities. Service by service percentage grants would go (Local Government Finance Act, 1958). That principle remains the basis of local funding to the present day. The education world, in particular, was furious. It lost. But, in fact, such was the pressure to spend more on education, that this change in the grant structure did not halt the rise in education spending.

Lowe argues that the Social Services Committee not only failed to achieve major cuts or changes in social policy but that it sharpened the capacity of the spending departments to resist the pressure for more spending cuts, which the new Chancellor Peter Thorneycroft demanded in 1957, in the wake of yet another economic crisis. It was this failure and defeat in Cabinet that lead Thorneycroft and the rest of his Treasury team to resign in January 1958. That, in its turn, along with a critical report from the House of Commons Select Committee on Estimates (HC 294 1958), lead to the appointment of the Plowden Committee. This was, in effect, a Treasury committee with an outside chairman. It was appointed to look at the way public expenditure was being controlled. It was that committee's report (Cmnd 1432, 1961) which recommended setting up the annual reviews of public spending, the Public Expenditure Survey, that has been with us, in one form or another, ever since.

The hard politics of the time were, however, that the Prime Minister, Harold Macmillan, was not prepared to support major attacks on the Welfare State or cuts that would be damaging electorally. Cutting taxes as a central plank of Conservative policy was abandoned. The Labour Party was beginning to take the initiative on the poverty of old people. The launch by the Russians of the first space vehicle, the Sputnik, had really worried politicians in the West. It suggested that the West was lagging behind the Russians scientifically. In the USA and in the UK and elsewhere, science budgets and higher education began to be looked on more favourably. Eccles, at the Ministry of Education, reaped the reward and was a powerful figure who gave that ministry its expansionist head. He was backed by the demographics of the period. The baby boom of the post-war years was going through the schools at this point.

As Macmillan's premiership continued so the pace of public spending grew. In the race to recover credibility in the run-up to the 1964 general election the budget was increased faster still, much as it was in the early 1990s. If there was a period of consensus or at least electoral competition on the basis of social spending, this was it.

Inflation and Full Employment, an Early Warning

The overheating of the economy in 1955 and the 'bonfire of controls' in the 1950s brought the first danger signal, a cloud on the horizon that was to become the major concern of the 1970s. Robert Hall, Economic Adviser to the government from 1947 until 1961, had become increasingly concerned with the growing wage pressures that were resulting from full employment (Jones, 1994). He saw that unless some way could be found to contain such pressure full employment would not be sustainable. That was the basis of the brief wage restraint policy agreed with the trade unions and the Labour government in 1948 and 1949. A White Paper on the subject was in train before the Labour government left office but the incoming Conservative government preferred to rely on monetary policy alone to tackle inflation.

By 1955 all the signs of economic overheating, which were to become so familiar, were evident. The Treasury persuaded ministers to produce a warning shot. The result was a White Paper entitled *The Economic Implications of Full Employment* (Cmd 9725, 1956). To emphasize its importance it was presented to Parliament by the Prime Minister, not the Chancellor. It pointed out that prices had increased by 50 per cent since the war. Though some of the rise had been the result of higher import prices and removing subsidies, most was internally generated.

> there has been in this country – to a greater extent than in many other countries – a continuing tendency for prices to rise as incomes increase faster than output. (para. 11)

In an extremely lucid and non-technical way the White Paper put the stark choice: if the country wanted to maintain the commitment to full employment in the 1944 White Paper it would have to find some way of stopping this inflationary process. To sustain full employment meant sustaining a strong demand for labour and goods.

> If the prosperous economic conditions necessary to maintain full employment are exploited by trade unions and business men, price stability and full employment become incompatible. (para. 26)

In the absence of such restraint the goal of full employment would have to be relaxed. It was a warning that was not heeded. The White Paper was so much exhortation and Hall considered it a useless and poorly timed exercise not accompanied by action (Jones, 1994: 146). But it had put its finger on the fundamental problem: full employment, without some form of pay restraint, would in the end fail. (See Cairncross, 1992 for an account of the experiments with pay restraint and economic planning in the 1960s.)

Social Services: Wasted Years?

In terms of individual social services the record of the period 1951 to 1964 was mixed. The Labour Party was to accuse the government of 'thirteen wasted years'. In retrospect, this is not an entirely fair judgement. Indeed, it now looks like a period of enviable organizational tranquillity. It is true that policy did not develop greatly in any field except housing, where some very important changes took place.

Housing success and failure

300,000 houses a year   The government began with a promise to raise house building to the 300,000 a year target. Macmillan and his junior minister, Ernest Marples of later Transport Ministry fame, approached the task with great enthusiasm, fighting off the Chancellor's attempt to freeze the house-building total (Jones, 1992 and Seldon, 1981). We have already seen that to achieve the target the size and standards of houses were reduced and few if any social amenities accompanied this building. The whole thing was approached like a wartime campaign driven from the centre, using local authorities to do the building. In January 1954 the total was reached a year ahead of target. It was a great electoral success, rather akin to the Conservatives' sale of council houses in the 1980s.

After the boost in council building had delivered the target the government turned to its promised relaxation in controls on private building. Building licences still existed but instead of private builders getting only a quarter of the total they were to get half in England and Wales, less in Scotland. There were plans to encourage the sale of council houses but they were dropped and not taken up again until 1960.

The clearest break with the policies of the 1945–50 period came with the publication of the White Paper on the future of housing policy and its subsequent implementation over the next four years (Ministry of Housing and Local Government, 1953). Its origins lie in the work done in opposition. It said that local authorities' true role, once the shortages caused by the war were over, should be a residual one. They should clear and replace unfit, or slum property. Private landlords should be the normal suppliers of rented property and hence rents would have to rise.

Controlled rents would have to be revised, council rents raised and a free market introduced in stages.

The first step in that direction was taken in the Repairs and Rents Act of 1954, which enabled landlords to charge more rent if they kept their houses in good repair and had recently spent a given sum on repairs. This only tested the water, however, and after the 1955 election was safely won the government embarked on what it knew would be probably its most unpopular social policy: phasing out rent control altogether. It went hand in hand with the phasing out of the general subsidy to local councils to build accommodation to rent. Private landlords would have no reason to continue in the market if local councils were renting property at subsidized rents.

Rent Act 1957 This was to be the most contentious and bitterly fought legislation of the period. The government's logic was sound. If a free market in housing was desirable and its long-term aim, private landlords had to be able to charge rents that would give them an adequate return. Rents had been controlled at the outbreak of war and not increased again. Landlords had to be able to charge a free market rent. There had to be a free contract between buyer and seller. Landlords should have the right to let to whom they wished for what period they wished, otherwise they would be afraid to put their property on the market for fear that the tenant would become a permanent fixture. That was precisely the position many landlords were in. The number of privately rented properties was already declining and would continue unless controls were ended. The main provisions of the Act were:

- Property valued at over £30 rateable value (£40 in London) was decontrolled; landlords could charge what they could get.
- All new tenancies would also be decontrolled, i.e. when someone moved.
- Where tenants' rent remained controlled it would still rise to twice the then rateable value. Rates had been revalued in 1956.
- The minister was given power to decontrol property at any time with the consent of Parliament.

The bill and the eventual Act provoked an enormous outcry. At this time there were about 6 million private landlord dwellings, mostly let to poor people. Controlled rents rose in London from 14*s.* (70p) a week to 22*s.* 4*d.*

between 1957 and 1959. Outside London they rose from 9s. 4d. to 13s. 1d. (Cmnd 1246, 1960). This was not people's only or main criticism. The potential loss of security of tenure was the most worrying for many. That threat was all the greater because of the reserve power the government had taken to decontrol more property without further legislation.

So great was the outcry and the perceived electoral effect that the government backed down on two occasions. The full effects of decontrol above the valuation limits was delayed for three years by the Landlord and Tenant (Temporary provisions) Act 1958. Eviction powers were weakened. Then in their 1959 election manifesto the Conservative Party promised not to use the powers to decontrol further in the next Parliament.

In many parts of the country without a grave housing shortage the issue subsided somewhat. But in London, especially, it would not go away. There had been a flaw in the legislation. Landlords could charge much higher rents for decontrolled property in an area like London. Property became decontrolled when a tenant, or tenant family, moved. If they could be induced to move the owner would reap a large capital gain as the property rose in value to reflect its new rental income. There was a very substantial incentive for landlords to get rid of old tenants. The most unscrupulous did so by terrorizing their tenants. The most notable cases were in London. For some time this aroused little press attention. Then towards the end of the period when Macmillan was Prime Minister a scandal broke involving the Minister of War and a call-girl racket, which also implicated the most notorious of the landlord evictors, Rachman. He was to introduce a new word into the English language, 'Rachmanism'. This finally did attract press attention. A committee of enquiry – the Milner Holland Enquiry – was appointed to investigate and was sitting when the 1964 election took place.

Decontrol: did it work?   One way to see rent policy in this period is a government courageously applying a painful but necessary cure. There is a good deal of truth in this view. If a private rented market was necessary there had to be some break with unprofitable rents that were at pre-war levels. The Labour Party rejected the need for private landlords and argued for the almost complete take-over of all rented property by local councils. In retrospect one can see how disastrous that monopoly land-lordism would have been. The idea of expanding housing associations as alternative social landlords does not seem to have been seriously discussed. The Conservative Party favoured a completely free housing market, the Labour Party a nationalized or 'municipalized' one. Little consensus here!

The difficulty was that the Rent Act did not succeed in reviving the private landlord and it failed politically. In 1953 there had been nearly 6 million private landlord dwellings in England and Wales. By 1961 the figure was 4.5 million and by 1971 the figure was 3.3 million.

There were several difficulties with the government's logic, not least that it did not go far enough. The private landlord was not only disadvantaged because of rent control, he was also disadvantaged by the tax laws compared to other forms if investment (Nevitt, 1966). This was to be made worse during this period. Owner occupiers had originally been fairly unimportant in tax affairs. They were treated as if they were landlords of their own property and hence drawing a rent on it. They benefited by not paying rent to a landlord. Low as the tax was, owner occupiers thought the whole thing crazy.

In 1963 the Chancellor gave in. The tax on owner occupiers was abolished but they continued to get tax relief on the money they borrowed. When tax relief on other kinds of interest payments was abolished they continued to get tax relief on their mortgages. As a party seeking to encourage owner occupation all this made sense. As a party in favour of encouraging the private landlord it did not. The capital gains to be made by a landlord selling his property to an owner occupier became irresistible. In the 1950s and 1960s alone, something like 2 million private landlord properties were sold to owner occupiers (Holmans, 1987).

The government also miscalculated the degree of resistance there would be to the loss of security of tenure, an ancient right in British law. It also made eviction attractive in areas of housing shortage such as London. Thus, in the run-up to the 1964 election, rent policy, and especially security of tenure, were still lively political issues.

Health service reform 1950s style

The Conservative government approached the service with great circumspection. It had acquired great popularity. (For an account of the period see Jones, 1992 and Webster, 1988, ch. VI). Crookshank, the new minister, was however not particularly interested in the Health Service. He was more concerned with broad economic matters. In the autumn came the normal discussions on next year's estimates and Butler wanted to hold the line on more public expenditure. As we have already seen a series of proposals were discussed between officials and the Treasury: imposing a charge of a shilling (5p) on each prescription, a boarding charge for being in hospital, a £1 charge for dental treatment and the complete abolition of the ophthalmic service. The ministry officials managed to get the Treasury to drop the boarding charge but the rest went to Cabinet. The proposals were too much for them, with the exception of prescription charges, where the Labour Party was on weak ground having approved them in principle before it left office. However, backbench Conservatives were furious that a tougher and more strategic approach was not being taken against health service spending (Jones, 1992).

The revenue from the charges was soon to be eaten up. The Labour government had agreed to the external adjudication of the doctors' claim for a pay increase and Judge Danckwert's award came after the Conservatives had been elected. It essentially accepted the BMA case and cost nearly £10 million. Coming on top of the prescription charges this was not a good start for the Conservative government.

Crookshank left, not missed as a minister, and Iain Macleod, the backroom boy of the 1940s, and goad from the backbenches in his first year as an MP, took over as Minister of Health in 1952. He presided over what Webster has called 'a new stability' (1988: 200), which lasted far beyond his period in office. Webster puts this down to Macleod's 'One Nation' views. Jones (1992) has another emphasis. She argues that Macleod did want change – his work in opposition suggested that – but he was cautious because he knew he was dealing with political dynamite. The Conservative backbenchers were calling for a Royal Commission on the NHS. His battle with the Chancellor over more cuts in the hospital building programme, which he lost, together with the cost of the Danckwert's award probably convinced him that something had to be done about the finance of the Health Service.

The Treasury pressed for an independent enquiry into the cost of the NHS. Macleod wanted it to cover the whole of social service spending. Butler resisted, arguing that this would look as if the Conservatives were attacking the whole Welfare State. The outcome was the Guillebaud Committee, an independent enquiry into the cost and finance of the NHS. Guillebaud was a Cambridge economist. He was chosen, over safer political nominees, because he could be claimed to be genuinely impartial. So it turned out.

The decision to appoint the committee proved a strategic blunder for those who wanted radical change in the NHS. (Perhaps this is why Mrs Thatcher firmly rejected such an independent committee in 1987.) The Ministry of Health warned at the outset that it might backfire: 'Treasury are here playing with fire and are liable to get very badly burned' (Ministry internal note quoted by Webster, 1988: 204). Indeed, the ministry was aware that needs were outrunning the supply of services and that the service was very tightly resourced compared with 1948 or even the pre-war years. Impartial observers would be convinced of this.

The committee asked the National Institute for Economic and Social Research to undertake the technical work for it. It was very dependent on the institute's findings for its own view of the economic problem.

> This investigation was undertaken by Brian Abel-Smith, a young Cambridge economist, using Professor R. M. Titmuss as a consultant. Their contact with the Guillebaud Committee was minimal, but their memorandum first read by Guillebaud in January 1955, was fundamental to setting the tone of the Guillebaud Report, and in its separately published form the elegant work of Abel-Smith and Titmuss overshadowed the pedestrian Report, and achieved stature as a minor classic of modern social analysis. (Webster, 1988: 207)

What Abel-Smith and Titmuss showed was that the cost of the NHS to public funds as a percentage of the GNP had *fallen* since its inception in 1948 (from 3.75 per cent to 3.25 per cent). Capital expenditure on new and improved hospitals had fared worst. It had been *three times as high* in the pre-war period before the NHS existed. Capital spending had declined compared to current spending and even to keep up with depreciation and maintain the capital stock would require higher spending. The committee recommended a capital programme of £20–30 million. The ministry had been proved right. Not only did the report endorse the view that there was no evidence of waste and extravagance, the repeated claim of backbench Conservatives, but it also argued that charges might be acting as a deterrent to use:

> It seems to us that the charge for dental treatment is impeding a number of people from making use of the general dental service.

> It seems to us that the level of charge for spectacles is such as to constitute
> a barrier to a proportion of the people who need to make use of the service.

The government was deeply depressed by the report. It had put off doing anything fundamental about the NHS while waiting for it. Now the report said, do not do anything; the NHS is cheap and good value for money. It does not need structural change. What it does need is more money spent on it, especially on its outdated hospitals. Conservative backbenchers were furious ('Now our hands are very largely tied' (Jones, 1992: 328)) and the Conservative Party Research Department was critical. The government was stuck with the NHS, for the time being. This did not stop further economies being demanded in the new economic crisis of 1956.

Another independent committee was appointed to investigate the cost of prescribing. It was equally unhelpful:

> We consider the present charge is a tax which stimulates avoiding action
> and is resented by patients and doctors as a tax on illness . . . we conclude
> that besides stimulating the wrong incentives, the charge per prescription
> has proved disappointing financially. (Hinchliffe Committee, 1959)

Come the next economic crisis, though, in 1961, prescription charges went up again.

The Guillebaud Committee did, however, produce results. The ministry, with the backing of this independent review, and a campaign by the Opposition for the 1959 election – 'no new hospital built since the war' – was able to convince the Cabinet to begin to institute a major hospital building programme. It was announced by Enoch Powell, the Minister of Health, in 1961. The district general hospitals that we now see all over the country mostly date from plans begun at this time.

The chance fundamentally to change the NHS had gone for a generation.

Beveridge abandoned

The Conservatives had been as critical of Beveridge as they had been of Bevan's National Health Service and wanted to make changes that would target benefits on the poor and move away from the universality they deplored in Beveridge's plan. That universalism was really a myth, and was basically flawed (Lowe, 1993; 1994), but the aspiration to move to adequate flat rate benefits for all remained both in the popular consciousness and in Labour's pantheon of ideals. National Assistance, on this model, was only a temporary necessity for all but those on the fringe of society. The Labour Party did not know how it was ever going to implement this ideal and struggled through the 1950s to find a way of achieving it. It was important for the new government to distance itself from the ideal altogether. The problem was, how to do it without rejecting Beveridge, whose report still had the status of a biblical text?

It adopted a similar strategy to that used in the case of Guillebaud: appoint a committee to give external legitimacy to the rethinking. This time, however, the government did not make the mistake of appointing someone whose views it could not predict. Phillips, who had undertaken the critical official review of the Beveridge Report in the war, was asked to chair the committee. His report said what the government hoped it would. The attempt to provide all pensioners with a basic pension that was adequate to live on, regardless of their means, was 'an extravagant use of the community's resources' (Cmd 9333, 1954, para. 212). At the end of 1954 the government officially accepted this view and with it rejected the Beveridge Report, even as an ultimate goal. National Assistance was destined to become not a gradually declining bureaucracy, but a growing one. In the years between 1951 and 1963 the numbers on National Assistance were to rise from 1 million to 1.5 million.

In the big review of public spending we discussed earlier social security came under considerable scrutiny. The Treasury was determined to stop a growing contribution to the National Insurance Fund coming from general taxation. This was necessary if the finance of the scheme was to be sustained. Without it higher burdens would be put on the low paid if the flat rate contribution was raised. So benefits could be frozen, but that was then thought unacceptable; alternatively ways could be found of raising contributions that would not fall on the low paid. Other countries, notably Germany and Sweden, were developing wage-related schemes, with the higher paid paying higher contributions for higher benefits. The Labour Party was conveniently exploring the same idea. What the government proposed to do was to add on to the basic scheme an income-related additional contribution which would earn pensioners, eventually, a higher pension – in practice a very small one. The scheme had the great virtue that the revenue came in long before any pensions had to be paid. The whole was more a form of revenue raising than a pension scheme.

People could opt out of it if they had an occupational pension scheme, much against the wishes of the Treasury (Lowe, 1993: 143)! Nevertheless, what had been agreed was a way of increasing the funding of the scheme while not cutting present benefits, a result that contrasts with what happened in the 1980s.

As the 1959 and then the 1964 elections approached the Conservative government felt obliged to counter Labour accusations – that the old were slipping further into poverty – by increasing basic pensions. The result was that by 1963 the retirement pension and other benefits for a married couple stood at a higher percentage of average earnings than they had in 1948 (33.7 per cent compared with 30.5 per cent), though sickness, unemployment and National Assistance benefits were still lower in relation to average earnings than in 1938!

Even so, the Conservatives had essentially maintained and slightly improved on the social security benefits of 1948, funding them more from contributions than had been planned. This trend was to continue. They also officially abandoned any pretence that the social security scheme was designed to meet a person's needs without supplementation by a means-tested addition, if all that individual had to live on was the state pension or other benefit. In terms of their 1940s agenda this was not bad going. But the Conservative Party did not approach the 1964 election with any more radical proposals for the 1960s. It was not prepared to means test all benefits or to propose anything radical. The Labour Party seemed, now, to have all the good ideas.

Educational expansion comes

More kids   The sheer demography of the rising child population drove much of education policy during this period. Those born in the 'bulge' years after the war began to enter primary school in the early 1950s, the secondary schools in the late 1950s and to knock on the doors of colleges in the 1960s. Class sizes were already well above what most educational-ists and parents considered acceptable. Classes of more than 40 in primary school were common. Winning extra resources to accommodate these numbers became a major preoccupation. On top of that, however, the 1944 Education Act had required the separation of primary and secondary schools, the abolition of all-age schools. That had not yet been accomplished. Nor had a school-leaving age of 16.

New kinds of job   The social and economic structure of the country was changing and young people's expectations were rising. Job opportunities for graduates were beginning to expand, and many servicemen had been given university places on leaving the armed forces after the war. Staying on at school and going to university was no longer an outlandish ambition. If the rhetoric of equal opportunity meant anything, it meant that if you could pass your exams you should be able to go to college.

The structure of secondary education also reflected a job market that was passing. Once, a small select group in the population would go into the professions and into a few clerking jobs. The rest would go into manual occupations, and the lucky ones would get apprenticeships at 16. That kind of labour market was changing, if slowly at first. It became more and more obvious as the sixties began that that was the world of the past.

These social and economic changes explain why education gained increasing political attention as the 1950s advanced but the new Conservative government began by needing economy, and as we saw earlier, education bore a large part of these cuts. They went down very badly in political terms. The feeling was that Florence Horsborough, the Minister of Education, had not handled the situation as well as she could have done, but there was probably as much male chauvinism in this as substance. It is an indication of the low priority given to education that Horsborough was not in the Cabinet, though personal dislike by Churchill played its part. The housing programme had been given top priority and there was little left for schools, despite the 250,000 extra pupils and the new housing estates being built where no schools existed.

Pressure for change   The first really politically damaging attack came from a House of Commons committee on which the Conservatives had a majority, the Select Committee on Estimates. The committee, in collecting evidence on the way public money for school building was being used had 'confronted overcrowding, lack of schools, heavy transport costs, a shortage of teachers and often rapidly deteriorating and even dangerous school buildings' (Eighth Report of the Select Committee on Estimates, 1952/3 para. 8; quoted in Jones, 1992).

The limits on school building were eased slightly in 1954 and this was the first wedge in what was to become strong external leverage to raise education spending, supported by a new and strong education minister, Sir David Eccles. Buildings were only a small part of the story. The regulations passed after the 1944 Education Act had set what were meant to be maximum sizes for classes in primary and secondary schools. These limits were 40 for primary classes and 30 for secondary ones. In the early 1950s over 40 per cent of primary pupils and nearly 60 per cent of secondary pupils were in oversized classes. These became the main focus of opposition, teacher and local authority attack and advice by the minister's own Advisory Committee on the Training and Supply of Teachers. Gradually more teachers were trained and oversized classes in primary schools began to fall. The proportion of secondary classes over 30, however, remained little changed up until the early 1960s. By the mid-1950s the scientific threat from Russia and general fears about Britain's poor technological performance began to make technical education an issue, largely ignored as it had been in the 1940s.

Technical education   A study purported to show that while Britain was producing 57 engineering graduates per million population, Russia was producing 280. Russia was also producing three times as many technicians per head of population. This greatly exercised Churchill, for the first time interested in education, and Eccles was able to turn it to his advantage. A White Paper on technical education followed in 1956, with the following results:

- A building programme for technical colleges began.
- Sandwich courses were introduced so that students could spend part of their time during their courses in industry.
- A 75 per cent grant was given to colleges to put on advanced technical courses.
- Eight of these colleges became Colleges of Advanced Technology in 1957, financed directly from central government.
- The National Council for Technological Awards was created.

A creative promotional ministry   The Ministry of Education learned that by mobilizing influential outsiders in criticizing the service for which you were responsible you could gather public and political support in Cabinet and win battles with the Treasury. The 1944 Act laid a duty on the minister to appoint an advisory committee to watch over the service. Through the 1950s and early 1960s the Ministry of Education made brilliant use of this machinery to focus attention on different parts of the service one by one. The reports by educationalists and interested lay people could be relied on to see deficiencies and call for more to be spent. A sequence of such reports, backed by increasingly sophisticated social science research thumped on ministers' and journalists' desks in the 1950s and 1960s and made the case for a better education system. They included:

- *Early Leaving* (Ministry of Education, 1954), which drew attention to the high proportion of able children leaving school at 15 and recommended a more generous system of grants;
- the Crowther Report, *15–18*, (Ministry of Education, 1959), which recommended an expansion of post-school education and the raising of the school leaving age to 16;
- the Newsom Report, *Half Our Future* (Ministry of Education, 1963), which called for improvements in secondary modern schools, especially in the poorest areas of cities;
- the Plowden Report, *Children and their Primary Schools* (Department of Education and Science, 1967), which favoured the more relaxed teaching methods in primary schools, called for extra resources for schools in poor areas and an expansion in pre-school provision for all who wanted it.

Alongside these advisory committee reports was a one-off report, the most influential of them all, on higher education: the Robbins Report (1963).

Although it is difficult to remember at this distance there was considerable opposition to the expansion of universities by those who taught in them, as well as by the Treasury who directly financed universities at this point through an intermediary body called the University Grants Committee. Yet increasing numbers of young people were gaining the qualifications necessary to gain a place in university and higher education more broadly. More were staying on into sixth forms and soon, as the sixties approached, the birth-rate-bulge boomers would come to be of student age. The Treasury increased grants to universities a little but by nothing like enough to meet the increasing demand. Increasing numbers of qualified school leavers, mostly from middle-class Conservative-voting homes, were failing to get places. Both the Treasury and the academics had to be convinced there were indeed enough able young people to justify expansion without reducing standards and that the whole thing was economically viable. A committee under the then Professor Robbins, a Conservative of considerable standing, made the case with a wealth of social statistics that became a classic of its time.

The education years   The mid-fifties to the end of the sixties was the time when education came into its own, much to many traditional politicians' surprise. This was a period in which the rising expectations of a much larger population of young people and the demands of a changing and expanding economy for their services combined to force education on to the political agenda as never before. In 1950 education had taken only just over 3 per cent of the GNP. By 1964 it was taking about 5 per cent, a figure not very different from its share in 1990. The big push came in the 1950s and early 1960s.

Rumbling through the period was a growing issue about the eleven-plus and comprehensive education, which we shall cover in the next chapter but it, too, reflected the deep social changes that were going on in the 1950s.

Conservative Achievements

These were far from wasted thirteen years. Controls and food rationing were gone and all but forgotten. A property-owning democracy was beginning to take shape. The destructive rent controls were partially eroded. Education had been expanded. The system of social security had been to a certain extent targeted and means tested. The new Conservative agenda worked out in the late 1940s had begun to be delivered. But the Welfare State was not costing less. In fact, it was all costing a lot more than it had in 1951. The Treasury had been seriously defeated more than once. Attempts to cut back, or fundamentally change, the services had run into much stronger opposition than Conservatives had foreseen. That is the true lesson of the 1950s. People wanted lower taxes but they did not want their services reduced either.

5 Completing the Post-war Agenda 1964–76, Part One: the Poor and the Poorest

An Old Agenda

The new Labour government that was elected in October 1964 came to power with a manifesto packed with social policy commitments, yet they were mostly extensions of the agenda the old 1945 government had left unfinished. The framework of ideas that was driving the 1964 government's social policies can be traced back in a fairly unbroken line to the 1920s and 1930s. Tawney would have recognized the debates about equal access to secondary education, the public schools and higher education. Beveridge would have recognized the issues in the social security debate even if he did not agree with the proposals.

Secondary education for all, achieving an adequate universal insurance benefit system, using local authorities as mass providers of housing – all this would have been familiar to the Labour politicians of the 1940s. Indeed, most of the leading figures in Wilson's administration had been young MPs in the Attlee period. Wilson himself had been a minister.

The legislative agenda of the 1964 government was interrupted by the Labour Party losing office in 1970. When the Labour Party returned to power again, early in 1974, it picked up almost where it had left off in 1970 for its first two years. Earnings-related pensions and child benefit finished off legislation that was in the pipeline in 1970.

The intervening Conservative government – 1970–4 under Mr Heath – was in power too short a time to reverse the tide. Indeed many of the Labour government's policies were merely taken forward by the Heath administration. Where they were reversed, as in the case of pensions, the legislation was repealed in 1974.

The really decisive break in the history of traditional social policy comes in 1976. Economic crisis forced new priorities on the Labour government and changed its thinking. Mrs Thatcher's election to the leadership of the Conservative Party in opposition in 1975 produced a sea change in the Conservative approach to policy.

These next two chapters therefore take the story up to 1976, the high tide of post-war welfare ideology. Some history books on the post-war period date the 'retreat from collectivism' much earlier, from 1948 or 1961 (Morgan. 1992). In social policy this will not do. Not only was the legislative agenda of the 1960s an intellectual extension of the 1940s but the expansion of social spending as a share of the national income continued to rise in a steadily steeper curve until 1976 (see Figure 5.1).

What is New?

Nevertheless, it would be wrong to portray the 1960s and early 1970s merely as a sequel to the 1940s, for the following reasons:

- First, social policy was even more central to the Labour Party's ideology in the 1960s than it had been in the 1940s. The Labour Party in the 1930s and 1940s put public ownership, full employment and anti-colonialism high on its list of concerns. By the 1960s economic prosperity and social policy were central for both parties. The politics of the 1960s *was* social politics.
- Second, the emphasis of Labour policy began to shift to a greater concern with equality in society rather than merely equality of access to state services.
- Third, a new social policy agenda was emerging, outside the normal range of party politics. It questioned the state's right to interfere in matters of personal concern: sexual relations between consenting couples of whatever sexual persuasion, the state's regulation of marriage and divorce, of women's right to abort a birth, the state's right to take

Figure 5.1 Welfare spending in Great Britain, 1900 to 1993

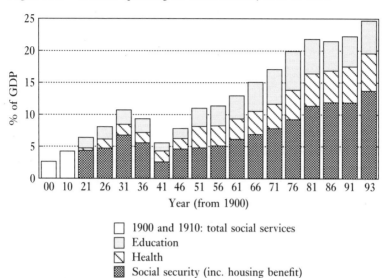

Source: Hills 1993 updated, Peacock and Wiseman 1961, for 1900 and 1910

life and its right to censor what people read. All these were challenges to paternalist and authoritarian state power. The fact that these ideas were associated with the left in politics and not the right tells us something about the peculiar mix of ideology that goes to make up Britain's political parties.

* Cross-party, single-issue groups emerged as powerful change agents. The Child Poverty Action Group was one. The most successful was the campaign to abolish capital punishment, which attracted large, growing and emotional audiences in the early 1960s. Homosexual law reform, abortion law reform and changes to the divorce laws were much debated in the run-up to the 1964 election. Though the Labour Party had shied away from committing itself, many individual MPs in the new Parliament felt strongly on these issues, especially the younger ones.

* Finally, immigration, race relations and the problems of the 'inner city' pushed themselves into political debate in the aftermath of the rapid

rise, from a very low base, in West Indian and then Asian immigration, which had begun in the late 1950s.

Thus the old politics of social policy began to give way to the new in the 1960s. We discuss this important period in the next three chapters. We begin with the battle of ideas that gripped the Labour Party in the 1950s and laid the foundation for its policy in this period.

Social Policy Moves Centre Stage

There had been a battle fought out over the Labour Party's soul in the 1950s, during its period in opposition. Social policy had been an important part of that battle.

The Labour Party has always been a broad coalition. The Labour government of 1945 to 1951 had forged a compromise between those in the party who saw socialism as being primarily about the extension of public ownership to most of the economy and those who saw its role as primarily concerned with social issues.

The 1945 government had taken forward both agendas. Were they to be equally pursued in the 1950s? Many in the party saw the social policy reforms of the 1940s as a distraction to its main purpose. The key changes brought about by the Attlee government had been the public ownership of the basic industries and they were only a beginning. As Barker puts it,

> However, it is not inappropriate that the post-war Labour administrations should be seen in the first place as the creators of massive public ownership. Nationalisation was the most characteristic single feature of Labour policy and it provided the fold within which, under MacDonald and his successors, the socialist lion, the trade union sheep, and the starry eyed child of liberal idealism had lain down together . . . By 1951 it was clear that a wholly new debate was beginning within the party, and a wholly new statement of its character was needed. (Barker, 1972: 82)

The central question was to become, was the Labour Party mainly concerned with extending public ownership or with attacking inequality through social policy? The debate was reflected in *The New Fabian Essays*, edited by Richard Crossman in 1952, and in the columns of *Tribune* and later the *New Left Review*. G. D. H. Cole (1957) in his last years was to argue, without much success, that the Labour Party should concentrate on democratizing industry, giving workers a greater say in the workplace. The old and the new left insisted that the Labour Party return to its fundamental battle with capitalism. The Welfare State had changed nothing. The alternative view was that the economy had been fundamentally changed by the capacity of government to regulate the macro-economy and by the creation of a Welfare State. Improving the quality and variety of people's lives should now be Labour's goal. In that pursuit social policy would play a central role.

The contribution of social science

Concern with social policy issues had already been growing in the later part of the 1940s, as we saw in Chapter 3. Some thinking politicians' interest was aroused by the first fruits and then a growing harvest of social science research which began to show that the supposedly perfect Welfare State institutions the party had been so proud of creating, were flawed. Jean Floud and Chelly Halsey, young sociologists working at the London School of Economics, were able to show continuing and substantial class differences in access to the new grammar schools. The examination taken at the age of 10 to determine which schoolchildren should attend was proving increasingly unpopular. A day's examination could decide a child's future. I can still vividly remember setting off, clutching a pencil and ruler for that day's exams in early 1946, and failing. The process seemed brutal and unfair to many parents, especially middle-class and aspiring working-class ones. Social scientists put flesh on this disgruntlement.

Hertfordshire tried to mollify parents by introducing a system of teachers' reports on a child's work and interviews spread over a longer period as a basis for the eleven-plus. This only worsened working-class children's prospects of entering grammar school. In 1954, in south-west Hertfordshire, 64 per cent of professional and managerial parents' children were going on to grammar school but only 12 per cent of manual working-class children (Floud and Halsey, 1957).

Yet the 36 per cent of middle-class parents whose children failed were also unhappy. They could not pay for a place in a grammar school any more and were deeply unhappy about sending their children to secondary

modern schools. Expensive private school places were the only alternative. Equal secondary education for all was turning out to be a myth and
the predictions made by some of those civil servants in the Board of
Education during the war were turning out to be true.

Other social scientists were uncovering extensive poverty amongst the
elderly, questioning established measures of poverty and the adequacy of
the levels of social support the new benefits system was providing (Abel-
Smith and Townsend, 1955; Townsend, 1954a, 1954b, 1957). Titmuss
was the first Professor of Social Administration at the LSE and an inspiration to this group. He had been the official war historian of social
policy, working in the Cabinet Office during the Second World War and
he wrote what is still the definitive account of social policy during the war
(Titmuss, 1950). The experience convinced Titmuss that universal social
institutions that met the needs of the whole population were the only way
in which a modern nation-state could be held together as an organic
whole (Titmuss, 1958). The forces of a modern market economy would
tear apart any allegiance individuals might have to some larger identity be
it family, neighbourhood or the state itself. In war a common external
threat might awaken a sense of altruism and allegiance (Titmuss, 1950);
in peace only institutions that fostered such altruism and solidarity could
achieve this sense of shared identity (Titmuss, 1972). Without it the
institutions of the market-place would collapse too because they depended on some acceptance of the rules of social order. Without a sense
of social solidarity the free political institutions would lose their legitimacy.

One unusual Labour politician, formerly an Oxford don, was Anthony
Crosland, who read not only this material but the new sociology coming
out of the United States and the new economics of industry. It was
uncommon for a politician to read social science so avidly. He was to
produce a seminal book, *The Future of Socialism* (1956), which influenced
a generation of young people just entering politics, journalism and the
academic profession (Lipsey and Leonard, 1981). He was very close to
the new Leader of the Labour Party who succeeded Attlee, Hugh Gaitskell.
What Crosland did in this closely argued book was to reject the claims of
the Marxist left that economic prosperity and social change depended
on transforming the ownership structure of industry. Macro-economic
planning could ensure full employment and the new large private corporations were capable of delivering economic growth. Further public
ownership was pointless. What socialists *ought* to be worried about was

the quality of life individuals could lead, the respect that was accorded to them and the opportunities they had to develop their potential. Education played an important part in achieving these goals.

A bitter battle followed Gaitskell's leadership and his attempt to get the Labour Party to abandon that part of its constitution that proclaimed its belief in public or common ownership. He failed, but to a very large extent the main thrust of Crosland's case was accepted. Social policy became the main element in the new Labour Party's detailed agenda.

Rethinking policy

Working parties and policy subgroups of the party's National Executive Committee were set up with sympathetic academics on them. Detailed policy proposals were produced on education, pensions and social security, housing and social and youth services. Social policy was now moving centre stage. It was given another push by another influential book, this time written by an American, John Kenneth Galbraith, called *The Affluent Society*. In it Galbraith coined the phrase 'private affluence and public squalor'. It had the attraction of offering a structuralist critique of modern capitalism which Crosland had not and it appealed to the non-Marxist left. In a vivid passage Galbraith describes an American family setting out for a picnic:

> The family which takes its mauve and cerise, air conditioned, power-steered, and power-braked car out for a tour passes through cities that are badly paved, made hideous by litter, blighted buildings, billboards, and posts for wires that should long since have been put underground. They pass into a countryside that has been made largely invisible by commercial art . . . They picnic on exquisitely packaged food from a portable icebox by a polluted stream and go on to spend the night at a park which is a menace to public health and morals. Before dozing off on an air mattress beneath a nylon tent amid the stench of decaying refuse, they may reflect vaguely on the unevenness of their blessings. (1958: 207–8)

This passage appears in a chapter introduced with a quotation from Tawney.

The message was that public expenditure on the environment and social goods was being neglected while private consumption was running to excess. While that vision of the United States may have carried credence, the latter stages of the Macmillan administration had seen a rapid growth in public spending to which Galbraith's admonitions scarcely applied, at least not to the same extent as in America. Nevertheless, it struck a chord with both left and right in the party and provided a binding theme that underpinned the new Labour Party programme entitled *Signposts for the Sixties* (Labour Party, 1961).

The contribution of demography

Ideas do not germinate in a vacuum. Demography was providing a fertile ground for this new concern with education and pensions. The number of families with young and teenage children in school, coming up to the age at which they might wish to go to university, was rising fast. The number of elderly was rising too. In 1941 the number of young people under school age plus the number over retirement age had been smaller than 50 per cent of the total working population. By the mid-1960s the percentage had risen well beyond 60 per cent and was continuing to rise. The United Kingdom was to experience the impact of a more dependent population, young and old, earlier and on a larger scale than other advanced economies. The political constituency for social policy was thereby created.

The weak link

Despite the growing interest in social policy the economy remained *the* focus of much everyday political debate and Harold Wilson's point of attack. He criticized the stop-go cycles of the 1950s and the country's poor growth record. Though, to the reader from the 1990s, an underlying growth of 2.5 per cent, single figure inflation and unemployment in the 1–2 per cent range looks rather good, other countries' growth rates in Europe had been more than double that and Britain's standard of living was being rapidly overtaken by her neighbours. Wilson, the Labour leader who took over when Gaitskell died in 1963, was an economist and particularly effective in criticizing this *relatively* poor performance. He, unlike his predecessor, believed in a strong state role in industry and the economy, encouraging new technology and planning for growth. He managed to capture popular and technocrats' support for this emphasis (Pimlott, 1992). Yet it was a rhetoric based on little or no policy substance.

The result was that the new Labour government came to power in 1964 with a detailed social programme and a presumption that the country's growth rate could be boosted to levels nearer our continental rivals to pay for this programme. It was to be done through the mechanism of something called 'economic planning'. No one could adequately articulate what that meant, except by producing paper plans that would try to convince companies that faster growth was possible. None of the real underlying constraints on growth, notably Britain's poor export performance, was addressed. Therein lay the reason for the disappointments of the next six years.

Reforming Beveridge

Ground work in opposition 1955–64

The most detailed policy work done by the Labour Party in its period in opposition had been on reforming Beveridge's flat rate social insurance plan. It had begun with two new lecturers in Titmuss's social policy department at the LSE, Brian Abel-Smith and Peter Townsend, who were convinced that Beveridge had made a major blunder in basing his plan on a flat rate principle. They worked on their ideas and lectured to Fabian groups in London and finally produced a Fabian pamphlet arguing a new basis for social insurance (Abel-Smith and Townsend, 1955).

The case for a change

Abel-Smith and Townsend were drawing on ideas about national pensions schemes that were developing in Germany and Sweden. They accepted that insurance-based contributions should remain as the basis for entitlement to benefit. Where Beveridge had gone wrong, they argued, was in seeking to finance the scheme out of flat rate contributions. Since these imposed a heavy burden on the lowest paid there was a limit to how far they could be raised. This had set an effective ceiling on the levels of pension that could be afforded since the Treasury was reluctant to see the insurance fund further subsidized from general taxation. Higher contributions would have to come from higher earners. If higher contributions were to be acceptable they would have to be seen to earn higher pensions. But *part* of those higher contributions could go to raising the pension floor for those on low earnings.

In principle, moreover, flat rate poverty line benefits were not a good basis for setting pensions. The relative drop in the standard of living suffered by a moderately good earner forced to retire on a low basic pension was that much greater than for a low earner. Occupational pension schemes took this relative deprivation principle into account. What was emerging therefore were 'two nations in retirement' as Titmuss (1958: 74) put it. Occupational pensions were still not within the reach of most people. They tended to tie people to existing jobs. Most ordinary workers in occupational pension schemes were paid very low pensions because private schemes could not guarantee future pensions against rising prices. Most workers who were covered were tied into their firms' pension scheme and they lost pension rights when they moved, often only taking with them their own payments into the scheme.

Beveridge, too, had been deeply suspicious of the irresponsibility of the large private insurance companies that he saw exploiting poor families. However, Beveridge was a strong believer in voluntaristic, trade union or friendly-society-based pension schemes. That is precisely why he had wanted only a low basic state pension.

What Townsend and Abel-Smith and Titmuss wanted was a single national superannuation scheme that would provide for most people what the top company pension schemes offered for their managers. The British pension scheme should move much closer to the continental ones being developed at the time, especially the German and Swedish models. This meant two things: first, linking benefit entitlements to previous earnings and second, not using actual past earnings as the basis for entitlement but increasing future pensions in line with the general improvement in earnings in the economy. In this way pensioners' living standards would keep pace with the rest of the society.

The 1955 Labour Party Conference debated pensions, and a motion called for an increase in the basic pension as usual. Richard Crossman was called on to answer the debate. He knew from Peter Shore, who was working in the Labour Party Research Department and was later its head, that some interesting work was going on at the LSE on these issues

(Ellison, 1988). He called on the Conference to approve the creation of a special study group to consider the future of pensions. A committee on social security and old age was set up and the LSE group of Titmuss, Townsend and Abel-Smith was co-opted. The group went on working for many years.

Right from the outset the idea of wage-related benefits was opposed by representatives of the Trade Union Congress. To them flat rate benefits embodied an egalitarian principle that should not be abandoned. Flat rate pensions should simply be raised. The Titmuss group's response was that raising flat rate contributions to pay for this increase would fall heavily on the poorest and was hardly egalitarian. The Treasury would effectively block any massive subsidy from the Exchequer, so the revenue had to come from higher contributions from the higher paid. If the state scheme went on being such a low benefit one there would be growing inequality between those on state pension and those on occupational pensions. Here was the real inequality.

The new plan

In the end a detailed scheme was agreed that added a wage-related benefit on to Beveridge's old flat rate pension. It would give a combined pension equal to about half the average worker's pay over his lifetime and rather more, proportionately, for the lower paid. Borrowing ideas from Germany, these lifetime earnings would be 'dynamized', that is, increased in line with earnings in the economy at large. Thus a worker who had been on average earnings through his life would retire on a pension equal to half average earnings at the time he retired and the pension would be inflation proofed after he retired.

Richard Crossman, chairman of the subcommittee, drove this plan through with great enthusiasm. A technical appendix setting out how the scheme would all be financed was written by members of the social policy staff at the LSE, 'the skiffle group', as civil servants were to call it (Labour Party, 1957). The problem for the Labour Party was that it would take many years to come to fruition, even when implemented. What were they to offer to existing pensioners?

The Labour Party's scheme was, however, enough to worry the

Conservative government. It legislated a very watered-down version of the scheme in 1959, as we saw in Chapter 4.

An alternative route?

Logically the Labour Party or the Conservative government might have taken a different route to pension reform at this time. They could have responded to the 'two nations' problem of workers excluded from occupational pension rights by legislating that all workers should be members of occupational pension schemes and that their pensions should be transferable between employers. It says something about the climate of ideas at the time that this option was not developed. It was to be, by the Heath Conservative government in 1971 (see p. 112).

Extending the wage related principle

Having settled on a new pensions policy the Labour Party committee went on to extend the principle of wage-related benefits to cover sickness and unemployment benefit too. Here the arguments took on a more economic focus. If unemployment benefit were set much closer to a worker's past pay he or she would be much less resistant to moving jobs and this would increase labour mobility and hence the technological revolution Wilson was so keen to see.

Labour Comes to Power

As we have suggested, the problem with selling these ideas for long-term pension reform to an electorate was that it would take a generation for the new pensions to be payable. The Labour Party executive was under much internal pressure to promise a large immediate increase in the flat rate pension if it won the 1964 election, despite the fact that the Conservatives had already increased pensions in 1963 as part of their attempt to stay in power. The Labour Party did promise a further immediate increase in the flat rate universal pension and honoured the pledge in March 1965 by raising the flat rate pension by 12s. 6d. The government had been elected with a tiny majority and Wilson knew he would have to go to the electorate again soon. He wanted quick results and immediately popular policies.

Between 1948 and 1962 the level of the basic single pension had roughly kept pace with rising male industrial earnings. It had been equivalent to about 19 per cent of average earnings in 1948 and a little less in 1962. By May 1965 the pension had been increased to just over 21 per cent of average male industrial earnings. Though this may seem a far from revolutionary step it cost a great deal of money in a budget already swollen by the commitments of the previous government and during a period of gathering economic crisis. It effectively put the more fundamental reform of pensions on to a back burner until the very end of the Wilson government.

However, the government did press ahead with introducing wage-related unemployment benefits for the reasons outlined above; the rationale fitted into the government's broader economic strategy. If unemployment benefit had to be wage related for economic labour mobility reasons so, too, did sickness benefit. It would be difficult to defend paying workers a higher benefit if they were unemployed than if they were sick. One is struck, rereading the discussions of the day, how completely topsy-turvy and transitory are the arguments used to justify social policies. Twenty years afterwards Mrs Thatcher's government was to abolish these benefits on the grounds that people would only return to work if their benefits were so low that they would have no incentive to remain on benefit. The objective was the same, the means opposite.

Means tests and a supplementary pension

There had been a different subplot to the social security discussions while Labour was in opposition. It was clear to some, as it was clear to me while working in the Labour Party Research Department at the time, that it would never be possible to raise the basic pension far enough to lift great numbers off National Assistance. The new pension scheme would take many years to come to fruition. Much more attention should be paid to making the National Assistance scheme more humane and less stigmatic. This might be done by making the system of income testing a more or less automatic process 'very much like income tax in reverse' (Glennerster, 1962: 33). A system of means-tested supplementary pensions could be created leaving the National Assistance Board to concentrate on the really difficult cases. It was not a message many in the party wanted to hear but the need to do something for existing pensioner voters forced its serious consideration (see below and Hall *et al.*, 1975).

Child poverty

Largely ignored at this time was the whole question of child poverty. Most families were evidently better off. Millions of new council houses had been occupied by families who were able to buy new furniture, televisions and even refrigerators from steadily rising real wages. The Conservative Party was proud of the prosperity the free enterprise economy was producing and the Labour Party was reluctant to concentrate on poor families' plight. They were to a large extent hidden from view. The family allowance, one of the first and most radical innovations of the 1945 government, had been allowed to decay and decline in real value, never having been increased since 1952. The Labour Party ignored the issue. There was not a single mention of family allowances in the speakers' guide for Labour candidates at the 1964 election (Labour Party, 1963a). Its only mention in the 1961 policy document of the party had been in relation to using the allowances to encourage staying on at school. Politicians argued privately that family allowances were deeply unpopular with ordinary Labour voters, who saw them as handouts to the feckless large family.

The best-laid plans

The politician who had most to do with the revised Beveridge plan in opposition, Richard Crossman, was a close colleague of Wilson, the new Prime Minister. He was also an immensely energetic and forceful person who was to be an unusually effective minister. He had been Wilson's campaign manager in his leadership bid. Prime Ministers tend to put such people in what they see to be their key Cabinet posts. Crossman did not end up in social security but in housing.

Social security policy, partly as a result, fell into a quagmire for the next four years. Wilson appointed separate Ministers of Health and Social Security, neither of whom were in the Cabinet, a situation that is barely conceivable in the 1990s. Instead, acting as a kind of overlord for these ministries and social policy overall, was Douglas Houghton, an ex-tax collector and a sceptic about Crossman's social security plans while in opposition. This can only have been deliberate on Wilson's part.

The big gesture was made. A large increase in the basic pension was approved as part of the first Queen's speech, pre-empting resources that might have been devoted to a deeper review. Crossman looked on appalled as he saw what was happening in his old policy territory. At the first annual review of public spending in the Labour period that took place in July 1965, Crossman recorded in his diary a set of comments that were to capture the essence of that early strategic mistake:

> And then we came to Pensions . . . under cross examination they [Herbison and Houghton] got into a horrible mess and confirmed my fear that the whole strategy of our pensioneering, worked out for years before the election, had been jettisoned, almost without noticing it by the Minister under the *diktat* of Douglas Houghton. The basic idea had been that we should switch as soon as possible from flat rate to earnings related contributions and in this way pile up enormous funds in the pensions fund which we could use to dynamise the existing flat rate pension. That was cardinal. However, Douglas and Peggy had turned things upside down, by first of all conceding an enormously increased flat rate pension financed by increased flat rate contributions. The net result is the worst of all worlds as we can't raise the flat rate contributions any higher without imposing an intolerable burden on the lower-paid worker. Even worse, the income guarantee we had pledged ourselves to introduce would now be at an absurdly low level as a result of the money we had wasted on the huge initial increase of the flat rate pension. (1975, Diary entry for 17 July 1965)

Shades of 1946. These factors help explain the relatively meagre legislative outcomes of the 1964–70 government on the social security front. The rumbling economic crisis of the time explains the rest.

Social security legislation 1964–70

The 1965 and 1966 changes included the following elements:

• The flat rate pension and other benefits were increased in March 1965.
• Earnings-related benefits were added to the basic benefits for sickness,

unemployment and widow's benefit. They amounted to a third of previous wages in a band of earnings that took in people well above the average wage. The benefits were only to be paid for six months.

The total benefit was never to rise above 85 per cent of previous earnings. In return all workers paid an additional 0.5 per cent of their earnings in social security contributions. The earnings bands were extended and employers contributed more too after 1969.

- The old Ministry of Pensions and National Insurance was abolished and replaced by the Ministry of Social Security.
- The old National Assistance Board was abolished and replaced by the Supplementary Benefits Commission; it came within the scope of the ministry but was to administer a supplementary pensions scheme and supplementary allowances in a supposedly more humane way.

A new national pension scheme?

All in all this was a modest legislative achievement after the years of work that had gone on in opposition. It might just have been different. In 1968 Wilson had a change of heart. He gave Crossman the job of running a combined super-department taking in both the old Ministries of Health and Social Security; the Department of Health and Social Security (DHSS).

Crossman called back into service the old LSE skiffle group, or most of it, and work that had been underway in the civil service on the National Superannuation scheme moved into top gear. It was a very bad time to be coming up with an expensive scheme, in the aftermath of a massive economic crisis and devaluation. The line Crossman took was reminiscent of that taken by Beveridge. The scheme would come in gradually over twenty years. By phasing in a gradual rise in pensions in line with earnings on a formula basis, the Treasury would be less likely to be faced with recurrent demands to increase pensions. That would not, however, be a line of argument that would appeal to the backbenches on his own side: 'My pension plan is not in fact wildly extravagant but unfortunately we dare not say so' (Crossman, 1977: 137).

Crossman made sure he consulted the CBI and the TUC every inch of the highly complex way and managed to carry them with him. A White Paper incorporating the basic principles, worked out ten years previously in opposition, was produced in January 1969. It had been steered through the Cabinet Social Services Committee with little opposition:

> This afternoon the Social Services Committee met under my Chairmanship and my complete pensions plan went through without any serious questioning except from James Callaghan, who after being Chancellor knew a great deal about it. The rest of the Ministers spent nearly all of their time asking about the effect of the scheme on the pensions of the civil service. It's mainly because Ministers get so ministerial that we have such appallingly ineffective discussion of great social issues. No one looked at the main economic impact of the scheme, its social impact or its effect on women or its effect on trade unions. (Crossman, 1977: 217)

This White Paper came out in the aftermath of a sterling crisis, a devaluation and a massive split in the government over a White Paper on trade union legislation, *In Place of Strife*. The complex legislation went ahead and was passing through Parliament when Wilson decided to call an election, mistakenly convinced by public opinion polls that he could win a snap election. He did not and the bill fell.

Conservatives Reverse Engines 1970

During their period in opposition the Conservatives had begun to take stock and revise their social policies. They were very worried by the new scheme the Labour Party had nearly got on to the statute book. It would have been a continuing and growing drain on the Exchequer in a period the Conservatives were pledged to roll back taxation. It had the potential to build up huge accumulations of funds from workers and use these to invest in private companies. It would offer more generous pensions than the private pension schemes could, especially inflation-proofed pensions, and might threaten the existence of private pension schemes and hence the source of much private capital for industry. The party, therefore, gave high priority to developing an alternative.

When it came to power it asked those civil servants who had spent six years working on Labour's complex scheme to devise another based on almost the opposite principles. Private occupational pension schemes, provided by the workers' own employers, should be the basis for future pensions. If this were simply left to employers there was no reason they would provide such pensions. Why should they not just 'free ride' on the state and expect it to provide means-tested pensions for their workers? If the state wanted to give up, eventually, the basic responsibility to provide adequate pensions for all, the thinking went, it would be necessary to *require* employers to provide adequate company pension schemes. The government would also have to find a way of meeting the objections that critics such as Titmuss had made of occupational pension schemes, notably that they inhibited free movement of labour and gave poor pensions that lost value when inflation occurred. The Conservative government did very quickly legislate part of the previous government's White Paper, i.e. the proposals that had been a response to the new campaign for the disabled and their carers.

The National Insurance (Old Person's and Widow's Pensions and Attendance Allowance) Act 1970 introduced a new benefit, the Attendance Allowance, from December 1971, for people being cared for at home by relatives who needed 'frequent attention throughout the day and prolonged and repeated attention during the night'. The government also followed the previous one in increasing the level of contributions paid by employers towards the costs of social security.

The break with the past and a harbinger of Conservative policies in the 1980s was the new government's pensions White Paper of 1971, *Strategy for Pensions* and the subsequent Social Security Act 1973. The White Paper saw the employer as the main pension provider of the future, not the state.

Flat rate contributions, the principle that had underpinned British pensions from the beginning and had been made into the central plank of Beveridge's scheme, were to go. There was to be a basic pension scheme provided by the state whose level was to be reviewed from year to year. It was fairly clear that this would be gradually eroded in significance. It was to be financed out of *earnings*-related 'contributions'. This was a further departure from the notion that what you paid in contributions was somehow related to your benefit. This was a simple graduated social security tax levied to pay for basic pensions. Employees would pay 5.25 per cent of their earnings up to one and a half times average earnings and employers would pay 7.25 per cent of their employees' earnings over the same income range. Every one would receive the same benefit.

All employees, over 21 and up to retirement age, would either have to be a member of an occupational scheme approved by a government agency, or a member of the government's Reserve Scheme. This was based on essentially the same principles as private schemes, though not threatening them, and it was available if an employee could not join a scheme run by his or her employer. Steps were taken to ensure a degree of transferability between these schemes when a worker changed jobs.

The Act was passed into law but like its Labour predecessor was never to be enacted. The miners' strike and Mr Heath's defeat intervened and one of the first things the new Labour government in 1974 did was to repeal that legislation. Pensions were back on the drawing board.

Labour Tries Again

The same group of civil servants, or some of them, dusted down their 1960s files and began work again. Richard Crossman was by this time dead, but in his place was a close friend – Barbara Castle – advised by one of the architects of the original Labour plans, Brian Abel-Smith. They began to reinstate the old scheme but recognized that it was crucial to try to get broader agreement. Simply reintroducing the Crossman scheme would not carry the Opposition and it might simply get repealed after the next election. It also had to carry the occupational pensions lobby, which included many trade unions; membership of these schemes now covered over half the population.

The resulting White Paper, *Better Pensions*, and the eventual Act, the Social Security Pensions Act 1975, went a long way towards incorporating some of the principles of the previous Conservative legislation and won Conservative support when it was passed. It introduced the State Earnings Related Pension Scheme (SERPS), which began to take effect in April 1978.

Social Security Pensions Act 1975

The main provisions were:

- The pensions paid under the scheme were to build up over the next 20 years, with the full pensions being paid in 1998.
- There were to be earnings-related pensions and contributions. Up to a

'basic amount' of weekly earnings a person was entitled to a pension of the same amount – a 100 per cent replacement rate. This basic amount was equal to the then basic pension and would be increased year on year in line with earnings.

- For the next band of earnings, up to an upper limit, the individual would earn a pension equal to 25p for each additional pound. For those around average earnings this in total meant about half pay.
- Lifetime earnings would be dynamized as in the old plan but the period chosen for this calculation would be the 'twenty best years' of a person's working life. This was done to enable women who were often not in the labour force as long as men to receive pensions related to their shorter paid working lives.
- In another element designed to give more equal treatment, a person who stayed at home to bring up children was to be counted as a contributor to the scheme. The same was true if he or she were in receipt of Attendance Allowance and therefore caring for a elderly relation or a partner, for example.

These elements made the scheme, at this point, the most 'advanced' in the world in terms of equal rights for women and carers. At the same time occupational schemes that could provide equivalent rights could qualify a person to 'contract out' and employees and employers concerned would pay a lower contribution to the state as a result. Guaranteed minimum pensions would have to be transferred to the new job or maintained in some way, and inflation proofed, or the employee would have to be bought back into the state scheme. Thus occupational pension schemes were to be preserved but subject to strict quality control and transferability rules.

The end of the story?

At last, in 1978, just over twenty years since the Labour Party had first published its original *National Superannuation* proposals, legislation implementing something like it took effect. Too late. If implemented in 1965 the scheme might have gathered support from those who were drawing its pensions by the time Mrs Thatcher came to power and the political climate changed. But the delay had been so great that it was barely in operation and the scale of the pension benefits built up so small, that the new Conservative government felt able to propose the whole scheme be scrapped. But that is for the next chapter in the story.

Child Poverty Again

In 1951 Rowntree, whose famous survey of poverty in York at the turn of the century had been so influential, and whose second survey had had so much influence on Beveridge, published his third survey of poverty in York (Rowntree and Lavers, 1951). He used the same standard for poverty as in his previous study and concluded that there had been a remarkable improvement as a result of the coming of the Welfare State and full employment. Almost no one in York was now living below his tough basic primary poverty line and less than 2 per cent of households were living below his rather more generous secondary poverty line. Those who were still poor were almost exclusively old people. Child poverty in working families had essentially disappeared. This view was to colour public perceptions for the next fifteen years.

Rowntree's definitions of poverty were later to be criticized by Townsend and others but they did not come out with dramatically different conclusions for the years of 1953–4 (Abel-Smith and Townsend, 1965). There had indeed been a real improvement in the living standards of poorer families.

Rowntree showed that without the impact of the Labour government's welfare measures, including the introduction of family allowances, a fifth of the working-class households in York would have fallen below the poverty line. That would have made sense to my parents' generation. People carry around with them two very different but equally valid notions of poverty. One is absolute. People in 1950 remembered life in the 1930s and recognized that it *was* better in 1950. Another view is that poverty is a measure of relative disadvantage. Young families might be better off than in the 1930s, but less well off relative to others. The Rowntree study fixed in politicians' heads the idea that poor *young* families were a thing of the past.

Though politicians' and public perceptions were that most families 'had never had it so good', in a phrase that was attributed to the Conservative Prime Minister Harold Macmillan, evidence was beginning to accumulate that many young families with children were not sharing in the general improvements in living standards.

There had been no study of household income levels since 1950, in contrast to the many there had been in the 1930s. Inland Revenue statistics had been analysed and suggested some increase in poverty but they were not a good basis. Evidence of falling standards of nutrition had emerged in a reanalysis of the British Food Survey (Lambert, 1964). Social workers in the field were becoming convinced that poverty faced by young families was growing. The Society of Friends (the Quakers), called a meeting at Toynbee Hall in the East End of London, the university settlement where Beveridge had first learned about poverty at the turn of the century. The meeting was addressed by Brian Abel-Smith, who with colleagues at the LSE was studying new material on trends in poverty since the 1950s. Those there were so distressed by the results that they decided to form an action group (Field, 1982; McCarthy, 1986).

Brian Abel-Smith and Peter Townsend had hit on the idea of using the Family Expenditure Survey to investigate what had happened to families' income over time. The survey was designed to provide the basis for calculating the government's cost of living index. Since the early 1950s it had collected information about a national sample of households, their expenditure, and as a check, their incomes too. It gave the only available source of information on trends in family income over time but it had never been exploited before.

The results were striking. Abel-Smith and Townsend took the National Assistance levels set by the Government as the basis for defining a poverty line. If government set this as a basic minimum income it was legitimate to say that those who fell below it were in poverty. Over the period since 1953 the numbers of families falling below this line had risen and had risen particularly amongst young families with several children.

This way of calculating poverty was to cause considerable controversy. Critics argued that to use the government's own National Assistance scale to define poverty was misleading. If the government chose to increase the National Assistance scale rate it would automatically increase the level of poverty on these measures. Generosity by government would lead to *more* poverty. This was a perfectly valid criticism in theory and later studies of low incomes were to use different methods. In practice, however, the government's basic assistance levels had kept fairly close to increases in earnings in the economy. What Abel-Smith and Townsend were showing was that, compared to the average household, families with children had been falling behind in their living standards and that many families with a low-paid head of household were trying to bring up their children on an income well below that which they would get if that person was unemployed and on benefit.

The two academics played their publicity cards carefully. They arranged to have the results published just before Christmas when the newspapers were looking for human interest stories.

The report, *The Poor and the Poorest*, was to become famous. It did attract a lot of press and television coverage and forced child poverty back on to the political agenda for the first time since the 1940s. So as not to lose the political momentum the action group (see above) was urged to become a national organization. Tony Lynes, Titmuss's research assistant, was appointed to run the central office more or less single handed. The organization was called the Child Poverty Action Group (CPAG).

This was an interesting development in its own right and was to set a precedent for other similar small pressure groups campaigning for particular social groups in the late sixties and seventies: the Disablement Income Group, Shelter and its campaign for the homeless, a revived MIND pressing the rights of the mentally ill, and many others. This constellation of groups came to be called the 'poverty lobby' and took its inspiration from CPAG.

The first fruits of their lobbying was to persuade the government to look again at the level of family allowances. It was not, however, a very propitious time. The economy was running into one of its periodic foreign exchange crises. The economy was not growing as fast as had been hoped and the public expenditure plans were going to have to be cut back before long. To add another major commitment was not going to be easy. The minister, Margaret Herbison, tried with little success to get the Treasury to give her a larger budget to meet the costs of an increase in family allowances. In October 1967 she was given a tiny sop. Family allowances were increased for *fourth* and subsequent children by a small sum equivalent to about 1 per cent of average earnings. The trade-off the Treasury demanded was an increase in the price of school meals and milk. Herbison gave up in despair and resigned. Faced with the difficulty that an across-the-board increase in family allowances cost so much money the Treasury argued that if the government must act on child poverty it should introduce a special new means-tested benefit for working families;

this was the kind of plan that was being discussed in the United States at that very time.

CPAG and its backers were convinced that the stigma and administrative problems that would surround such a scheme would lead to many, perhaps most, of those for whom it was intended never receiving it. Family allowances did reach virtually everyone entitled to them and they reached mothers. CPAG then came up with an ingenious way of targeting the money on the poorest families while keeping family allowances. Let the mothers draw the benefit and tax the extra benefit away from the average taxpayer. The Treasury and the Inland Revenue objected, defeating the idea in 1967, but in the end the Cabinet came to accept it after intense lobbying by the CPAG and, significantly, some trade union leaders. In 1968 family allowances were increased to a level higher than they had been in 1945, in relation to the average pay packet, but the standard rate taxpayer had the increase taxed away. This was the beginning of a new debate about how and whether to target support for poor families that has not been resolved in the 1990s.

The CPAG became so fed up with the government's response and to the fact that it was letting the value of other benefits slip back again that it let off a broadside in the run-up to the election whose catch phrase title was to stick: 'the poor are getting poorer under Labour'. It did have an immediate impact on the Labour Chancellor, who in 1970 concentrated most of his tax cuts on the poor. The attack also endeared the group to the Conservative Party. The group's proposals to increase the level of family allowances and reduce the scale of the tax relief richer families with children got was put to the shadow Tory Chancellor Iain Macleod. Field describes the occasion (Field, 1982: 38–9). Macleod, despite suffering from advanced arthritis, displayed what Field called 'the best political probing mind I ever came across'. Macleod committed the Conservatives to do something about child poverty, and more than that, to implement the CPAG plan.

In fact, when they came to power later that year, the Conservatives did not do so. Macleod had died in July 1970. Instead they took off the stocks the new means-tested benefit for working families the Treasury had tried to persuade the Labour government to introduce. It was enacted in about six months as the Family Income Supplement Act 1970.

This was to be a 'temporary' measure, making the maximum impact from spending a small sum of money. It was targeted on those in work on very low pay and with children. As their incomes rose, however, so these families would lose their benefit. This could encourage families not to raise their incomes and trap them in poverty, critics argued (Field and Piachaud, 1971). It was an argument that was to become a major focus of debate in the 1980s.

What is striking in retrospect, however, is that a government could be so embarrassed by an attack from a small group that was campaigning on behalf of poor families and that the Conservative Party should see this as a cause worth taking up. Far greater child poverty was to occur in the 1980s with little or no political embarrassment or outcry.

The coming of child benefit

While in opposition the Labour Party had time to reflect again on the issue of family allowances and child poverty. It was opposing the means-tested family income supplement, so what would it do instead? It pledged in its 1974 manifesto to go for what Eleanor Rathbone had advocated after the First World War, a benefit for each child. The manifesto did not say how this would be paid for. The Child Benefit Act was duly passed in 1975. By then the oil crisis was hitting the economy and the government put off implementing the scheme. Instead it introduced a benefit targeted on single parents (See Chapter 7).

Barbara Castle, who had been a strong advocate of child benefits and took the bill through the Commons, was removed from the post of Secretary of State for Social Services when Wilson resigned and James Callaghan took over as Prime Minister. He had opposed the move to increase family allowances in the previous government if Margaret Herbison's account is to be trusted. Frank Field, who was closely involved in the events, relates that what happened immediately after Castle lost her post was that the Labour whips began a devious campaign to undermine the government's own statute (Field, 1982: 18). Backbenchers were told the trade unions were against implementing the measure. The trade unions were told the backbenchers were against. The plan was to offset the increase in the cash child benefit by abolishing the tax relief parents got for each child. This relief was worth nothing to poor families and a great deal to rich families. However, it also had the feature that trade unionists were supposed to oppose: the loss of tax relief came off the pay packets of men and the child benefit would go to mothers. The Cabinet discussions on the matter, and this objection among others, were leaked. With a furious Barbara Castle operating from the backbenches (Castle, 1980) and the CPAG lobbying ceaselessly, the Cabinet was shamed into implementing its predecessor's legislation. Child benefit for each child replaced the perversely targeted child tax allowance that Titmuss had attacked thirty years or more earlier.

Balance Sheet So Far

The first Wilson Labour government had left office with the tag 'the poor are poorer under Labour' hung round its neck. Was that fair? Professor Atkinson's account remains the most balanced:

> There can be little doubt that social security received much more attention from the Labour Government of 1964–70 than it did during the preceding thirteen years . . . What is more controversial is whether the Labour measures were sufficiently large – or even of the right kind – to make a significant contribution to the reduction of inequality in Britain. (1972: 12)

Notice the shift in the goal posts, here, from Beveridge's criteria. Atkinson, in tune with emphasis of the time, was asking whether overall inequality had been reduced, not whether the absolute standards of living of the poor or their basic incomes had been improved. At that time the idea that *absolute* living standards of the poor would decline was not even considered. It was to happen in the 1980s when the 'poor becoming poorer' was to take on a new meaning.

Effort

Labour had planned a faster rate of growth in public spending when it reached office than the previous government: 6.6 compared to 4.8 per cent per annum in real terms. It achieved a 6.5 per cent increase per annum in real volume terms, pretty good shooting in the economic climate of the time with a sterling crisis intervening in between. The social security budget increased from 7.2 per cent of the GDP to 9.3 per cent between 1964/5 and 1969/70. The government cannot be faulted in terms of sheer expenditure. But to some extent these figures were misleading. Unemployment was beginning to rise – a point to which we return. There were more old people and part of the increase in family allowances had been clawed back in tax increases. Adjusting for these factors, however, there was still an increase in the percentage of the GDP going to social security from 7.2 to 8.6 (Atkinson, 1972) so the additional effort was real enough.

Between May 1963 and November 1969 basic insurance benefits had risen in value by 14 per cent. Most of that increase had happened in that first March 1965 rise and beneficiaries had suffered from not having their benefits uprated in the aftermath of the sterling crisis until November 1969. Take-home pay had suffered as a result of the rise in flat rate contributions, as Crossman had noted at the time in his diary. So the low-paid worker with a family was only 7 per cent better off in 1970 than in 1964. The new earnings-related benefits were of relatively little help to the poorest paid. Supplementary benefits had been made more generous, however. Here was the first move to targeting by a Labour government boxed in by public spending pressures and its promises to the poor.

Despite spending so much more on social security the Labour government had left office with little credit, quite unlike its 1945 predecessors. On both occasions the main beneficiaries of the government's innovations were not the very poorest but the rather less poor.

In 1974–6 the achievements, in the Labour Party's own terms, were more considerable. The final implementation of the national pensions plan and the introduction of child benefit were real achievements in a period of world economic crisis, even if child benefit had to be prized out of the government. This was to be the furthest the 1945 social policy agenda was to go. It was its high water mark.

6 Completing the Post-war Agenda 1964–76, Part Two: from Equal Access to Equality?

Health Care

If social security and child poverty had become contentious in 1964–70 the Health Service experienced minimal changes to its structure but real growth in spending. The Labour Party came to power with no really new ideas. It was sufficient to restore the NHS to the glory it had once been in 1948. Then it had been completely free at the point of use. There had been no charges on prescriptions, or dental, or opticians' services, or spectacles and dentures. The party had fiercely opposed the prescription charge increases of 1961 and was committed to abolishing them altogether. It did so very early in its period of office, in February 1965. It was to be a short-lived nostalgic return to the 1940s.

By 1967–8 the economy was in deep trouble. The pound had to be devalued and cuts in public expenditure were called for by the Treasury. Rather than cut the hospital building programme the Ministry of Health offered the Treasury a restoration of prescription charges – at a higher rate than they had been when Labour took office: 12.5p per item. This was a blow to the party faithful and to the government's self-confidence.

More new hospitals

The big hospital building programme had been begun by the previous Government in 1961. Given the lead time on hospital design this programme really got into full swing only in this Labour period. Many of today's district general hospitals, especially the really big ones, date from this period, suffering from much of the same design brutality as many of the housing estates of the same period. Yet, to its credit, the government did hold to that programme, more or less, despite the sterling crisis and devaluation. Other later governments might not have done! On reaching office Labour committed itself to increase Health Service spending in real volume terms by 4.8 per cent a year. This was cut back after the economic crisis of 1967 to a rate of increase of 3.8 per cent but it was still higher than the previous government's plans. The Labour government could claim it had given higher priority to health than in previous years (see Table 6.1).

A GP charter

There were the normal fisticuffs with the doctors. The BMA put in a claim for a 30 per cent rise and were given 10 per cent in 1965. They talked of resigning from the service. In the course of discussions they proposed a charter for the family doctor service. Kenneth Robinson, the minister, negotiated an agreement that gave more financial support to GPs' basic practice costs and some more obligations to provide a basic service. More health centres were built, in which groups of GPs could work with others such as community nurses and health visitors.

Scandal

Ever since the Health Service had been created, and indeed for long before it, the long-stay services in hospitals for the elderly and mentally ill and handicapped had been a disgrace to a humane society. They were becoming worse, as the very costly staff needed to keep them bearable became more difficult to recruit. In 1961 the government had assumed,

Table 6.1   Planned and actual expenditure of Conservative and Labour governments 1963/4 to 1976/7

(i) Planned average annual growth rates in constant prices

| Service | *Volume terms, growth in percentages per annum* | | | | |
	Conservative plans 1963/4 to 1967/8	Labour government plans 1964/5 to 1969/70	1968/9 to 1971/2	Conservative plans 1970/1 to 1974/5	1972/3 to 1976/7
Housing	3.8*	7.1	3.2	−0.4	−4.4
Education	5.7	5.7	3.8	3.3	3.4
Health and Welfare	3.0	4.8	3.8	3.3	3.4
Social Security	4.8	6.6	5.1	2.1	1.3
Roads	6.9	7.2	7.5	6.1	5.15
Defence	2.7	0.0	−1.9	−0.9	1.4
All public expenditure	4.1	4.2	3.0	2.6	2.2

* includes Environment

(ii) Actual as against planned growth rates in constant prices

| Service | *Volume terms, growth in percentages per annum* | | | | | |
| | 1964/5 to 1969/70 (Cmnd 2734) | | 1968/9 to 1971/2 (Cmnd 4234) | | 1970/1 to 1973/4 (Cmnd 4578) | |
	Actual	Planned	Actual	Planned	Actual	Planned
Housing	3.8	7.1	−1.6	3.2	5.9	0.0
Education	4.9	5.7	4.0	3.8	4.9	3.5
Health and Welfare	3.4	4.8	3.2	3.8	5.2	3.2
Social Security	6.5	6.6	9.7	5.1	4.0	2.5
Roads	5.7	7.2	5.5	7.5	3.9	6.2
Defence	−2.4	0.0	−3.1	−1.9	−0.8	−1.4
All public expenditure	4.1	4.2	1.4	3.0	5.5	2.0

Note: The figures show increases in the amount of services provided, not their cost.
Source: Glennerster 1975

on the basis of recent reductions in admissions to mental hospitals, that many could be closed. This helped to keep down the apparent cost of the new building programme. It was to be mainly devoted to building new large district general hospitals and not to replacing these very old institutions, many a hundred years old. Conditions in them were appalling. One remarkable campaigning woman, Barbara Robb, finding out from personal experience how bad they were, put together a series of accounts in a book called *Sans Everything* and used it to launch a campaign to improve, or else close long-stay facilities.

Shortly afterwards the brutality and poor care being meted out in Ely, a long-stay hospital for the mentally handicapped in Cardiff, were opened to public scrutiny by a nurse writing to the *News of the World*.

Kenneth Robinson had asked a Conservative lawyer to undertake an official enquiry. He was Geoffrey Howe, later Mrs Thatcher's Chancellor. His report was devastatingly critical of conditions, staff morale and management and arrived on Richard Crossman's desk to be dealt with. The civil servants were keen to give the whole thing as little publicity as possible and do nothing. Crossman saw this as a way of extracting more resources for his department and especially of improving conditions in these long-stay institutions, which he had become convinced were an outrage and would prove a political embarrassment. Instead of burying the report he decided to maximize publicity for it. He telephoned Fleet Street editors, gave 'exclusives', told them a dynamite report was on its way (Crossman, 1977: 418, 421, 425–30). As an old journalist he knew how to manipulate a scandal for his own purposes. Against his department's wishes he established an inspectorate, actually called the Hospital Advisory Service, to monitor conditions in these institutions. We see, here, the first cracks in the popular edifice of the NHS. These were institutions hidden from public view, dealing with people with no ability to complain, who were incapable of exercising any power of exit or market sanctions. The employees, many poorly paid and with little or no training, had excessive power over the patients. The fact that they were being looked after as part of the popular and politically sensitive NHS had made no difference. They were out of sight and out of mind and it was in the interests of the bureaucracy and the professionals to keep them that way. The series of scandals that came to light in this period tell us something about the decline in standards that can take place in any institution that is hidden from public gaze. Theoretical democratic control was not enough to save these patients. Press exposure and the fear that there might be more such did begin to put a tighter form of accountability in place. There were wider lessons here for the service at large. It was a cloud on the horizon for those who could see it.

At the end of Crossman's period of office a White Paper had been drafted setting out a phased plan for improving the services available for mentally handicapped people, and building up community facilities. It will seem somewhat old-fashioned in approach to today's readers. It relied on fairly large hostel accommodation but it was the first attempt to look long term at the needs of this group (Glennerster and Korman, 1983). It was adopted and published by Crossman's Conservative successor, Sir Keith Joseph, with virtually no changes (Cmnd 4683, 1971).

A new structure for the NHS?

It was during this period too that, prompted originally by the Royal Colleges, the government started to think again about the structure of the NHS. The medical profession had never been entirely happy with the local authorities continuing to have health responsibilities and had pressed for the local health services run by local councils to be brought within the ambit of the National Service and thus more effectively within the profession's sphere of influence.

In 1968 the Minister of Health published a Green, or discussion, paper setting out a possible reorganization of the NHS, the first of many in the next twenty years. It was a hurried document which was, as much as anything, a response to the big changes that were being proposed for social work. Social workers were then often part of the empire of the local authority Medical Officer of Health. This first Green Paper was really a last minute attempt by the Ministry of Health to counter the loss of social work functions which this committee – the Seebohm Committee – was proposing (Cmnd 3703, 1968).

Social Work

It was the Seebohm Committee that created the modern social work profession. It is therefore worth looking at its origins (Hall, 1976).

On one level these are demographic. The rapid increase in the number of births immediately after the Second World War had resulted in a much larger than normal teenage population in the late 1950s. They became the focus of commercial attention, from pop groups and record companies to scooter and motor-cycle manufacturers. They also committed crimes, as all teenage groups had done, crime being concentrated in that age group. Teenage delinquency became a matter of public concern and political interest. Part of that concern was channelled into a debate about families with difficult children and families at risk. The Ingleby Committee (Cmnd 1191, 1960) had made tentative proposals to co-ordinate preventive work between the multiple agencies concerned with family welfare. At this time social workers were trained by numerous specialist bodies. Probation officers had one kind of training, organized by the Home Office. Child-care workers had another, mental health workers another, hospital social workers another, those working mainly for welfare departments with the elderly mostly had no training at all. Social workers were employed by a variety of public and private agencies. They were fragmented and very weak as a group. Part of the agenda was to increase the professional status and power of this disparate collection of professionals.

Some reformers argued that there *was* a common thread of principle that underlay all these activities, at least at the level of basic training. New courses had been set up, like that at the LSE, which taught this generic base and gave a common qualification in social work. The children's service had done extremely well. Could this not be the forerunner of a larger social work department?

The groups of specialist social workers were badly divided. Many wanted to retain their independence, others saw the case for merging. There was also conflict at the level of central government departments. The Home Office did not want to lose control of its child-care and probation service. The Ministry of Health did not want to lose control of its welfare officers and of the new, social work assistants it was training.

The government decided to appoint a committee to review what it called 'local authority and allied personal social services'. The committee, chaired by Lord Seebohm, had only one representative on it from the medical profession: Professor Jerry Morris, an epidemiologist, joint author with, and personal friend of, Professor Titmuss. Another member of Titmuss's department, Roy Parker, was on the committee and was to play a particularly influential role.

Seebohm's logic

The unquestioned assumption was that social work would remain a pre-dominantly public sector, local authority responsibility. If you wanted social work to acquire status anything like the status of medicine it would be necessary to create a unified and large social work department with a powerful chief officer, like the Chief Education Officer or Medical Officer of Health. It would give social work not only bureaucratic power but a career structure. To do that meant putting together enough foot soldiers to justify the appointment of a general. So, to the existing responsibilities of the Children's Departments, the committee added the various social workers in the existing health and welfare departments, their home helps and the residential care of elderly and disabled people. Though many of these were *not* professional social work activities in the full sense they added numbers and budget size to the departments and hence their power in the local authority hierarchy. It was an exercise in bureaucratic and professional power politics.

To back up the claim to professional status a single training body for social work was to be created, modelled on the General Medical Council and later professional statutory bodies; it was to be the Central Council for the Education and Training in Social Work (CCETSW).

The new social services departments

When the Ministry of Health officials woke up to the significance of these recommendations for the Medical Officer of Health's role they rushed out their own Green Paper suggesting that non-social work services like home helps should not be taken away from the local authority Medical Officers of Health. The Home Office was also unhappy. It wanted to and did keep probation out of the new social service departments. The report was published in July 1968, almost at the same moment as the Russian invasion of Czechoslovakia and got less than massive attention in the press. The resulting bill was introduced and passed with little debate and no opposition from the Conservative front bench. It had cross-party support and was passed not long before the Labour government lost office in 1970. Crossman, who took over responsibility for the report when he became Secretary of State, was bored with the whole thing, whereas he had had a lively interest in the pensions plan:

when I got to my room at 70 Whitehall I found an official from the Home Office with a long and official virtuous draft on the kind of speech they thought I ought to deliver. After an hour's talk with them trying to get it straight, I left these three officials to do it for me while I went across to the House to listen to the final part of the Common Market debate. (1977: 835–6, Diary entry 25 February 1970)

The new 'Seebohm' social services departments of local authorities, as they were called, came into operation in 1971 and were encouraged by the new Conservative Secretary of State, Sir Keith Joseph, to submit to him ambitious plans for expansion. Here, certainly, was a clear example of consensus between the parties. The battle had been between the professions and the central government departments with whom they were most closely associated. It is an example of what Dunleavy (1991) calls the 'bureau shaping' activities of government departments and civil servants in their own interests.

Social work had carved itself out a new empire and a hierarchical career structure. It was a similar story, but on a larger scale, to the creation of the Children's Departments in 1948. There was a difference. Those had provided a career structure and senior posts for women. The new highly-paid directors of social services were to be mostly men! The idea that social work might be anything other than a primarily statutory, state-employee-based profession was not seriously debated.

There were also some genuine concerns for the groups in need. The Seebohm Report took as its guiding principle the notion that there should be one department that offered help and support for families in need at any period in their lives. The new departments should not be seen merely as a place where bad parents or sick and damaged people went. It was to be, so far as possible, a universal service providing support at periods in the life cycle when it was needed.

One single department concerned with most aspects of 'welfare' as the public generally understands the term, is an essential first step in making services more easily accessible. (Cmnd 3703, 1968, para. 146)

This report represents, perhaps, the high tide of post-war universalist ambitions. It was a bridge too far. The new social services departments would, in the tighter economic climate they would soon inhabit, inevitably spend most of their time with the poor and the frail and the ill. They would never become the general recourse for the ordinary family. It was romantic to believe it could ever have been otherwise.

NHS Reform Again

A second go

Crossman had not been satisfied with the hurried Green Paper on Health Service reform that had been produced by Kenneth Robinson as a pre-emptive strike against Seebohm. With Seebohm nearly on the statute book what was to become of the NHS? Crossman produced a second Green Paper (DHSS, 1970). He accepted the medical profession's pressure for the inclusion within the NHS of all medical and related professional activities. The local authorities' health departments, weakened by the loss of functions to the new social work and social services departments, should be removed and responsibility for the community health services transferred to the NHS. Area health authorities would be created that would run the local hospitals *and* the community services. To encourage collaboration with the new social services departments they would cover exactly the same geographical area.

The private hope of Crossman and his adviser Abel-Smith was that at some time these area health authorities would merge with the local authorities, bringing both the social work and the medical services under the democratic control of the same agency. That was precisely what the BMA feared. The area health authorities were to be directly responsible to the Department of Health and Social Security. The intermediate regional layer would go. It was by far the neatest and most streamlined structure to be proposed for the NHS since the Second World War. But it removed the layer that the profession had pressed Bevan to put in place and on which it had most leverage: the regions, then called regional hospital boards. The second Green Paper fell with the government.

A third go

The Conservative government accepted the BMA's objections. A regional tier was introduced into the plans set out by Crossman. Below the areas were to be district authorities charged with the operational management of the services. They were based, essentially, on the catchment areas of the large district general hospitals built in the 1960s and 1970s. Areas were to be planning units, not the driving force, of the system. The medical profession had thus removed power from those bodies with the strongest local authority links and placed it at the point where they could have most impact. The loss of direct local authority control of services was partly recompensed by local authority representation on the area authorities and partly by the creation of community health councils that were composed of lay people appointed to act as consumer watch-dogs. Again the Conservative government fell before these changes could be implemented but they were so nearly in place that the Labour government of 1974 decided not to revoke them, merely increasing the powers of the community health councils.

Byzantium

The resulting structure was the most Byzantine ever imposed on a UK public service. There were regional health authorities with a team of multi-professional officers supposedly acting in unison. There were area teams of officers doing the same and district teams below them. As Roy Griffiths, Mrs Thatcher's adviser, was to say ten years later, Florence Nightingale would have paced through this maze 'searching for the people in charge' (Griffiths Report, 1983, para. 5).

Layers of this edifice have gradually been removed in the 1980s and some of the most recent changes in the 1990s will remove the regions and amalgamate the districts into entities that look remarkably like the area health authorities of the second Green Paper. Richard Crossman is no doubt sitting somewhere looking on with a hearty chuckle.

What Seebohm and the new NHS had done, however, was to separate into two statutory camps the social workers and the medical and related professions, like nursing. Social services departments would employ the one and the NHS the other. There would be a joint consultative machinery to link the two services but for those dependent on both, like the elderly, the mentally ill and the handicapped, the results were not to be good.

Planning and rationing health care

When the Conservatives returned to power in 1970 they were committed to containing public expenditure but not to reducing or cutting back services like the NHS. How could that circle be squared? The Heath government believed that the application of new planning and budgetary tools invented in the United States in the 1960s would help get more out of the given budget, just as it was hoped that the internal market would do this in the 1990s.

A pilot programme budget for health and social services was drawn up in 1971 and subsequently developed (Banks, 1979). Crossman had found that when he wanted to give more priority to services for the mentally handicapped no one knew what was already being spent on them. How would you ever know whether you were succeeding? The department wanted to make a better case to the Treasury for resources. How could it do so when it did not know what priority groups were getting what or what the implications of an ageing population were? So far from being a tool to cut health spending the DHSS was using the programme budget to sharpen its weapons in the battle for funds with the Treasury.

By the time Barbara Castle became Secretary of State this planning and budgetary tool had been well developed. She decided to use it not merely to battle with the Treasury but to give explicit planning guidelines to the lower tiers in the NHS to shift priorities towards the groups that had been the focus of the *Sans Everything* and the post-Ely policies in the last administration: the elderly, the mentally ill and handicapped. She published a priorities document setting out budgetary and service targets for each. This was a courageous exercise in open planning that was not to be repeated. The difficulty was that the NHS was not like a large company or the armed services. The lower tiers were run by medical politics and no one was clearly charged with managing the changes (Glennerster and Korman, 1983). They frittered away as they trickled down the complex hierarchy we have described. This was the height of optimism about the capacity of rational planning to solve the problems of the NHS, what Klein calls 'paternalistic rationalism' and it was to decline steadily thereafter (Klein, 1989: 105).

The final part of this rational plan for the NHS was the attempt to allocate resources more fairly between areas of the country. We saw in Chapter 3 that health resources in the 1930s and before followed the capacity of consultants to attract private fees and benefactors to give hospitals endowments. The coming of the NHS had changed matters much less than might have been expected. Budgets in the post-war period had tended to be rolled forward in an incremental way, perpetuating the inequalities of the past. The 1964 Labour government had not helped matters by approving a lot of hospital building in London. Research by Culyer and colleagues at York, and others, had attracted attention to this issue. Since the main losers were the northern regions where Labour was strong, equity and political advantage seemed to coincide. The government set up a working party to find a way of allocating health service budgets on a more scientific basis than last year's budget plus or minus 'x per cent'.

The Resource Allocation Working Party did so and produced a formula that came to be named after it, the RAWP formula. It allocated money on the basis of a region's population and its relative health needs – actually death rates from different conditions. Though criticized, it was probably the most sophisticated system of its kind anywhere in the world. It remained in use for more than a decade, shifting resources to the north and other deprived areas. It has been replaced by district-based allocations of a similar kind in the 1990s. It must be counted one of the real technical achievements of the period.

Education and the Pursuit of Equality

Abolishing the eleven-plus

Education had been central to Anthony Crosland's vision of a fairer and more equal society. Class divisions stemmed, in large part, from Britain's segregated education system. He was to become Secretary of State for Education in Wilson's government in 1965 and charged with implementing the changes he had pressed on the party in his book ten years earlier.

In the 1960s education was the political talking point. Bad landlords and high private rents might worry the poorer and older voters but they were of declining electoral importance. Younger educated and middle-class parents cared about education and their numbers were growing. The labour force was changing. The numbers of pupils staying on into sixth form and applying to university was growing rapidly, as we saw in the last chapter. Secondary modern schools that provided no school-leaving qualifications were less and less relevant to this new population. These schools themselves began to build up examination courses. The pressure to obtain the restricted grammar school places intensified. Abolishing the eleven-plus had an increasing electoral appeal.

Yet many Labour councils with ex-grammar school pupils on them, who were proud of their grammar school provision built up since the 1920s, were less sure. Wilson himself seemed equivocal. He was interested in expanding technical education and higher education of a vocational kind. Where he stood on grammar schools, as an ex-grammar school boy, tended to be obscured in pipe smoke.

Pressure

That, at least, was how it seemed to two ex-employees of the Labour Party Research Department as they discussed matters after lunch on Boxing Day 1964, with their wives nursing two children of under a year. Were they going to have to sit the eleven-plus like their fathers? The grammar school defence groups were already forming. The likelihood was a Wilsonian compromise and fudge around the corner. A ginger group was called for. This was almost a year before the CPAG was to be formed on the same logic. Various people known to be interested and expert were approached. One parent who had older children at comprehensive school lived nearby and had been interviewed on the radio; she was the wife of Tony Benn. Perhaps she could be roped in. A group of interested people collected together and decided to launch something called the Comprehensive Schools Committee. An article in the *Guardian* with an address to write to elicited hundreds of letters wanting to know more about comprehensive education. Local groups were formed and Caroline Benn became the best-informed person in the country on the subject. Her regular reports on the subject sold out rapidly and were sent for on the morning of publication by the Department of Education, by taxi. She briefed her husband and later one senior civil servant remarked, not altogether happily, 'it is like having another bloody Minister of Education in the Cabinet'. The civil service persuaded ministers not to legislate on the matter, probably wisely, as it turned out. A circular, the famous Circular 10/65, was issued to local education authorities saying that it was government policy to abolish the eleven-plus examination system and selective secondary schools. The government wanted local authorities to produce plans for secondary education of a non-selective type and would they please do so within a year. LEAs were given a choice of how to do it. Schemes that had been tried by existing local authorities in the 1950s were described. Existing buildings could be used and grouped into lower and upper schools or middle and senior schools with every child moving on from one to another. 'Let us get a few of the really good authorities that everyone respects to play ball and the rest will follow', was the civil service advice. There would be no permission to build new grammar schools.

It worked. By the 1970 election nearly all local areas were well on their way to switching to comprehensive education. The circular was withdrawn by Mrs Thatcher when she became Secretary of State for Education in 1970, but authorities of all political persuasions continued the change and more comprehensive schools were founded in her period than in the time of any other minister. Reintroducing the eleven-plus, denying most children access to grammar schools and hence access to the booming clerical and semi-professional jobs that were being created, was simply not practical politics. Nor did it make sense to the chief education officers of the day. Building one secondary school for local children was more economic in rural and small county town areas, the Conservative heartlands.

When the Labour government came back to power it did introduce legislation to require local councils to abolish selection but the battle was, by then, all but won. Whether it achieved the egalitarian results Crosland and other reformers had hoped for is more debatable and would be difficult to judge until much later. We shall return to the point in the last chapter.

Raising the school leaving age to 16

This had been legislated for in 1944 but no government had been able to free the resources to do so. The Conservative government had promised to in 1968. That coincided with the economic crisis of 1967–8 and one of the economy measures was to put off the change until 1971.

Educational priorities and disadvantage

The government had not come to power with any strong policy for primary or pre-school provision, except reducing class sizes. The Central Advisory Council for Education, whose reports had been so influential in the Conservative period, produced one more on primary education – the Plowden Report – in 1967. It endorsed and encouraged the child-centred, relaxed and informal approach to primary teaching that had developed in the late 1950s and 1960s and had become much admired abroad. It also began to come to terms with important changes in the social structure and accepted more explicitly than any previous report that equal access to services was not enough to ensure equal benefit. Despite all the improvements to the basic standards of schooling that had been achieved since 1945, and the excellent results achieved by the most able, differences in achievement between the highest and the lowest were greater than in most advanced economies. (Similar results have been found in the 1990s (Green and Steedman, 1993).)

Standards in many inner-city schools and other deprived areas were particularly disturbing. Members of the team had visited the United States as part of their investigations and were influenced by what they saw, in particular the programmes of compensatory education. It was not enough simply to provide ordinary average schooling in these deprived areas, they argued. What was necessary was distinctive and *better* education than normal to compensate children for the lack of stimulus their environment and their families could give. Schools in such areas should be given special help, their teachers paid more.

This idea did not go down well with the teachers' unions, and sociologists talked about the ecological fallacy: not all or most poor children were in schools designated as poor. But it was the first attempt by an official committee to come to terms with the problems set for schools by poverty and deprivation. (The Newsom Committee, 1963, on secondary modern schools a number of years before had recognized some similar issues but not developed a coherent response.)

Plowden urged that pre-school education was vital and especially for children in such areas. It should be made available to all families who wanted it for their children but it should come first in the poorest areas. The report was followed by the sterling crisis later in 1967 and there was little money to implement its proposals. In 1972 Mrs Thatcher produced a White Paper proposing a phased introduction of pre-school provision for all parents who wanted it. It is a goal that still has to be reached.

Higher education

The big breakthrough in the expansion of higher education had been achieved in the period of the 1959–64 Conservative government with the Robbins Committee Report (1963), as we saw in the previous chapter.

Most of the actual expansion fell to the Labour government to implement. What the Labour government added was the creation of a public sector of vocationally and technologically based institutions – the polytechnics – and the Open University.

The binary system created

Hugh Gaitskell had set up a study group to settle what Labour's policy towards higher education should be and to attempt to pre-empt the Robbins Report (Labour Party, 1963). We discuss later its distinctive contribution, the Open University. In other respects the committee said much the same as Robbins, stressing the case for university expansion of the traditional kind. It had supported the merger of the Colleges of Advanced Technology into the university system. As chairman of Labour's Home Policy Committee Wilson had other ideas. A separate committee was set up to work on further and higher vocational education. It opposed the wholesale expansion of the universities. These were not capable of delivering the officer class that would lead Wilson's technological revolution. Nor would they attract working-class children. A new kind of institution was called for that linked with local industry, like the further education colleges, but doing work that would be of higher educational standard. These institutions would span the range of work from part-time vocational courses to top rate research and teaching that would outdo the universities (Robinson, 1968). Here was a quite distinctive and opposing philosophy to Robbins or to the Crosland wing of the Labour Party.

Though the Labour Party accepted the Robbins Report and made no public commitment to a different policy, when Wilson became Prime Minister this alternative was pressed forward. In 1966 Crosland published a White Paper proposing the creation of a separate but equal system of new polytechnics (Cmnd 3006), run by local authorities but drawing on a national recruitment of students. The demand for student places was thought to be growing faster than Robbins had forecast and the polytechnics were to provide the extra places. They grew rapidly, not least because government came to see them as a cheaper way to expand higher education. By the 1980s they were taking equivalent numbers of students to universities.

The polytechnics did not retain the very distinctive character their more enthusiastic proponents hoped for. They gradually moved nearer and nearer to being cheaper and more teaching-based universities. The Conservative government accepted the logic of the drift (Cm. 1541, 1991) and merged the two parts of the binary system into one. The polytechnics became 'new' universities.

A University of the Air?

How could university education be extended to that part of the population who were past normal university age and were already in work or were at home bringing up children? As early as 1960 Professor Sir George Catlin had suggested a 'university of the air' (see Hall *et al.*, 1975 for an account of this story). Michael Young, that most original of ideas men, founder of *Which?* and much else, was experimenting with and writing about using television to educate people in their own homes. About the same time Harold Wilson had returned from the Soviet Union, much enthused by the idea of using correspondence courses on a mass scale to teach university degrees. Acting as secretary to the Labour Party study group as I was at that time it occurred to me that these two ideas might be put together. What the eventual report said was,

> We propose that, as an experiment, the BBC sound radio and television and the ITA should be required to cooperate in organising a 'University of the Air' for serious adult education. [There would be correspondence courses and] Wherever possible students should meet regularly at area colleges for the equivalent of university tutorials. (Labour Party, 1963b: 34)

That remains the basis of what is the Open University today.

The idea became Wilson's own particular passion. He gave the job of implementing it to Aneurin Bevan's widow, Jennie Lee, when he won the 1964 election. The DES thought the whole idea barmy and resisted it throughout. It was only her direct line to Wilson that got the Open University on to the statute book and into reality (Hall *et al.*, 1975).

More higher education

Thus, up to about 1972 higher education expanded faster than it had ever done before, not merely catering for the big increase in the number of 18-year-olds but substantially increasing the proportion of the population going to higher education. The Labour government expanded higher education as a whole faster than Robbins had recommended. More teacher training places and more advanced further education and polytechnic places were created. In the 1960s higher education doubled in size. The percentage of the age group entering full higher education rose from 7.7 per cent in 1958 to over 13 per cent in 1972.

It was not an achievement to be underestimated and it slowly began to change the nature of the of the labour force in a major way (Glennerster and Lowe, 1990). After 1972 the expansion ran out of steam for a period. The salaries that new university graduates earned fell relative to the 1960s as the supply of graduates rose. The government cut the real value of student grants in the early 1970s, so both the rewards fell and the costs rose.

Private education

The public schools had long been an obsession with those on the left in British politics and for good reason. Tawney had advocated their reform. There had been a committee of enquiry on ways of integrating the public schools more closely with the state sector during the Second World War (the Fleming Report, 1944). (In the absurd ways of the English, 'public' schools mean private schools. To be more precise, they mean the very small group of elite private schools that belong to the Head Masters' Conference.)

These schools had for long been the entry gate to the class elite that ran British society. In 1964, 87 per cent of the Conservative Cabinet had gone to public schools, 76 per cent of Conservative MPs (15 per cent only of Labour MPs), 76 per cent of judges, half the positions at the top of the civil service, nearly 60 per cent of the directors of the leading firms, and so the list went on (Glennerster and Pryke, 1964). Three-quarters of all sixth formers in 1967 were in this small number of schools. All sections of the Labour Party were keen to break this class stranglehold which fitted ill with the meritocratic technological future Wilson was presenting.

There was, however, no agreement about what to do, despite much agonizing in opposition. Some wanted to make the schools illegal and take them over, as Bevan had done with the teaching hospitals. Others felt this was wrong in principle and electorally suicidal. The debate was often conducted in terms of the clash between the pursuit of equality and people's individual freedom to educate their own children in the way they wished. The reason for the indecision was therefore not pure lassitude but reflected a genuine principled dilemma of a very sixties kind. The best the party could come up with was the phrase in its manifesto that a Labour government, if elected, would, 'set up an educational trust to advise on the best way of integrating the public schools into the state system of education'. (I well remember the hours of debate that went into that wording!)

The result was the Public Schools Commission. It was a typical committee of the great and the good with representatives of the public school sector and state schools and local authority people on it. It divided its work into two phases. The first would deal with the group of schools that aroused most passion, the elite boarding schools such as Eton and Harrow. The second would consider the future of those private grammar schools that had, since 1902, received a direct grant from central government in return for offering free places to some pupils.

Neither report was unanimous. The majority First Report (DES, 1968) recommended removing the schools' tax advantages unless they collaborated with the state sector in providing places for state school pupils who needed boarding education for personal and educational reasons. The direct grant schools were to lose their grants unless they became comprehensive schools though they could opt into the local education system fully if they wished to. No action was taken by the Labour government before 1970 on the integration policy but tax advantages that parents gained in paying their children's fees were withdrawn in successive Finance Acts, from 1968. (In practice rich families found their way round these curbs too!) When that government left office there was a Green Paper on these issues in draft called *Education for a New Generation*, which never saw the light of day (Glennerster, 1972).

When Labour returned to power it did abolish the direct grants to private grammar schools; they were phased out by the time of the 1976 Education Act. About a quarter of the grammar schools, mainly the Catholic ones, became local authority comprehensive schools and the rest became independent day schools.

More equality?

Whom did all these changes benefit? We discuss some of the longer-term trends in the last chapter of this book. Immediately, however, the new comprehensive schools did expand the range of subjects and school-leaving qualification opportunities available to the average child who would before have gone to a secondary modern school. This shows up in the much higher qualification rates and higher staying on rates in the 1970s and 1980s. The effects are difficult to disentangle from the longer statutory school life introduced at the same time. But overall the research suggests that the averagely able and below average children definitely gained from comprehensive education. The achievements of the most able do not seem to have been affected at all significantly, though there is dispute about this (Glennerster and Low, 1990). If this is true the long-term impact was to some degree egalitarian.

The rapid expansion of higher education places in the 1960s did increase participation amongst all classes or social groups, though the trend had been in progress since the 1930s or earlier (Halsey *et al.*, 1980). The 1960s expansion seems to have benefited most, not the top professional and managerial classes nor the working class, but the intermediate groups, clerical, service occupations and lower professional groups like teachers' children. These were groups growing rapidly in social significance and electoral clout.

The bastions of class privilege, the public schools, had escaped. The picture is, therefore, mixed but overall it was middle England that had gained again. In an early evaluation of this period I allocated the total increase in education expenditure between 1962/3 and 1968/9 between the social groups who could be said to have benefited (Glennerster, 1972). There had been an overall increase of 85 per cent. The professional and managerial group had benefited by an increase of 136 per cent, manual working groups by about 75 per cent. The expansion of higher education and the larger numbers from these classes staying on at school explained this.

If the middle class had gained disproportionately from the education changes of the period, did the working class gain from the housing policy?

Housing

We have already seen that Wilson chose to appoint Richard Crossman to the housing ministry and not to social security or education, which had been his previous briefs, because of the central importance the Prime

Minister placed on housing. The Labour Party had promised to increase house-building to 500,000 houses a year.

Rents and the private landlord

Top of the agenda, though, was the repeal of the 1957 Rent Act and the restoration of some kind of security of tenure to those in privately rented housing. This had been thought to be a potent electoral asset at the election and it was important to deliver on it. Whether the politicians were right is another matter (Banting, 1979).

The committee of enquiry discussing the problems in London where Rachman had operated had still not reported and swift action was needed. An emergency Act restricting landlords' eviction powers was passed. For the larger legislation Crossman called in outside experts, notably Arnold Goodman, Crossman's solicitor and general fix-it man, and David Donnison from the LSE, whom Titmuss had suggested he consult. The ministry did not take kindly to this outside interference at first. Crossman describes a typical encounter at which he was presented with a paper to approve, as he left the office for home, which was supposed to be a summary of proposals drawn up by these outsiders. Somehow, the paper included almost none of them, only the proposals the Ministry had already put to him (1975: 90).

The outside group was to be influential in shaping the legislation, since the party had come to power with no clear idea of how it was going to deal with the issue of rent control and security of tenure despite having made it a central plank in its election campaign. (See Banting, 1979, for the best brief account.) The party believed that landlords were evil people, or at least that the system was evil, and that it was enough to simply freeze rents. The advisers argued that this would make private rented property unsustainable and it would disappear, to the disadvantage of poor people. There had to be a means of enabling landlords to increase rents from time to time and the rents had to be high enough to keep landlords in business. The ministry wanted a formula. The advisers thought a flexible approach was much more workable, with a local rent officer setting rents. The rents of existing tenants, which had remained controlled at the very low 1939 level, would have to be raised. Despite having campaigned on the basis of stopping rent increases the Labour Party's new Rent Act would permit their more general increase.

> The Ministry officials were both surprised and delighted: It was a bill to raise rents. It was something the civil service would never had dared to suggest. For the first time we had a Minister prepared to put some flexibility into the rent control system. It's odd that it should have been a Labour Minister of Housing. (Banting, 1979: 50)

The part of the bill that caused most difficulty was the clause that gave the minister power to remove the controls on the existing very low rents on a region by region basis. He faced such backbench opposition from his own side that he had to amend the bill in committee, limiting the increases that could result. In the event no minister was to use this controversial power.

This compromise between rent control and the market lasted, with modifications, until Mrs Thatcher's era. It did not succeed in halting the decline in private landlord property – which had all but disappeared by the mid-1980s – but it may have slowed it down.

The council housing drive

Wilson had instructed Crossman to launch a 'housing drive', language reminiscent of the 1940s. The party had, it will be recalled, committed itself to increase house-building to 500,000 a year. The White Paper of 1965 pledged to do that by 1970. How was this to be achieved?

Crossman began by having dinners with the leading building contracting firms (1975: 30, 81). If the government wanted to build more quickly, they told him, it would have to concentrate on the large cities and undertake comprehensive redevelopment there. It would have to use industrial building methods. This would also fit the futuristic technological image Wilson was so taken by. Crossman visited the ministry's architects and was encouraged by their enthusiasm for mass-produced housing. In Oldham 750 houses were being built by these methods. 'Why not rebuild the whole thing? [i.e. 300 acres of the city centre] Wouldn't that help Laing?', he asked (p. 81).

Wilson's support for the housing budget was crucial. Crossman describes the Cabinet discussion (1975: 153–5). The Cabinet was told by the

Treasury that it could not spend more in the next four years than the previous Conservative government had planned to do in its pre-election expansion plans for higher education, hospitals and roads.

> The one social service they felt it was popular to cut back was public sector housing . . . It was my contention that whereas the other Ministers could fairly be asked to be content with the amount of money in the Tory estimates that was unreasonable in the case of housing. (p. 153)

Crossman proposed raising the target to the figure Wilson had suggested, using industrialized types of building to keep the costs down and use factory capacity that existed. There then ensued a sharp debate with the Chancellor and other ministers who were being told they could have no more money. Wilson took a vote, announced it tied, argued strongly for an increase and declared that that was what the Cabinet had decided.

It was the number of units built that mattered for political purposes. The capacity to say that the number was bigger than the Tories had achieved was what really mattered, just as it had for Macmillan after 1951. What those houses were like to live in, whether they would last, what they would cost to maintain, whether fungi would grow on the walls, how the local authorities could manage such large stocks of houses effectively – these questions were not asked (Power, 1988). They were not important to the politicians.

The influence of the construction industry on the Ministry of Housing and on local councils to build high-rise accommodation in this period and before is documented by Dunleavy (1981). One is tempted to make an analogy with the American Military–Industrial complex. What had grown up in the years of vast public housing schemes was a public housing–construction industry complex, a production process that kept building housing units for the benefit of the construction industry and politicians regardless of their social worth.

In the event the sterling crisis put paid to Wilson's ambitions. In 1967 over 400,000 houses were built in a year in Britain for the first time and in 1968, 413,000. There it stalled, cut back by the measures that were taken to meet the sterling crisis in 1967/8. By the end of 1969 the number built had fallen to 370,000. Instead attention began to shift from the destruction of old houses to renovation, with the White Paper *Old Houses into New Homes* (Cmnd 3602, 1968).

Owner occupation

Owner occupiers had always been considered Tory voters by Labour politicians. Yet as their numbers rose steadily it began to dawn on them that this attitude was merely electoral suicide. In 1966 the Labour government produced a significant White Paper, *Help Towards Home Ownership* (Cmnd 3163). It pointed out that the tax relief owner occupiers gained was a kind of subsidy which went disproportionately to higher-income mortgage holders. Those who did not pay tax got no help in becoming owner occupiers. Though academics had been making this point for many years this was the first official recognition of the equity problem involved. The proposal that followed was designed to help low-income families who were wanting to buy. It reduced individuals' mortgage interest with a direct subsidy so long as they gave up the right to claim tax relief. Though it did not last and did not reach many people it was the first attempt to rationalize the rather perverse way owner occupation has been supported by government.

Race Relations and the Inner City

One of the really important and lasting changes that affected the social structure of modern Britain began in the late 1950s and became a nasty political issue in the 1960s. It was the scale of immigration from the Caribbean and then East Africa and the Indian subcontinent.

Until the late 1950s Britain was an overwhelmingly white society. Even immigration from white Europe was strictly limited. The exodus from Russia and Eastern Europe of Jews in the early part of the century had lead to the 1905 and 1914 Aliens Acts, which had given the state wide powers to control entry, demand work permits and powers of deportation. Few of those who gained entry were black.

One of the consequences of the very high levels of employment in the 1950s was a shortage of labour. This lead to the increasing employment of women in traditionally mixed and women's employment – teaching and clerical work – but it did not lead to the employment of women bus drivers. Instead London Transport went to the West Indies to recruit. The restrictions on entry did not cover those from the Commonwealth.

They were considered British. London Transport had trail-blazed and many individuals from the Commonwealth followed, lured by the considerable job opportunities in Britain at that point.

Those who came settled in the traditional areas to which newcomers had gravitated in the past, such as Notting Hill in London, excluded by price and discrimination from living in most other places. Living along side poor white families they rapidly became the object of sharper discrimination and prejudice as their numbers grew. Notting Hill experienced the first race riot in 1956 and a largish vote for a Fascist candidate at the 1959 election. (For a vivid brief account see Kullmann, 1960).

Immigration became a political issue. It was not that the numbers of people entering the country at that point was large. Net immigration between 1951 and 1961 was less than 200,000 over the whole decade. The problem was that the immigrants were black. The Conservative government felt it had to respond and passed the first Commonwealth Immigrants Act in 1962. Vouchers were issued only to those who had a job to come to or who had educational qualifications or training likely to be useful to the British economy. Wide-ranging discretionary powers were extended to the authorities.

The Labour Party, initially, took the high moral ground and opposed the second reading of the bill. The Leader of the Opposition, Hugh Gaitskell, said,

> The immigrants are healthy, law-abiding, and are at work. They are helping us. Why then do the Government wish to keep them out? We all know the answer. It is because they are coloured and because in consequence of this there is a fear of racial disorder and friction. This is the real question. Why do we have so much hypocrisy about it? Why do we not face up to the matter? (Hansard, 16 November 1961)

It was not an hypocrisy confined to the Conservative Party, however. Many Labour councils were arranging their priority council house waiting lists to exclude immigrants. When the Labour Party came to power in 1964 it did not repeal the Act, after a very sharp lesson in the feelings of the electorate. In a mixed constituency a Conservative candidate was able to make very effective use of the race issue, so defeating the intended Foreign Secretary, Patrick Gordon-Walker.

What the new government did was to introduce a measure designed to make certain kinds of blatant discrimination illegal and to discourage others. (See Bindman and Carrier, 1983 for a discussion of this and later legislation, and Husband, 1982. A contemporary and widely read account was Rose, 1969.)

Race Relations Act 1965

> The 1965 Act made discrimination – defined as 'treating a person less favourably than another on the grounds of colour, race, or ethnic or national origins' a civil wrong when done in relation to the facilities of 'certain places of public resort'. Effectively this covered discrimination in pubs, dance halls and hotels but little else. It failed to touch at all on the critical areas of employment and housing. Furthermore, the sanction for breach of the law was to prove so nebulous as to be actually non-existent. In the event of a failure to conciliate a dispute by the Race Relations Board, set up to administer the law, the case could be referred to the Attorney-General who had power to obtain an injunction in the County Court. But not a single case reached the court in the lifetime of the Act. (Bindman and Carrier, 1983: 126)

A pattern had been set, however, for social policy in this field. A clamour for more restrictions on immigration would be acceded to, followed by a measure to protect more fully those from ethnic minorities who were already in Britain. It was, indeed, raised to the level of a principle by James Callaghan, the Labour Home Secretary a few years later when the Labour government was faced by an upsurge in immigration from East Africa. Here Asians were being expelled by the African governments. If we want to preserve good race relations, Callaghan argued, we must stem the inflow and balance it with positive measures to help eliminate discrimination for those who are here already.

The 1968 Commonwealth Immigrants Act further restricted entry but it was balanced by the 1968 Race Relations Act, which substantially extended the 1965 Act to cover employment and housing and strengthened the enforcement procedure. This Act was based on American experience with civil rights legislation but it fell short of it in several respects. Individuals had to take action to claim discrimination had taken place against them. In the United States class action could be taken on behalf of a whole group. The courts could not insist on target quotas or affirmative action to ensure equal opportunity. Nor was there any concept of 'indirect discrimination', practices that would in general tend to discriminate against a group, such as an employer's power to require certain kind of uniform. The concept of indirect discrimination was included in the later 1976 Race Relations Act but it has been very narrowly interpreted by the courts. The year 1968 was not only one of tougher action to stem immigration, it was also one of massive race riots in the United States. Though the problems were on a much larger scale and different, analogies were drawn and fears raised. Enoch Powell made a widely reported speech predicting 'rivers of blood' as a consequence of the growing population of ethnic minorities.

The Home Office, inspired by American experience and by an uncommon civil servant, Dereck Morrell, thought that special measures should be taken in areas where there was poverty and a high proportion of incomers. The aim was to stimulate local people in these areas to work together and create a new multi-cultural civil society. Their poverty made this a rather Utopian remedy and it ended in disillusion.

The next approach was to see the problem as economic. These areas needed help in generating jobs. Incentives were redirected from encouraging firms to leave city centres to return to them. The somewhat dubious concept of the 'inner city' became common parlance and an official inner-city policy was born in the late 1970s (Cmnd 6845, 1977).

These were all mealy-mouthed ways of saying that certain areas attracted large concentrations of non-white British and made the white majority uncomfortable. They were seen to be prone to riots and to need some kind of extra help. Various kinds of special programmes directed at such areas have been invented including the original grants made under Section 11 of the Local Government Act of 1966, Urban Aid; other versions followed. (Edwards and Batley, 1978; Higgins, 1978). A powerful critique of the government's poorly co-ordinated approach was mounted by the House of Commons Home Affairs Committee Report on Racial Disadvantage in 1981 (House of Commons, 1980). There was little response.

The worst riots came at the time of high unemployment at the beginning of Mrs Thatcher's period in office. The most notable were the disturbances in Brixton which lead to a report by Lord Scarman on policing that took its brief much wider, to discuss the whole range of disadvantages suffered by those living in the area (Cmnd 8427, 1981).

Despite garden centres and tree planting nothing amounting to a coherent or high priority policy could be said to have followed. More money was taken out of the poorer urban centres by changes to local government finance than was gained by them in special grants. The 1980s experienced increasing geographical concentration of poverty, as studies for the Joseph Rowntree Foundation showed in 1994.

Equal Pay

Social policy is traditionally thought of as a redistributive device, taking the incomes earned in the market-place, taxing them and giving benefits to families and individuals. It has rarely, in Britain, been concerned with regulating wages for social purposes. Wages councils did strengthen groups of workers in certain industries with weak bargaining power. They were abolished in the 1990s. Britain, despite trade union pressure, the Webbs's and Rowntree's advocacy, has never had a minimum wage.

Increasingly in the post-war years women moved into the public sphere of paid work. Yet their rewards were consistently less even when they were doing identical work, such as teaching. On top of that they tended to be employed in 'women's occupations' that were traditionally paid less. Unequal rewards for women for equal work became less and less acceptable though change was very slow.

Social policy is not just a matter of government legislation. Inaction is just as definite a policy as action. For many years governments did not accept that unequal pay for men and women was a legitimate cause for concern. A tacit or *de facto* policy of inequality existed.

There had been a Royal Commission on Equal Pay as early as 1949 and in 1951 the International Labour Organization had passed a convention calling on member states to adopt equal pay. It took twenty years before legislation was passed in the UK. Bruegel (1983) notes some of the contributory events that preceded the passing of legislation in 1970. There was a strike by women workers at Ford, Dagenham, in 1968 and trade union pressure was exerted through a National Joint Action Committee in 1969. The Minister of Labour at this point was Barbara Castle. But probably as important, employers knew that membership of the EEC, which they favoured, would require equal pay anyway. The CBI was, thus, not too resistant to the idea. As in other areas of equal opportunity Europe has been an important lever for change.

The Equal Pay Act

The eventual legislation made a distinction between earnings that were the consequence of different *worth* and earnings that were different despite *equal* worth. It was the latter that constituted discrimination.

There are two ways of measuring worth that are embodied in the Act. The first is that the person be engaged in 'the same or broadly similar work' and the second relates to work of 'equal value'. A woman doing the same or similar work as a man who was paid more had to show that any differences between her work and that of this comparable man were of no practical importance (Bruegel, 1983). The Act only dealt with differences or injustices within a firm. If a firm paid very low wages to a primarily female staff, in a laundry for example, it could not be caught by the Act and many firms with low wages were of this kind.

Where women were doing different work it was possible to call for a job evaluation to judge whether the work was of equal value. Firms were not obliged to undertake such an evaluation though. Moreover, even where a job was deemed of equal value the tribunal could determine that different pay was justified because of 'material difference' in the circumstances. The man might have longer service or do more overtime. Both were likely to tell against women.

Redress lies with the individual or the union acting on the individual's behalf. In the past unions were male dominated and might not have been supportive, though this has been changing. In the immediate aftermath of this legislation and the demand for women in the labour market, women's hourly earnings rose quite sharply. The median average hourly pay of women relative to men rose from 63 per cent in 1972 to 73 per cent in 1976 and then rose more gradually reaching 79 per cent in 1991 (Machin and Waldfogel, 1994).

The Sex Discrimination Act 1975 gave women the theoretical right to equal access to jobs and to equal treatment within them. The legislation did not, however, deal with indirect discrimination and the consequences of a segregated labour market. Women continue to work in lower-paid and part-time employment. Assumptions about the gendered division of paid and unpaid work and the absence of child-care facilities make the remaining differences very difficult to tackle. This is where equal pay legislation on its own can do little without further social policy intervention.

In the 1940s day care provision had been rapidly run down after the war. Pre-school provision has been very slow to develop and has never been designed for working mothers' convenience. Most working mothers with young children have relied on family members and child minders. Women's role as carers weakens their position in the labour market and their lower earning power in the market-place justifies their position as carers. Thus the rights to equal pay and access to the labour market were important both practically and symbolically but, given the gendered division of work, these were not substantive rights.

The 1975 Employment Protection Act introduced statutory maternity provision. Subject to being employed for two years over 16 hours per week, 5 years for those working shorter hours, a woman had the right to stop work for 11 weeks prior to the birth and to return to work 29 weeks after it. Pay was given for 6 weeks at 90 per cent of the woman's average earnings minus the statutory maternity allowance payable under the 1975 Social Security Act, and for 12 weeks at statutory sick pay. The 1975 legislation guaranteed reinstatement to similar work (not the same job). Various entitlements e.g. to pensions, were not continued through the period of leave. Though these formal rights were an important breakthrough many women found the lack of affordable child care a barrier to their practical return to work.

As with social security legislation, women had made some progress towards equal treatment in the public world of paid work but the implications of the private world of the family and gendered roles within it remained largely unchanged or beyond the reach of social policy.

Feminist analysis has provided a different perspective on many issues in social policy and it revived its vitality and policy relevance in the 1970s and 1980s. Just as Marx had tried to 're-fuse' (Gough, 1979) the forces of production and the relations of production, to get people to see how capitalism affected class relationships, so feminists were trying to 're-fuse' the relations of production in the public sphere with the relations of reproduction in the private sphere, to get people to see the interaction between the two. Equal pay policy is a good example of the need to do just that.

7 Morality, Family and the State: the Legacy of the Sixties

Economists and market liberals more generally often discuss the excessive power of the state almost exclusively in terms of its powers to tax, provide services and regulate the economy. More directly intrusive, however, is the state's power to regulate personal behaviour. The state sets the framework within which couples live in a legal relationship called marriage, it determines the age of consent to sexual intercourse, it makes certain kinds of intercourse criminal acts, it forbids or regulates the grounds on which abortions can be undertaken legally. The courts set precedents and rules which determine what happens when a marriage breaks up. All of these functions profoundly affect the quality of people's lives and are part of social policy. They interact with the more traditional forms of social policy, such as social security and social work.

Social policy, as we saw in Chapter 1, is not only concerned with pieces of social legislation. It concerns various functions performed by the state (local and national), the tax system as well as cash benefits, and also functions of the courts, the police and the penal system. One of the most difficult areas of all for governments to tread is the boundary line between the family and the state's legitimate functions. Another is between the state and the employment market. Each affects the other, as we have seen in the case of equal pay. The role women can play in the family is constrained not just by social norms (*de facto* policy if government does not seek to change them) but by the employment market and by government provision or support for child care. More care of children and frail and dependent people is undertaken by family members than the state could ever undertake, or should. Indeed, in so far as government merely assumes families will take the strain this is a *de facto* policy. There is much that governments cannot change about family or individual behaviour. But at the basis of Anglo-Saxon social policy has been the view that the family is a private world in which the state should have no role. Like the market, the state regulates its existence, the contractual basis of marriage, and indeed supports and encourages the institution, but should not actively intervene within it. In fact, it has been drawn in to protect children within families that are harming their children. That has been the case since the late nineteenth century. Whether it should protect the woman as the weaker partner was one of the issues that came to be part of policy debate in the 1970s, both with regard to divorce and to domestic violence. The issue concerned not just provision of refuge from violent males but the whole question of policing and its role in domestic situations.

The 1960s marked an important phase. The state's right to intervene in sexual matters was questioned and modified. Initially the debate remained outside the party political contest and was taken up by private Members of Parliament. It was in the 1990s that the Conservative Party sought to move the issues back to the centre of party politics, asserting the state's duty to set a moral climate and support the traditional family.

Though it is commonplace to see the 1980s as the decade of individualism and rolling back state power, in the field of morals and personal life it was the 1960s that reduced the intrusiveness of the state and extended individual freedom, while the 1980s and 1990s did the reverse. Jane Lewis (1992) has called the 1960s 'the permissive moment' emphasizing the fleeting nature of the trend. Yet the legislation passed in that period was 'momentous' in that it has lasted and has directly affected very large numbers of people, probably more deeply and personally than the changes to the structure of pension schemes or the National Health Service.

The younger generation of the sixties had grown up during the Second World War. The war had opened up a ferment of debate and fundamental questioning about society. More of this generation had undergone secondary and higher education. It was an era of optimism and economic growth as well as the security of knowing that jobs were available for young people. The very shortage of labour had attracted women into the labour force in growing numbers, not least in teaching, nursing and social care. This increased their economic and intellectual independence.

Contraception was not only limiting the time women spent having children but made exploratory sex more safely possible and, because less guilt ridden, more enjoyable. AIDS had never been dreamed of. A number of trends therefore combined to make this a period of moral questioning and change which fitted alongside the economic structural changes we have so far discussed.

The faith of many intellectuals, reminiscent of earlier thinkers such as Hegel, Mill and Durkheim, was that collective welfare, full employment and education would facilitate individual growth and autonomy, 'moral individualism'. In harmony with this goal the state should match its role of collective provision with a withdrawal from spheres that were not properly its province – regulating sexual behaviour, for example. What this thinking did not take on was the task of questioning the role of women in the family and the state's part in this. That was for feminist writers in the 1970s and 1980s to do. The first concrete official expression of this questioning of the state's role in relation to sexual behaviour comes with the Wolfenden Report in 1957.

Homosexual Law Reform

At the end of the Second World War a new Director of Public Prosecutions was appointed, Theobald Mathew, who with approval of the Home Secretary and support of senior officials began to take a much tougher line against homosexual practices, which were a criminal offence. Fear of prosecution made individuals a security risk. The defection of two known homosexuals – Burgess and Maclean – from the Foreign Office to Soviet Russia only heightened the pressure to do something. The number of convictions for gross indecency rose from 800 a year pre-war to 2,300 in 1953. The convictions often involved the police acting as *agents provocateurs*. The popular press broke the previous taboos in 1952 with a series of lurid accounts of the practices of 'evil men' (Weeks, 1990). There was a series of highly publicized trials. The whole criminalization process seemed, in its own right, to be creating an assault on public decency. It was probably this which lead the Home Secretary, Maxwell-Fyfe, after a particularly high profile trial, to appoint the Wolfenden Committee in 1954 to look at both homosexuality and prostitution. It also followed a report from the Church of England's Moral Welfare Council in 1952 that recommended reform.

Wolfenden Report 1957

The committee's report contains what remains a classic statement of principle about the appropriate role for the state in relation to the private lives of individuals.

> Our primary duty has been to consider the extent to which homosexual behaviour and female prostitution should come under the condemnation of criminal law . . . We have therefore worked with our own formulation of the function of the criminal law so far as it concerns the subject of this enquiry. In this field, its function, as we see it, is to preserve public order and decency, to protect the citizen from what is offensive or injurious, and to provide sufficient safeguards against exploitation and corruption of others . . . (para. 13)
>
> It is not, in our view, the function of the law to intervene in the private lives of citizens, or to seek to enforce any particular pattern of behaviour, further than is necessary to carry out the purposes we have outlined. (para. 14)

The law should protect young people, those with some mental defect and any individual from abuse but should uphold 'the importance which society and the law ought to give to individual freedom of choice and actions in matters of private morality' (para. 61).

It took ten years for the recommendations on homosexual law reform to be enacted. It was discussed as a possible element in a Labour Party policy document in the early 1960s but it was considered too politically dangerous. Crossman noted in his diary a remark by Harold Wilson:

> HW   That boy [Peter Shore, head of the Labour Party Research Department] is trying to put in everything, including a passage on Wolfenden, which would cost us, at a rough estimate, 6 million votes. (Crossman, 1981: 944)

However, the law was being made to look an ass by the mid-1960s and it was this, as well as the more liberal climate, which lead to legislation in 1967.

Sexual Offences Act 1967

Homosexual acts between consenting males over the age of 21 were decriminalized. Despite pressure from the Homosexual Law Reform

Society, conspiracy to commit and seeking to commit or facilitate homosexual acts was still an offence. These sections have been used to prosecute magazines for publishing contact listings. No legislation was passed concerning lesbian activity. It had never been criminalized. Victorian assumptions that it did not exist, or if it did it was not harmful, persisted.

A backlash

For many years, throughout the late 1960s and 1970s, this change in the law came to be accepted. Gay rights groups campaigned to change public attitudes to sexual orientation, with some success. A number of local councils began supporting gay organizations and this became a peg on which to hang a more general attack on 'looney left' councils. One council, Haringey, was attacked for having in its library the book *Jenny Lives with Eric and Martin*.

What really began a backlash, however, was the coming of AIDS. Fear, and the popular association of AIDS with homosexuality, began to refuel anti-homosexual feelings. An editorial in *New Statesman and Society* (vol. 115, no. 2963, 1988) captured the way the issue had become a party one:

> The Conservatives have already reaped untold electoral benefit from the 'looney left' campaign. Labour are indelibly seen as the gay party. The Conservatives are now positively coming out as the anti-gay party to milk for all it is worth the growing hostility towards homosexuality felt by the majority of people in this country.

This backlash did result in one piece of legislation. Section 28 (1) of the Local Government Act 1988, or 'Clause 28' as it was referred to in the campaign for its abolition. Under it,

> A local authority shall not
> (a) intentionally promote homosexuality or publish material with the intention of promoting homosexuality;
> (b) promote the teaching in any maintained school of the acceptability of homosexuality as a pretended family relationship.

In 1977 the gist of this section had been included in a bill in the House of Lords. The government of the day had rejected it on the grounds that it was not possible to legislate about the proper content of teaching on such a subject. It is a mark of how far politics had moved in the next decade that the legislation was passed in 1988.

A counter-move?

In 1994 an amendment to the Criminal Justice Bill was moved to lower the age of consent for homosexuals to 16, the same as for heterosexuals. This had been discussed by the Wolfenden Committee on the grounds that most countries have the same age and that any difference was discriminatory. Wolfenden had taken the view that young men needed a longer period of protection from the possible attentions of older men, and in which to make up their minds over such an important decision. In the end, the House of Commons compromised on the age of 18, once again bringing it into line with the age of majority; Wolfenden had used this age (21 at the time of his report) as a yardstick, but it had been reduced to 18 after his report. The House of Lords rejected an attempt to reinstate the age of 21.

Abortion

The Abortion Law Reform Association (ALRA) had been campaigning since the 1930s but had made little headway. A House of Commons debate in 1952 lasted one minute. The 1961 thalidomide tragedy raised the issue and put it into a different, public health category, a move enhanced by the growing awareness of the hazards of back street abortions.

In 1962 an opinion poll showed that 73 per cent of the public favoured abortion when a foetus was deformed (Potts *et al.*, 1977). The ALRA stepped up its activities and lobbied private members. Kenneth Robinson in 1961 and Renée Short in 1963 both had their bills talked out, but the Lords gave serious attention to a bill introduced by Lord Silkin in 1965. Medical opinion was divided. GPs seemed to favour wider scope for abortion but the BMA and the Royal College of Obstetricians and Gynaecologists opposed it, believing they might be forced to act against their consciences, and fearing being dictated to by patients and government. They then moved to arguing that there should be a conscientious objection clause in any legislation (Simms, 1985).

In 1967 a new Liberal MP, David Steele, drew the right to introduce a private member's bill and chose abortion law reform. It was similar to the bill introduced by Lord Silkin earlier and this time it passed.

The Abortion Act 1967

The Act did not introduce abortion as a right or on demand. It extended the previously very restricted categories of women who could be given an abortion. Doctors, two of them, had to give their approval. A woman could have an abortion up to twenty-eight weeks of term if two doctors agreed that either the child would be handicapped or

> the continuance of the pregnancy would involve risk to the life of the pregnant woman or of injury to the physical or mental health of the pregnant woman or any existing children of her family, greater than if the pregnancy were terminated.

Saving the woman's life was no longer the sole criterion.

Yet the decision was still a medical one and the decision to stop a pregnancy was different in nature to one to continue:

> If a woman plumps for motherhood, no member of the medical profession will ask if she is emotionally or financially ready for such a commitment, whether she has given it enough thought, whether her relationship can stand the strain. (Suzanne Moore, *Guardian*, 8 October 1992)

This was very far from abortion on demand, therefore. The Lane Committee (1974) found that about 70 per cent of women seeking abortions had been accepted by the NHS, a further 10 per cent by private clinics and 20 per cent were not accepted. Women have also been treated later than might ideally be the case because facilities have not kept pace with demand.

This was always a measure that raised deep moral issues though it has never become *the* dominant social policy issue that it has been at times in the USA. In the period from 1968 to the early 1990s there were sixteen attempts to change the Act, which all failed.

Attempts to modify the legislation have been varied, from trying to control the charitable sector's right to perform abortions, to shortening the period in which abortion was legal. The only change to have succeeded concerns this last point. The maximum term was reduced from twenty-eight to twenty-four weeks by the 1990 Human Fertilization and Embryology Act, on the grounds that, owing to medical advances, foetuses are viable at an earlier stage of development.

Divorce

The reform of the divorce laws can also been seen as part of a more general attempt to remove the state from intrusive control over individuals whose marriages had broken down. In the 1960s such individuals could not free themselves legally without going to degrading lengths. They had to be caught in an adulterous act, a prearranged one if necessary. As well as the number of 'hotel divorces', the number of couples who were cohabiting while still locked into an official marriage with someone else was growing. The Law Commission, a new body set up by the Labour government to review existing laws, reported on the divorce laws. It argued that to release couples from such a false situation would facilitate remarriage, help reduce extra-marital affairs and support the institution of marriage, not undermine it (1966). It is therefore wrong to see this legislation as driven by libertarian instincts to break up the family. It was driven both by respect for the traditional institution of marriage and a belief that it would be better served by honesty and mutual respect rather than by state enforcement.

The Divorce Reform Act 1969

The Act introduced 'no fault' divorce. This did not mean that fault was no longer an issue but it did mean that there were now two criteria for divorce available that did not imply fault. The sole ground for divorce was now to be 'irretrievable breakdown'. There were five proofs of such a breakdown: adultery, unreasonable behaviour, two years' desertion, two years' separation if both parties consented to divorce, or five years if the divorce was contested.

Under Section 4 of the Act a respondent could plead that she or he would be caused 'grave financial or other hardship' if the marriage were dissolved. In this instance the court could take account of the conduct of the parties and not grant a decree. This section and the five-year delay was put in to protect women who feared that after years of support they would be left high and dry for a younger woman. The bill was attacked as 'a Casanova's Charter' by Lady Summerskill, an ex-Labour minister and feminist campaigner. She said that women, although they should not be trapped in bad marriages, needed some protection for their more vulnerable position. For this reason, too, it was agreed not to enact the 1969 Act until the Matrimonial Proceedings and Property Act 1970, which gave the weaker party more rights to property on divorce, was in place.

The various new pieces of legislation of the period were consolidated into the 1973 Matrimonial Causes Act. This added a three-year bar on petitions for divorce after marriage. The 'grave financial hardship' clause was elaborated to include 'the loss of the chance of acquiring any benefit which the respondent might acquire if the marriage was not dissolved'. This would cover, for example, a stake in a husband's pension. In dividing up property, present and foreseeable needs and ability to pay were to be taken into account. So, too, were unpaid contributions to the family's welfare. The Act's aim was to

> place the parties, so far as it is practicable and, having regard to their conduct, just to do so, in the financial position in which they would have been if the marriage had not broken down and each had properly discharged his or her financial obligations and responsibilities towards each other. (Section 55 (1))

While the spirit of the 1969 Act had moved away from issues of conduct, the 1973 legislation, and the way the courts interpreted it, moved conduct back in. The courts had notions of a woman's proper role in marriage. Women in cohabiting partnerships that broke up had to prove they had made greater contributions than a married counterpart (Smart, 1984). The law remained both supportive of marriage and of women's traditional role within it.

However, the rule that parties should be restored to their original financial position proved hard to implement. The maintenance requirements were very broad, and men who remarried had great difficulty in meeting them as well as supporting a new family adequately.

Rehabilitative maintenance or 'clean break' settlements had come to be introduced into case law in the early 1970s (Smart, 1984). It was

introduced into public policy in the 1984 Matrimonial and Family Proceedings Act. Maintenance would be paid according to the earning capacity of the recipient as well as of the payer. The older the child the greater
the expectation that the ex-wife should work.

The personal and the political

What we had, then, were some very important moves to reduce the
intrusiveness of the state in sexual matters in the 1960s. It was limited
and did not give free licence to abortions, or to sexual relations for young
men. Marriage was still carefully constructed in a traditional mould.
Lewis argues that, paradoxically,

> Deregulation of personal relationships effectively served to increase the
> privatisation of the family and ironically further to distance the personal
> from the political. (1992: 64)

Nevertheless, in the longer run, the greater freedom to break marriage
contracts had repercussions for the state and the taxpayer. If couples
could negotiate 'clean breaks' that left one ex-partner dependent on social
security, the state was brought back into the equation. Why should taxpayers, many of whom were couples who had not divorced, pay for those
who had? In a period of rising social security spending and tax resistance
the state would soon enter the arena of marriage breakdown in a very
heavy-handed way, at least where one of the previous partners tried to
turn to the social security system for support. Concern about the state of
the family would re-emerge in the 1990s as those worried about traditional family values reacted to the social changes taking place.

Single parenthood, in particular, whether because of broken marriages
or otherwise, began to become an issue of political concern in the late
1960s, though the emphasis was first on the needs of the single parent
rather than the taxpayer.

Lone Parents

The issue of the state's responsibility for lone parents has always been
tangled up with moral concerns. From the 1834 Poor Law onwards

widows have been in a class of their own. A widow had not caused her change of status. She was not at fault. Yet her circumstances meant that she was often unable to support herself. In many cases she might have been expected to enter the labour market, and often did, but the state did tend to assume responsibility, giving outdoor relief under the Poor Law and then in the 1920s introducing widows' pensions. Other types of lone parent were deemed 'at fault' in some regard: the separated, the divorced, the deserted and the unmarried (always the smallest group). Moreover, governments have always feared collusion. Couples would not actually be living separately, but would pretend to and draw benefit. Alternatively, benefits might 'double up' maintenance payments ordered privately through the courts. They feared that giving benefit would encourage lone parenthood, making it easier. The tangles facing the government in the 1990s were not new (Lewis, 1994).

Beveridge had deliberated long and hard over how to treat lone parents. Were they deserving or undeserving? Should they be treated as mothers or workers who should be required to seek paid employment? Society's attitudes to the last question have changed over time (Lewis and Piachaud, 1987). Increasingly the expectation has grown that single mothers should be in paid employment. In the 1940s the view was that motherhood came first.

Beveridge took the view that unmarried mothers were undeserving and should be the province of the National Assistance Board. He recommended that all other lone mothers should receive an insurance-based benefit high enough to preclude the need to work. The children would attract family allowance. This never happened because of the doubling up problem.

> Beveridge clearly acknowledged the importance of women's work as mothers, but his commitment to social insurance meant that he could only give them entitlements as wives, which in turn meant that it would inevitably be difficult to provide benefits for deserted wives whose husbands had a legal obligation to maintain. (Lewis, 1994)

Consequently widows retained their favourable status and others were obliged to rely on usually low or non-existent maintenance payments from their ex-husbands, topped up by National Assistance. But the role of mother still predominated. The National Assistance Board did not insist that lone mothers register for work in order to claim assistance.

Through the 1950s the number of lone parents had risen only slowly. Then the effects of the divorce law changes became very evident. By the late 1960s divorce and separation had become a more important reason for single parenthood than widowhood. In 1961 the number of persons divorcing for every thousand married couples was two. By 1971 it was six and by 1991 it was over twelve. In 1961, 2.5 per cent of households were lone parents with dependent children. By 1971 the figure had risen to 3.5 per cent, by 1981 to 5.8 per cent and by 1991 to 6.5 per cent.

The Labour government appointed a committee to investigate the problem in all its aspects. The Finer Report was published in 1974. It recognized discrepancies between public law (government policy) and private law (what the courts decided in individual cases). It wanted to unify the two, giving ultimate responsibility for the administration of maintenance to the state. The state would carry the prime responsibility for ensuring that the families' needs were met and would then recoup maintenance from the father. It would have made all lone parents eligible for a non-contributory guaranteed maintenance allowance. This would have had a non-means-tested children's component, and a carer's component, which would taper off to allow women to earn and receive some benefit and would disappear when the parent carer's earnings reached the level of male average earnings.

By the time the report was published political interest had waned. There was little debate in Parliament (Lewis, 1994) and virtually none of the recommendations were implemented. The economic crisis was upon the government and a new and potentially expensive benefit was not going to win favour. A few things were done. Lone parents were given an additional allowance when child benefit was introduced. A higher disregard was introduced to enable them to take some part-time work and keep in touch with the labour market. This policy was extended in 1980 with the introduction of the 'tapered earnings disregard'.

Finer's main concern was not pursued at the time; it was an attempt to fuse public and private law, and to reduce the overlap in responsibilities between the courts and the state for maintenance of the family's basic living standard, this maintenance being in the child's interest.

The next attempt to tackle that issue had to wait until the 1990s, when it was reinforced by the Treasury's need to save money. This change was also driven by concern about the rise in divorce and marriage breakdown. Divorce was too easy and those who left marriages should pay the costs, it was thought. While Finer was trying to put maintenance squarely in the public sphere, the legislation of the Major era aimed to re-privatize it (see p. 217).

Domestic Violence

Though the 1960s encouraged individual freedom in sexual matters, drawing the boundary between intervention and privacy was difficult. A good example of the ambivalence of the state towards the privacy of the family has been its attitude towards domestic violence. This includes rape and sexual assault within marriage, child abuse, elder abuse and wife battering. The issue that has had most prominence is 'wife battering' or violence towards the female partner and it has lead to the most policy response.

In 1972 a group of women in Chiswick, in West London, were conducting a high street campaign on prices in the shops and in the course of talking to women they discovered the importance of domestic violence. This, not inflation, was uppermost in many women's experience. One of the price campaigners was Erin Pizzey who saw the need to provide some kind of refuge or way of escape for women, together with support and advice. Chiswick Women's Refuge was a highly publicized response to this need. It was a self-help group which managed to raise enough money to keep a large house on the High Road as a hostel and place of refuge. It operated an open door policy and ran into continual battles with the authorities over public health and other regulations. This only served to increase public attention (Rose, 1985). The movement spread and made some local authorities consider providing refuges themselves. In the main, though, this has remained outside the statutory sector.

In 1975 a House of Commons Select Committee reported on violence in marriage. It reviewed existing ways of dealing with it, and found them wanting. While criminal law on assault was theoretically adequate to deal with domestic violence, it was not adequately enforced by the police because the home was not considered an appropriate place for them to intervene.

There was even more difficulty with the civil law. A woman could obtain a non-molestation order or an exclusion order but only as part of some other process such as divorce, damages or judicial separation. These were lengthy processes and fundamental ones too. For a vulnerable woman who was being regularly beaten, initiating divorce proceedings might well make the whole situation worse. Furthermore, only court bailiffs could serve or enforce injunctions and they only worked during office hours (McCann, 1985).

The Law Commission had been reviewing matrimonial law in the magistrates' courts since 1973 and recognized that existing law did not give adequate protection to women in these situations. In 1976 the Domestic Violence and Matrimonial Proceedings Act was passed. It was followed in 1978 by the Domestic Proceedings and Magistrates' Courts Act. The 1976 Act applied to both married and cohabiting couples. Non-molestation orders and injunctions could be obtained without recourse to other proceedings and without notification to the other party. Injunctions could involve the power to arrest. The 1978 Act was intended to give recourse to the magistrates' court and hence speedy justice. However, the powers of these courts was also limited. Magistrates could make personal protection orders which excluded the husband from the home, but unlike the 1976 Act, it could not bar him from the surrounding area (Kennedy, 1992).

Case law

A common tactic used by the courts is to bind *both* parties over to keep the peace. This disposes of the need for a contested case and is aimed at neutralizing hostility between the parties. The result is to brand the victim as violent and to place an equal responsibility for the disturbance on each party. It reflects a certain ingrained belief that the woman must have done something to provoke the attack. Exclusion injunctions have tended to be temporary, allowing the woman a limited period in which to find alternative accommodation and there has been a reluctance to grant exclusion orders because of the perceived conflict with the property rights of the husband (McCann, 1985). An exclusion order is deemed permissible so long as it is in the best interests of the *children*. A woman is given protection because of her status as a mother rather than as an afflicted party as such. Even so the courts have moved to give increasing protection to women, and more injunctions have had the power of arrest attached to them: 24 per cent in 1980, rising to 28 per cent in 1987 (Dobash and Dobash, 1992).

Policing

Law is not enough on its own, it must be enforced. The police were initially reluctant to get involved and were not trained to do so. In 1985 the Metropolitan Police Force's Working Party into Domestic Violence was set up and reported in 1986. It concluded that most officers' responses were inappropriate and unhelpful, that police policies were inadequate and that training was virtually non-existent. Training dealt with the issue under the heading 'domestic dispute', trivializing it rather than dealing with it as a crime.

A Home Office report in 1986 also emphasized the need to keep the criminal justice system out of domestic situations and the need for education for couples, to minimize conflict. By 1989, however, the Home Office had moved to recommend that special police units be set up to deal with domestic violence. This happened in London, West Yorkshire, South Wales, Northumbria and other places.

Provision of refuges

The 1977 Housing (Homeless Persons) Act gave local authorities powers to provide accommodation for *mothers* escaping violence. Authorities may only accommodate their own tenants. A woman wanting to move out of the area has no right to accommodation. Local authorities have since 1976 been under great pressure to spend less and few refuges have been set up by them. The main response has been by the voluntary sector. This lack of provision seriously restricts the capacity of the courts if there is nowhere for the woman to go. The whole complex area of policy illustrates the delicate balance that policy must keep when tackling the privacy of the family.

8 The Party Over, 1976–88

It was the economic crisis of 1976 that finally broke the continuity in the social policies of the post-war era. As Anthony Crosland, who was in the Labour Cabinet in 1975, put it, 'The party is over.' He was actually talking about the finance of local government for which he was responsible, but he was summing up a much deeper sense of change in the climate of ideas about social policy, which began in this period. Like all periodization, the choice of this point to mark the break is problematic. For many years after 1976 more stayed the same than changed in social policy. Major institutional change took more than a decade to come but the climate of ideas and above all the economic and social structure did begin to change decisively at about this time.

A check to growth

One clear discontinuity was in public spending. It had been dictated by the visiting team from the International Monetary Fund, on whom the Labour government had called for help. Such crises had happened before – in 1949, 1951, 1956, 1961, 1967, 1971. But once they had passed, the growth of public spending on social services as a share of the national income had continued. This time it did not, at least for a decade and a half. The share of the nation's resources going to social policy was to stabilize and then decline in the period from 1981 to 1990, the first time this had happened in the twentieth century except as a consequence of war (see Figure 5.1).

Social policy and the economy

In the longer run the strain of trying to contain the rising demands for health and other spending prompted politicians to search for fundamental structural change in the Welfare State, as we shall see in the next chapter. More immediately important, however, was a reappraisal of the relationship between social policy and the economy. In the 1940s and 1950s both the Labour and Conservative governments, and the civil servants advising them, had been acutely aware of the economic needs of the country. Stafford Cripps and Hugh Gaitskell, Chancellors in the first post-war Labour government, had been puritanical in their determination that the Welfare State should not take resources from the export drive. Butler had been determined that it should not take away from private consumers' spending power in the early 1950s.

The philosophy that drove the Wilson government was a reaction against perceived private affluence and public squalor. The system of public expenditure planning that had been introduced in 1961 may have actually made it more difficult for the Treasury to control spending than it had been in the 1950s (Glennerster, 1975; Wright, 1980). The Cabinets of the time set targets for government spending based on what were no more than *hopes* of how far the economy would grow. It rarely grew as intended. Moreover, departmental spending was preserved in real terms even when prices rose, something no private firm or household could do.

By the mid-1970s even Labour politicians came to believe that economic growth should be given priority over social spending. The British economy had consistently performed less well than its competitors since the Second World War, indeed for much longer. Perhaps it was, after all, true that this was the fault of the Welfare State. The basis of Labour support, manufacturing industry, seemed to be in terminal decline. Some economists were arguing that the reason lay in there being 'too few producers': too many teachers, social workers and doctors and not enough people producing goods (Bacon and Eltis, 1976). Others contested this view. The structural changes taking place in the economy were a result of changing consumer preferences. People in Britain, and other economies too, actually wanted more health and education and not more manufactured goods (Glennerster, 1976). But many economists argued that the government's first claim on capital and on labour was 'crowding out' other economic activity, not least wealth creation (for a contemporary discussion of this debate see Blackaby, 1979). These views became dominant and certainly shaped the thinking of the Conservative Opposition at this time but they also strongly influenced that of the Labour government. If the Welfare State was eating into the manufacturing base of the country it was also eroding Labour's natural base of electoral support.

There was a feeling, shared by those on the left and the right of politics, that capitalism was finally in crisis (Gamble and Walton, 1976; Gough, 1979; O'Connor, 1972) and the Welfare State was, in no small measure responsible, if rightly. The climate of economic thought in the 1960s had been favourable to social policy. Now that conventional economic wisdom was reversed. The Labour government decided not just to curb public spending but to shift the emphasis within it, supporting industry and economic growth more generally, shifting the emphasis within social programmes to policies that would foster economic efficiency.

The best example of this change of emphasis was the speech that the new Prime Minister, James Callaghan, made at the trade union college at Oxford – Ruskin College – in 1977. Education had become too concerned with giving children a good time, standards were too low and schooling was too little geared to the needs of a modern economy, he argued. 'A great debate' on the issue was needed. After a consultation period the resulting White Paper said,

> Young people need to reach maturity with a basic understanding of the economy and its activities, especially manufacturing industry, which are necessary for the creation of Britain's economic wealth. (DES, 1977)

This theme was to run through the education policy of not just that Labour government but the following Conservative governments too. Almost exactly the same sentiments can be found in the next Conservative government's White Paper on schools eight years later:

> By the time they leave school, pupils need to have acquired, far more than at present, the qualities and skills of a technological age. (DES, 1985)

Various attempts were made to link school and workplace and encourage technical and vocational training in schools and after. A series of schemes were adopted to subsidize employers to take on young people and give them a basic training, very rudimentary in the early versions.

Giving up Keynes

The impact of the crisis on established ideas about full employment was even more profound (Burk and Cairncross, 1992). This was not just any sterling crisis. The oil price shock, caused by all the oil producers raising their prices, had sparked world wide destabilization and, in Britain, this boost to inflation, as unions and firms tried to pass on the consequences, built upon the long-term accelerating inflation rates of past decades. It pushed inflation – not unemployment – to the top of politicians' concerns and it caused a fundamental reappraisal of the Keynesian approach to economic management.

In the twelve months from July 1976 retail prices rose by 17 per cent. It looked as if inflation was simply going to explode and the economy with it. The inflation caveat, entered so long ago in the 1944 White Paper on full employment (see p. 5), now assumed central importance. Full employment could only be sustained if inflation was held in reasonable bounds. It patently was not. The facts seemed to fit the predictions made for so long by the American economist Milton Friedman. Governments could not affect the long-run level of unemployment. They were power-less. If they tried to reduce unemployment below the market-determined level it would simply produce inflation. Ideas only take root when the soil is fertile. In 1976 the soil could not have been better prepared for such an idea to take root.

The Labour government tried, initially with some success, to reach agreements with the trade unions to restrain wage increases. The government used social benefits, 'the social wage', as part of its case to persuade the trade unions to moderate their pay demands. Restrain pay demands and we shall be able to keep full employment and sustain the Welfare State, it argued. It worked in the short run but this was not 1940. In 1978/9 the attempt to continue to hold down public sector pay provoked massive public sector strikes. This 'winter of discontent' would live on in the folk memory and in political discourse. The policy and the government crumbled.

The failure of the incomes policy route left the Labour Party without a policy on full employment or inflation. No convincing answers appeared in the 1980s. It was the Conservative Party that adopted a new economic philosophy with enthusiasm.

Monetarism rules OK

Mrs Thatcher, in opposition, and her Conservative advisers became convinced that conquering inflation was the key economic goal and that Friedman was right. This conviction was to lay the foundations for the economic policy of the 1980s. Nor was the change of heart confined to the Conservative Party. Callaghan told the Labour Party Conference in 1976 that full employment could not be restored simply by boosting public spending. That might temporarily reduce the numbers of unemployed, but if the UK remained uncompetitive and if inflation went on rising, that remedy would be worse than the cure.

Unemployment rose from about 3 per cent in 1974 to 12 per cent in 1982/3. This was simply without precedent in the post-war world. Though other countries followed, accepting higher unemployment in an attempt to get inflation under control, none followed such a Draconian course through the 1980s. Heath, in 1971, had recoiled when unemployment figures rose above a million. The numbers out of work rose to more than 3 million in the early 1980s. Yet it did not bring the government down or lose it elections. Most people were not out of work. To most, 17 per cent inflation was more frightening than seeing other people unemployed, mainly in the industrial heartlands of the country. It took a decade of lower prices and finally unemployment hitting the middle class in the south-east of England, for that view to begin to change.

Social policy in 1945 had been founded explicitly on the assumption of full employment. Now that had gone.

The labour market and inequality

In retrospect we can see that unemployment was not the only structural economic change taking place at this time. Comparative economic analysis since has shown that a common trend of historic importance was beginning to affect first the United States and then the UK at about this time. For nearly a century, and certainly since 1945, the United Kingdom had experienced a slow but definite equalizing in incomes and living standards. In the late 1970s, before Mrs Thatcher, this began to change, as it had done in the United States in the early 1970s and was to do in many other advanced economies in the 1980s (Atkinson, 1993; Gardiner, 1993). The dispersion of earnings became more unequal not only because of the decline of old prosperous industries but because within existing industries the spread between the high and low paid became much wider. Part-time work became more common; most of the new jobs generated in this period were part time. Female participation in the labour force rose sharply from 53 per cent to 65 per cent between 1973 and 1991 (though not in full-time jobs), while male labour force participation fell from 93 per cent in 1973 to 86 per cent in 1991.

Between 1971 and 1991 jobs in manufacturing nearly halved. At the same time roughly the same number of jobs were created in the services sector. While most of the jobs lost in the manufacturing sector were full time and male, over a third of those created in the service sector were part time. It was mostly women who gained the service sector jobs (Land, 1994). The trend to greater inequality was to be charted with devastating clarity by the Rowntree Inquiry into Income and Wealth (1995). It began in this traumatic period of economic change.

Taxes as a burden

It is not surprising to find these changes reflected in attitudes to taxation. In the period from 1951 to 1976 two-thirds of all Britain's economic growth had been devoted to increasing its public services. Other countries had done the same, but out of much higher growth rates, leaving their citizens significantly better off, privately, as well as publicly. Public opinion polls suggested that until the early 1970s most people in the UK were, however, reasonably content with this set of priorities. Conservative posters at the 1964 election had boasted 'the Conservatives are chalking up ten new schools a week'.

During the period of the 1964 Labour government, however, the percentage of the public supporting more spending on the social services fell from 44 per cent to 22 per cent. By the mid-1970s public opinion was receptive to cutting taxes, though support for the NHS and particular services remained high (Whiteley, 1981). The shift was scarcely surprising. In the mid-1970s average real take-home pay, after tax, actually fell for the first time since the war. In 1973 real consumer expenditure reached its post-war peak. It then fell in 1974 and again in 1975. It remained stable in 1976 and fell again in 1977. This was unprecedented since 1945. People were prepared to support improved public services as long as their private consumption patterns were improving too. That ceased to be the case from 1974 to 1977 and the repercussions for social policy were profound. The Conservative Party promised tax cuts at the 1979 election but did not propose any major changes in social policy to achieve them. The same political response to similar pressures happened in other countries, from California to Denmark, at the same time.

Demography and home ownership

Other basic social changes were under way. The big increase in the child population, those born in the 1940s and 1950s, was now through school and into the labour force, paying taxes. The big rise in the number of the elderly had taken place from 1940 to 1970. Then the numbers of elderly stabilized and will not increase until the next century. The rising population was the middle-aged middle-class tax payer. As Davies and Piachaud pointed out,

> Thus the dilemma arises that the households that are best off, and must be expected to bear the brunt of paying for improved social services, are the very households which benefit least from the social services. (1983: 52)

Standard rates of income tax were now affecting most families. In the 1940s only a minority of families were caught in the income tax system to any significant degree. By the mid-1970s nearly all families were in the income tax net. At the same time over half the households in the country were owning or buying their own homes. Early in married life, especially, this took a very high share of a family's income. Taxes threatened earners' capacity to house their families in ways to which they aspired.

So it is not hard to see why taxation and take-home pay now moved centre ground in home politics for demographic as well as economic reasons. Far from being seen as a boon to a family's living standards high taxes to pay for social benefits began to be seen as a threat.

On the eve of the election Callaghan, the Labour Prime Minister, confided to his political adviser, Bernard Donoughue,

> You know there are times, perhaps once every thirty years, when there is a change in politics. It then does not matter what you say or what you do.

There is a shift in what the public wants and what it approves of. I suspect there is now such a sea change – and it is for Mrs Thatcher. (Lawson, 1993: 19)

A Thatcher revolution?

In the light of all these factors the shift that took place in tax and social policy in the 1980s should be no surprise. Nor should Mrs Thatcher's appeal. Yet was her victory in the leadership election as important a turning point in Conservatism as she and many commentators have suggested? Whatever the case made in other spheres the claim as far as social policy is concerned is less clear, especially in the period 1979–88.

Mrs Thatcher claims, in her account of her years at Number 10 (Thatcher, 1993), that Conservatism had gone profoundly wrong in making too many compromises with socialism in the post-war period. She had been a spending minister, like all the others, of course, pressing for expansion in education in 1972 (DES, 1972). So had Sir Keith Joseph. But, she claims, after the miners' strike, and Heath's defeat, Joseph and those around her went through an intellectual rebirth that rethought Conservatism in fundamental ways.

> Welfare benefits, distributed with little or no consideration of their effects on behaviour, encouraged illegitimacy, facilitated the breakdown of families, and replaced incentives favouring work and self-reliance with perverse encouragement for idleness and cheating. The final illusion – that state intervention would promote social harmony and solidarity or, in Tory language, 'One Nation' – collapsed in the 'winter of discontent' when the dead went unburied, critically ill patients were turned away from hospitals by pickets, and the prevailing mood was one of snarling envy and motiveless hostility. (1993: 8)

A new social policy agenda?

Yet the Conservative Party did not come to power in 1979 with a shining new set of social policies. Its monetary policy *was* new, however, and it was pursued with a fierce determination no previous government had achieved. This had unexpected consequences on unemployment and hence on social policy. But for the most part, Conservative policy began in 1979 by returning to those principles thrashed out in 1947–50: home owner-ship, the right to buy council houses, and the concentration of public expenditure on those in need, combined with choice in education. R. A. Butler would have recognized it all.

What was different about the 1980s was that Mrs Thatcher did not need to temper these policies to meet a hostile public opinion. She was moving with the grain. She was able to make a speech praising inequality, 'Let them grow tall' (Conservative Party Centre, 1979). It was happening anyway. Social and economic change were on her side. Most people were now working in non-manual occupations. Most people were now owner occupiers. Council house sales proved highly popular. Most people now had occupational pensions. Even so, once mainstream services that most people used came under the hammer, the public showed how deeply they had become part of the social fabric. This was above all true of the National Health Service. Mrs Thatcher did not dare to touch it until her third term. It is not until the end of Mrs Thatcher's period and her third election victory that fundamental structural changes were tried. Almost drunk with political self-confidence, one Cabinet minister was heard to say, at a dinner in 1988, 'There is nothing we cannot now do.'

But that was nearly ten years away. Mrs Thatcher's social policy revo-lution only unfolded slowly. There were other prior goals: inflation, the trade unions, the nationalized industries and foreign policy. Neither Mrs Thatcher's nor Lawson's long accounts of their periods in office (Lawson, 1993; Thatcher, 1993) contain any more than very brief discussions of social policy. Though the key changes begin in Mrs Thatcher's era the critical break with the past comes in 1976.

Labour 1976–9: Cuts and Fag Ends

Most of Labour's period in office after the IMF visit in 1976 was con-cerned with the battle with inflation, the statutory limits to pay and cuts in public expenditure. Many of these cuts were in fact no more than reductions to previously planned increases in spending but they were a sharp psychological adjustment for public sector workers and managers used to a world of regular incremental growth.

New ways to control public spending

The Treasury introduced changes in the way public expenditure was controlled. The Treasury reforms introduced in 1961 had largely survived intact. A department's expenditure plans for the medium term, five, then four, then three years, were argued over, cut and then approved. Once approved the department could, in normal times, be fairly sure they would be kept to. If any price or salary increases occurred an additional sum would be voted to meet the extra costs. This gave public sector managers a stable climate in which to plan and provide services, more stable than the private sector. It did mean, however, that managers could simply accept wage increases knowing the costs would be eventually accommodated. This was one reason for the steady rise in the share of public spending in the national income, the Treasury argued.

In the wake of the IMF visit a new system of control was introduced that set cash limits to a department's budget. It was set in ordinary money terms. If prices or salaries rose faster than the amount allowed for in the cash limit the department would not get any more money. It would have to make savings, cut staff or otherwise keep within its budget. Certain services, notably social security, were excluded from this arrangement because it was impossible to forecast accurately several years ahead what the level of unemployment would be, for example. The Conservative government later developed this into a tougher system of cash planning targets set for several years ahead but the first step happened in 1976. Cash planning has remained in place, with modifications, since (Harrison, 1989; Thain and Wright, 1990). The process of planning public expenditure and setting the levels of tax were brought together in the Autumn Budget of 1993 for the first time.

The first cuts

The Labour government's plans in 1976 set out to deliver a small rise in social security spending (see Table 8.1). In the end spending rose much more because of the increase in unemployment in the period. The government planned a very modest increase in health spending: 5 per cent over the remainder of its period in office. This was the kind of increase

Table 8.1 Real public expenditure on selected programmes in the United Kingdom 1976/7 to 1982/3

| | *1976/7* | *1978/9* | *1980/1* | | *1982/3* | |
			Labour plans	*Conservative out-turn*	*Labour plans*	*Conservative out-turn*
Defence	102.0	100	107.7	106.5	108.0	115.3
Law and order	98.5	100	104.2	107.6	108.7	116.4
Education	102.4	100	101.8	98.5	102.3	95.5
Health and personal social services	97.0	100	103.5	102.0	107.8	105.3
Housing	124.3	100	109.8	90.9	114.4	62.2
Social security	87.1	100	104.9	105.8	107.7	119.1
Total public expenditure	101.6	100	106.1	101.8	110.7	104.2

Notes: The figures represent public expenditure in real (volume) terms with each programme indexed so that 1978/9 = 100. In this table, the programme figures for education and health and personal social services and housing relate only to expenditure in England; the law and order figure relates to expenditure in England and Wales; the social security figure relates to expenditure in Great Britain.

Source: O'Higgins 1983

that had taken place each year in the past, not over the span of a Parliament. It planned a small real cut in education spending and stability in housing. In fact, councils cut their building plans for schools and housing because of the costs of borrowing money. Health charges were raised. There were no new policies or a new strategy. The government tightened its belt and hoped for the best.

At the end of this period of cuts and at the end of the winter of discontent, Mr Callaghan had to go to the country – and lost. The Thatcher era dawned.

Containment, Continuity and Tentative Change 1979–88

As we have already said, Mrs Thatcher's two first administrations did not produce revolutionary change in social policy. Her government first returned to the principles established in the late 1940s: containing public spending, shifting the finance of services away from direct taxation, targeting social security, enforcing tenants' rights to buy their council houses. Structural change came later, not least because spending proved so difficult to check.

Containment

The economics of the mid-seventies found direct expression in the government's early pronouncements. Its first public expenditure White Paper began with the statement, 'Public expenditure is at the heart of Britain's economic difficulties' (Cmnd 7746, 1979).

In his first Budget speech the new Chancellor, Howe, painted a vivid and accurate picture of Britain's relative decline as a manufacturing nation. The answer lay, he claimed, in increasing personal incentives by reducing direct taxation and reducing the scope of state activity, 'to leave room for commerce and industry to prosper' (*Hansard*, 12 June 1979).

There were indeed dramatic shifts in tax policy. The standard rate of income tax that most people paid on their marginal additional earnings was cut from 33p to 30p. In later Budgets this was to fall to 25p.

That reduction was paid for not by a reduction in spending, however, but by an increase in the tax on nearly all goods, the Value Added Tax *and* by an increase in the National Insurance contribution. Over the period from 1980 to 1990 the Treasury contribution to the National Insurance Fund from general taxation was reduced from 18 per cent of the total to nothing at all in 1988/9. Indeed, before unemployment began to rise, the fund had moved into surplus (HC 617 1989/90). Pensions and contributory social security benefits were, by 1989, being paid for entirely out of contributions, just as Macleod and Powell had argued should be the case in the 1940s (see p. 74). What none of these measures did was actually *reduce* public expenditure. The government had inherited large awards (the Clegg awards) to public sector workers that had been necessary to get the previous government off its incomes policy hook. It had also come to power with promises to increase defence and police spending. Its tight monetary policy produced a sharp rise in unemployment and hence in benefit spending. Only very minor reductions in spending on the other social programmes were introduced. Housing was the one service where really massive reductions were made in capital expenditure and in subsidies to local councils. Education suffered with real cuts (see Table 8.1). For the rest spending continued to rise. One commentator in 1983 concluded,

> beliefs that it [the Conservative Government] would lead to radical changes in the welfare state are, so far, largely unfounded, not so much because the Government has changed its mind as because it has been unable to implement its rhetoric. (O'Higgins, 1983: 175)

Another long-term review

The Chancellor, Geoffrey Howe, was at that very time trying to induce the Cabinet to think big and long. Just like his predecessor, R. A. Butler, forty years before, he was struggling to make sense of a commitment to reduce taxation with no proposals to reshape social policy. The Treasury, as it had done on several occasions before, proposed a long-term review of public spending going well beyond the normal three-year period, looking at the coming decade and beyond. The task was entrusted to the Central Policy Review Staff, who then briefed Cabinet.

The results of this exercise suggested that unless something fundamental was done spending would go on taking an even higher share of the GNP than it had done under Labour. Various options were trailed (Lawson, 1993), including introducing education vouchers, replacing part of the NHS with private insurance. These were probably more by way of making the Cabinet think but in Lawson's words, 'The result was the nearest thing to a Cabinet riot in the history of the Thatcher administration' (Lawson, 1993: 303). The paper was shelved and to ensure its demise the 'wets' in Cabinet, so Lawson claims, leaked the paper to *The Economist*. Mrs Thatcher announced that none of the proposals were being pursued.

The Treasury did not give up, however, and after the election in 1983 a fuller, more cautious paper on the long-term prospects for social spending was produced and published as a Green Paper (Cmnd 9184, 1984). Lawson set a medium-term goal of stabilizing public spending in real terms and then modified it to a less impossible goal of a slower rate of growth than the long-term growth of the economy. But how to do it?

Social Security Reform

If spending constraints *were* to work, given Conservative policy on defence and law and order, they had to work on social security above all. It was the largest spending programme and rising the fastest. Here, the new Conservative government did make some early very important decisions.

Incentives to work

The first target were the wage-related sickness and unemployment benefits introduced by the Labour government in 1965. These, at least higher unemployment benefits, had been introduced, it will be recalled, to make labour mobility more acceptable. The Conservative government believed that they merely reduced the financial incentive to seek work urgently and encouraged people to stay on sick pay for longer than necessary.

The fact that if benefits are sufficiently high they will at some point discourage people from returning to work is not really in doubt. It has been a basic principle of poor relief policy ever since 1834. The debate is about the level at which the disincentive to work effect begins to have a significant effect. The belief in 1979 was that the short-term benefits dating from 1965 were that high. In consequence, the earnings-related supplement for unemployment and sickness benefits was abolished from June 1982 and from the next month unemployment benefit and supplementary benefit paid to unemployed people (except the additions for children) were made taxable. This created 'clear water' between benefits and wages for all but the very poor. Did it have the desired incentive effect and increase employment?

As it happened a long-term study of the unemployed was taking place at the point when these changes took place and some answer can be given. For young people under the age of 25 there was some effect. Standardizing for other economic changes taking place, one group of leading academics concluded that the reduced benefits were associated with young people returning to work faster. For those with families and for older people, however, there was little or no effect (Narendranathan *et al.*, 1983). The overall effect on employment was small.

Sick pay

The administration of sick pay was also changed. Until 1983 it had been paid, as Beveridge intended, as a cash benefit by the local office of the National Insurance or Social Security Department. The Social Security and Housing Benefit Act of 1982 made employers responsible for paying 'Statutory Sick Pay' for the first eight weeks of sickness, though the employer could recover most of the cost from the state by reducing the net National Insurance contribution paid. The period was later extended to twenty-eight weeks. (Some groups were excluded such as those under the lower earnings limit, the self-employed and those of pensionable age. It was not payable for the first three days off work.)

This change was presented as a simple administrative device. But many argued that it was a first step to making employers responsible for sick pay, as most have always been for higher-salaried staff. This prediction was borne out in 1994 when the government abolished its reimbursement of the costs of statutory sick pay, leaving employers to cover all the costs of their employees' sickness absence (except for small employers). The reasoning was not just to save tax but to encourage employers to police sickness absence more closely. The concern of many critics was that it would encourage employers to be more selective in hiring staff. People with a poor health record or a chronic condition would find it difficult to get a job because they would be more costly. This had always been the case for a statutory scheme and general risk sharing. (For the other changes to sickness and invalidity benefits in 1995 see below.)

Uprating

The most important change made in those early years of the new Thatcher government, however, was to alter the basis on which benefits were 'uprated', or increased on a regular basis. We have seen that in practice for most of the period since the Second World War social security benefits had been raised to match rises in the general level of earnings in the economy. Often this was delayed until just before an election, but by 1983 the real value of the basic pension for a married couple had more than doubled since 1948 and was at its highest point compared to the average after-tax income.

From 1982 the government was only to uprate pensions in line with prices. This meant that the basic pension became a lower and lower percentage of the average wage or average disposable (after-tax) income. It fell from over 23 per cent of average male earnings in 1981 to 15 per cent in 1993 and on reasonable assumptions will fall to 10 per cent by the year 2010. The basic state pension would then become an irrelevance and could be abolished.

Similar trends have been followed with other benefits. The savings have been enormous in public expenditure terms: the cost of the basic pension has been cut by a third in a decade. None of this tackled the basic structure of social security, however and Norman Fowler, the Secretary of State, initiated what was billed as the most thorough overhaul of the social security system since Beveridge – still, notice, the reference point.

The Fowler reviews

These were a series of four separate reviews of different aspects of the social security system, which were undertaken with painstaking care. Detailed studies were made using modern computerized modelling techniques. The economists in the DHSS produced studies of past trends in pensioners' incomes suggesting that old people had done better than many sections of the community if you took account of private pension income but those who had been hardest hit were young families (DHSS, 1985a). Improving their lot became part of the objective of the reforms. A Green Paper, backed by the results of the studies, was published (DHSS, 1985b) and a fierce debate followed. The process was a good example of the sort of informed policy debate that had characterized social security since Beveridge. It was a conscious attempt to live up to that tradition. It was also to show how difficult it is to change a complex system, not only because it serves many interested parties but because the problems it is trying to tackle *are* complex.

Targeting

This basic truth was best illustrated by the reviews' attempts to tackle the question of targeting. As in the Conservatives' discussions in 1947–50, the key objective was to save money by targeting and means-testing benefits. What the review team found was that the UK already had one of the most targeted social security systems in the world, with a wide range of means-tested benefits that had grown up over the post-war period. The means-tested Family Income Supplement introduced in 1971 and the housing allowance a year later, had been superimposed on top of existing means-tested charges for services. This had created a fearsomely complex web. The consequence was that when people moved off these benefits, as their earnings rose, they had to pay full rent, full prescription charges and tax. At some points the loss of these means-tested benefits produced a 'tax' on earnings equivalent to more than the extra earnings gained. The Green Paper concluded, having reviewed the options,

> A wholly means-tested approach to social security – including pensions and child benefit – would at best meet only one of the main objectives of social security: to concentrate help on those who need it most. This approach would, by discouraging self help and reducing incentives, undermine the importance of individual provision. (DHSS, 1985a, para. 6.9)

The dilemma of targeting could not have been more succinctly put.

Much energy and ingenuity was devoted by the review team to trying to reduce the effect of this poverty trap. Tapering off the means tests cost more money unless the basic benefit rates were cut. The politicians were not ready to do this. So a series of sensible but small adjustments were made which did improve the poverty trap slightly and did not cost too much but were nowhere near the hoped for breakthrough to simplicity (see Barr and Coulter, 1990, for a discussion of this).

SERPS

The other major attempt to save money was the proposal in the Green Paper (DHSS, 1985b) to abolish the State Earnings Related Pension Scheme (SERPS) introduced after such an anguished pregnancy in 1978 (see p. 114). Though it had then gained cross-party support the government now argued that the promises SERPS made to future generations of pensioners were too costly.

According to Lawson (1993) the civil servants on the review team came up with proposals that would have cut the costs of SERPS. This appears as one option in the Green Paper. Fowler, the Secretary of State, wanted to go further and abolish SERPS altogether. This option was included in the Green Paper as a second, but preferred, route. The basic flat rate pension should be retained, the Green Paper said, but,

> We should not place on our successors the responsibility for meeting all our financial expectations in retirement. Instead we should ensure that everybody is able to save and invest for his own additional pension. (DHSS, 1985b, para 7.13)

To prevent people simply relying on the state to keep them when they retired all workers would be required to contribute to a pension scheme of some kind a minimum of 4 per cent of their income. Tax reliefs would encourage people to opt into private schemes.

Lawson (1993, ch. 47) describes a furious row that broke out between him and Fowler when Lawson realized that no one was costing the loss of revenue these tax reliefs would cost the Exchequer. He blames Mrs Thatcher for insisting that there must be incentives for people to join private schemes and that the government could not simply remove SERPS and not help in return. When the Treasury did do their sums they concluded that abolishing SERPS would actually *cost* the Exchequer £1 billion! Lawson also opposed the idea of making membership of private schemes compulsory, which would add to employers' costs.

This whole episode illustrates the key difficulty a government faces if it wishes to scale down its future pension responsibilities. The responsibilities for existing pensioners are difficult to abandon. On top of that such a government must also ask the present generation to spend more on its own future pensions.

The proposal to abolish SERPS and put the responsibility on to individuals and employers was almost universally opposed, among others by the CBI and the private pensions industry who did not relish having to cater for the lower paid with poor job prospects. The campaign mounted after the publication of the Green Paper by the poverty lobby, groups representing the elderly, by the CBI and the insurance industry, stayed the execution of SERPS. It was retained but the pensions promised, above all to women, were cut. The government did also increase tax reliefs to those who joined private schemes.

The policy had close similarities to the failed legislation of the Heath era. Unlike Heath's scheme, in 1973 occupational pensions were not the only, or the most favoured, alternatives. Instead private individually tailored 'portable' pensions which an individual could take from job to job, were given particularly favourable tax treatment. The one option not seriously discussed was to raise the retirement age for women, primarily because Mrs Thatcher opposed it! She did this when it was discussed in 1989, when the Treasury supported it. It was to be proposed again in Clarke's first Autumn budget in 1993 and legislated when Mrs Thatcher had gone.

The Social Fund

Towards the end of the Labour government's period in office a committee was appointed to consider the tangle of discretionary payments that those on Supplementary Benefit could receive. A claimant might have special dietary needs or be in an emergency with no bedding or furniture. Claims were growing, as was the cost, but different offices and officers might be more sympathetic than others. The poverty lobby had pressed for clearer rights and a team of officials set to review the scheme proposed that the guidelines that already existed could be tightened up and turned into statutory rules approved by Parliament (DHSS, 1978). This was done in 1980 by the new government. The scope for discretionary payments by officers was greatly limited but payments began to grow again and the application of statutory rights proved very expensive. When people's rights became clear they claimed them! The number of furniture grants given rose three and a half times between 1978 and 1983, the White Paper complained (Cmnd 9691, 1985: 37). The way to stop this rising expenditure on exceptional extras, the government concluded, was to give people money to meet the cost of new bedding in an emergency, but only to give it as a loan. A new fund was set up to meet these costs – the Social Fund – but it was not to be open-ended. Cash-limited sums would be made available for specialist officers in each local office to allocate in any year. The local office would set the priorities within guidelines. The fund would help with maternity and funeral costs and there would be community care payments for those leaving hospital, but other elements would move to a loan basis. Funeral expenses would be recovered from the dead persons' estate where possible.

The Social Fund loans probably caused more dispute and anger than any other part of the reforms. Recovering loans made to poor people to cover emergencies seemed particularly harsh. The government claimed it would stop abuses of the system. The total sums of money involved, however, were quite small.

The resulting legislation, the 1986 Social Security Act, embodied these changes and smoothed out some of the perverse overlapping elements in the web of means-tested benefits that had grown up in the previous twenty years. Various changes were introduced during the passage of the legislation to mollify groups of losers, for example housing benefit recipients. It was *not* a brave new world but it was a slightly less idiotic old one. The provisions came into effect in April 1988.

The Social Security Act 1986

The main effect of the Act was that:

- Common rules were introduced to assess entitlements to all the means-tested schemes which had previously operated under different definitions and rules about income and capital.
- Family Credit was introduced in place of Family Income Supplement. It *was* more generous, and applied to low-paid families in work (24 hours a week reduced to 16 in 1992).
- Income Support replaced Supplementary Benefit. It had a simpler system of automatic additions to the basic rate to cover the costs of children or a disabled person.
- All recipients would have to pay a sum equivalent to 20 per cent of the rates and the new poll tax. This was part of Mrs Thatcher's personal crusade to force local voters to recognize the cost of local services but it complicated the otherwise laudable attempt to simplify the Income Support scheme. This 20 per cent requirement was abolished after Mr Major became Prime Minister.

Results

The consequences of this complex and detailed set of new rules have been assessed by Evans *et al.* (1994). They conclude that little changed.

The share of total spending going on means-tested benefits remained virtually constant. More help went to the elderly, to the long-term sick and to children, but less to the families of the unemployed. The Social Fund did result in a reduction of two-thirds in real spending on exceptional items. Spending on Family Credit did rise above the old FIS levels. The number claiming the new benefit rose from 3 per cent of all families with children, under the old system in 1986/7, to 5 per cent in 1990/1 under the new. A detailed look at which groups gained and lost suggests little overall effect on the level of poverty one way or the other. The main impact had been to churn up the incomes of the poor, some gaining, some losing. What it had *not* done was to reduce the social security budget.

Housing Reform

Council house sales

Undoubtedly the most popular and politically successful policy the government initiated in this first period was the sale of council houses. This had been on its agenda ever since the 1940s and individual councils had enabled their tenants to buy their council houses, but it had never been encouraged by Labour councils and it had never necessarily been an attractive option. What the government decided to do was to give council tenants of three years' standing a right to buy their homes at a generous discount under the 1980 Housing Act. The longer they had been tenants the larger the discount. The discount began at a third off the value of the house and rose by one per cent for each year up to a 50 per cent discount. By 1989 the discounts had been raised to 70 per cent in some cases. These were powerful inducements and they produced results. Sales reached a peak at nearly a quarter of a million a year by 1982. More than a sixth of the total stock of council houses was sold in the period 1979–87. Between 1979 and 1994 the share of the total housing stock owned by local councils fell from nearly a third to little more than a fifth. Sales began to slow down as most of those who had the capacity to buy, and some that really did not, had bought their houses. This left behind in local authority and housing association tenure mostly the poorest groups in society. In 1974 just under half the tenants in social housing were in the bottom 40 per cent of the income distribution; by 1991 the proportion was three-quarters and only 40 per cent of them had jobs.

Diversifying social housing

Though councils did not get the full value of the houses they sold they did get some. But the government did not want the council sector they were busy reducing to grow again and stopped councils from spending most of their receipts on new building. It did, however, follow the trend set by the previous Labour government in switching financial support to non-profit housing associations. By the 1990s these had become the main suppliers of new social housing units for lower income renting.

The final strand in the 1980s housing policy was to withdraw the subsidies councils received to keep down the level of council house rents. Councils were forced to raise their rents nearer to the fair rent levels set for private and housing association tenants. Poorer tenants, the great majority, could claim housing benefit from the Department of Social Security. This was still a subsidy from the central government but it came targeted on the poor and indifferent to the form of tenure. Housing benefit was available to all tenants on a means-tested basis. The policy begun in 1972 had been taken to its full and logical conclusion.

Though making sense as a housing policy, it was steadily pushing up the social security budget and adding to poverty trap problems that social security reforms were wrestling with at the very same time. For a full account and an evaluation of the housing policy of the period see Hills and Mullings (1990).

Continuities

The first two terms of Mrs Thatcher's government saw changes in direction and portents for the future but there was more continuity than change. In education the financial squeeze was tightest on the universities. Overseas students had to pay the full cost of their education, extending the logic of the policy begun previously. At one point, in 1984, Sir Keith Joseph proposed to make home students pay towards the costs of their university education. He saw this as a way of getting more money for the universities in his annual battle with the Treasury. Within weeks he had to withdraw the proposal in the face of outraged opposition from Conservative backbenchers. What would their middle-class parent constituents say and how would they pay for their private schools if they had to pay for university too? There was a wider political lesson. Touch those parts of the Welfare State that most benefit the middle class at your peril.

Keith Joseph had also become keen to introduce some kind of voucher scheme. This would have given parents the equivalent of a luncheon voucher that could have been taken to any school of the parents' choice, public or private, and cashed for their child's education. The DES officials patiently pointed out that for state schools this would have meant no advance on what could be achieved already if there were places available. There were few spare places and it would increase the administrative costs considerably. To extend the scheme to private schools would mean that parents who now paid for their children's education would become eligible for vouchers and public money. This would increase the education budget by 6 per cent at a stroke and the Treasury would never entertain the idea (for an account of the dilemmas see Blaug, 1984).

What did happen was a very limited scheme that went some way to replace the loss of support some direct grant schools had suffered after 1976. Parents with low incomes could apply to send their children to a restricted list of independent schools and fill a quota of 35,000 places in all. The state would then pay the fees on an income-related sliding scale. This was called the Assisted Places Scheme.

For the rest, though in straightened circumstances, the education system went on much as before, focusing on links with industry, criticized for its standards, beginning to lose custom to the private sector. For a detailed account and evaluation of the period see Glennerster and Low (1990). In the Health Service too there were changes designed to reduce costs and increase managerial efficiency. The complex layers of administration introduced in 1974, of regions, areas and districts, were slimmed down. Area health authorities went. Sir Roy Griffith was brought in from Sainsbury's to advise on how to improve the management of the NHS. He could see no one in charge and proposed that there be a system of general management in place at each level to run hospitals and districts rather than leaving the service to be ruled by multiple professions. These changes took effect from 1983 on. Beyond that nothing fundamental changed in the NHS. What did was the fierce rigour with which cash

9 New Directions, 1988–95

Mrs Thatcher's third election victory was important for the institutions that deliver social policy in the UK, the National Health Service, schools and local government. The first priorities on the Conservatives' agenda had been accomplished. The trade unions had been tamed, the miners defeated, and inflation brought under control. Now, as their third election approached, the Conservative Party could contemplate something more radical. Mrs Thatcher's memoirs capture the logic:

> The manifesto was designed to solve a serious political problem for us. As a party which had been in government for eight years, we had to dispel any idea that we were stale and running out of ideas. We therefore had to advance a number of clear, specific, new and well-worked-out reforms. (1993: 572)

There is a general and disturbing lesson to be drawn from these remarks from a consummate politician. Seeking to win votes by promising to spend more on social programmes was thought to be impossible and, in her case, undesirable. Parties cannot, however, merely promise to keep the status quo. It looks boring. 'New ideas' have to be put on show in each manifesto. Perpetual change becomes a consequence of the political market-place.

A Radical Manifesto

A series of policy groups had been set up in 1986 to prepare the ground for the next election, each chaired by ministers. The input from Mrs Thatcher's own Number 10 Policy Unit and through it, from external 'think tanks', was significant. Mrs Thatcher claims that, 'The manifesto was the best ever produced by the Conservative Party' (1993: 572).

In terms of its coherence around a central theme and the radical nature of its proposals, this is a not unreasonable claim. The first eight years of Mrs Thatcher's government can be seen as completing an old agenda that can be traced back to the period 1947–50. The 1987 election set a new agenda and a new direction for Conservative social policy.

It is usually claimed by political opponents and many social policy commentators that this change began the breakup of the Welfare State. For some in the Conservative Party this was probably the ambition. But it can be seen as the very opposite – the beginning of a revival in the social institutions that deliver social policy. Therein lay the political skill of the proposals. They appealed to both sections of the Conservative Party and had an appeal beyond.

On balance, the evidence is that it was the reformers and not the abolitionists who won. Middle England still needed the basic social services too much for a Conservative Party that wanted to win to abolish them. Yet their increasing cost was a threat to the central goal of reducing taxation. Could the circle be squared? It is worth seeing how Mrs Thatcher herself saw the changes:

> The manifesto went to the heart of my convictions. Those we wanted to empower were not . . . those who could afford their own homes or private schools for their children . . . but those who lacked these advantages. (p. 572)

Reversing long-run decline?

What Mrs Thatcher saw, with her populist insight, was that there was growing dissatisfaction with state services that gave little choice to their users, in which the professional view was dominant and the parent or patient in the waiting-room seemed to count for little. In a growingly sophisticated consumer society this compared poorly with the market sector. The Labour Party, in the 1960s and 1970s, had experimented with forms of consumer participation to remedy the same defects: a few token lay representatives were placed on consultative bodies. This had satisfied no one.

What had gradually happened was what Durbin had feared more than fifty years before. The professionals and service providers had come to be too insensitive to their clients. Services that lack an effective sanction against abuse will come to abuse. Ultimately, the most effective sanction is for the user to say, 'I have had enough. I am taking my custom elsewhere.' Institutions that lack such external discipline eventually decline, be they corporations, governments or social services (Hirschman, 1970). The cosseting of the British economy through imperial protection and the captive markets of the empire in the early part of this century may explain the long-run weakness of British firms. The same decline can be said to have afflicted the institutions of the Welfare State. It took a long time, but by the 1970s some of the signs were on the wall.

Some of the earliest were visible on the vast public housing estates built in the 1960s where the 'consumers' had least capacity of all to make their voices heard or to exit. Until the 1940s, at least, council housing had been both much sought after and well managed. Then, as politicians saw success and votes in building houses, regardless of the quality of the living environment, or the capacity of the councils to manage the stock, standards fell. Housing managers, caretakers and other staff left the estates for cosy central offices and left the tenants and the stock to fend for themselves (see Power, 1988, for a vivid description of this process of long-term decline). The tenants left behind, especially after the encouragement of owner occupation, had even less leverage and purchasing power. Some estates became hard to let, despite a housing shortage, and provided an environment of squalor and crime that made them social ghettos. This was happening long before the right to buy policy came into force (Glennerster and Turner, 1993).

Education also had its warning signs. One of the most dramatic and well publicized concerned a primary school in a poor area of Islington.

> In the autumn of 1973 William Tyndale was an ordinary enough junior school in a run down part of north London; within just two years the school had fallen apart and striking teachers, angry parents and helpless politicians were confronting one another through the headlines of the national press and the current affairs programmes of television. (Gretton and Jackson, 1976)

The poverty of the area and the extreme difficulty of appointing good staff on the salaries available were the predisposing factors at work in this school. Yet it also showed how powerless the system and parents were when a school fell into the hands of teachers who took the law and the children into their own hands. The politicians had given up exercising control, the inspectors only advised, the governors were ineffective and the parents powerless. In the end, there was an independent enquiry and teachers were dismissed, but the whole episode alerted the wider public to the fact that there was something very wrong with a system that could let this happen. Gretton and Jackson, in their powerful account, concluded,

> All these issues we have mentioned – the powers and responsibilities of local authorities, the control of the curriculum, the criteria for assessing a school's efficiency, the aims of primary education, the need for testing, the role of the inspectorate, the function of managers and the professionalism and accountability of teachers – are proper subjects of consideration by the Secretary of State for Education . . . After William Tyndale [he – though all his predecessors have] can no longer pretend that it is all happening somewhere else. (1976: 125–6)

This 'scandal', like the Ely Hospital scandal of the 1960s (see p. 125), shook a complacent system. It came on top of the publication of a very influential set of papers by Conservative academics – the Black Papers (Cox and Dyson, 1969) – highly critical of modern methods of teaching and standards in state schools. This theme had been picked up by the previous Labour Prime Minister James Callaghan, in a famous speech at Ruskin College, Oxford in 1976. Work had then begun within the DES on devising a National Curriculum (Centre for Contemporary Cultural Studies, 1981; Glennerster and Low, 1990).

Lawson's account of the origins of the education reforms is worth noting. He, too, perceived that voters were worried about standards.

> When I became Member for Blaby . . . I found the biggest single issue to be parents' dissatisfaction with the standards of education and conduct in the schools most of their children were obliged to attend. (Lawson, 1993: 602)

Nor was Blaby unrepresentative. As Halsey concludes, in his review of a series of public attitude surveys in the 1980s, 'Public perceptions of the performance of secondary schools in particular are decidedly gloomy' (Halsey, 1991: 57). There was comparative evidence from abroad to support such instincts (Green and Steedman, 1993).

The continuing concern for education standards was later illustrated by the considerable attention given in the press and television to a critical speech made to the British Association by Sir Claus Moser in 1990 about the standards of British education. The result was private support to set up a National Commission on Education, which reported in 1993. It contains the best review of the education system as it was in the 1990s.

Lawson and Thatcher had thus listened to middle England when the Labour Party was stilled tuned to the wave length of the NUT. Education, after health, was next to top priority for voters (Halsey, 1991).

Radical ideas

When the policy groups reported in 1987 and the Conservative manifesto emerged it contained radical proposals on housing and education. There was nothing on the National Health Service. No radical ideas had crystallized and Mrs Thatcher decided that it was too hot a political potato to handle anyway in the manifesto (Thatcher, 1993: 571). Nor was there any fundamental change to the policy on community care. Both were to come later.

Housing Choice

> Municipal monopoly must be replaced by choice in renting. (*The Next Moves Forward*, Conservative Party, 1987)

It was clear by 1987 that there was little extra mileage in the sale of council houses to individuals, at least as a way of significantly reducing the size of the council sector. The remaining tenants were too poor. Why not give tenants the right to transfer the ownership of their house to a private landlord or housing association if they were dissatisfied with their council? If the estates were so bad that no one wanted to buy them a central government agency could take them over, improve them and sell them off.

Ultimately, if there was to be real choice the private landlord market had to be revived and this meant giving landlords the right to let at free market rents. The tenant would have some security at the end of the lease, the right to appeal if a rise in the rent was unreasonable or beyond a normal market increase. This last provision was an improvement on the situation in the 1957 Act, which had no provision for appeal and no element of security. Taken together these ideas amounted to the most coherent housing policy the Conservatives had had since 1953.

These were the ideas embodied in the manifesto and the 1988 Housing Act:

- Rent control in the private sector was removed. New tenancies would be either assured leases with renewal rights or short-hold.
- Central government could designate an area of public housing and create a Housing Action Trust to manage the houses, eventually disposing of them.
- The notion that individual tenants could get a landlord to take over their house was dropped as impractical and replaced by an arrangement which put the onus on private landlords or housing associations. They were given the right to bid to take over an estate or part of it and the tenants had a right to vote on the proposal and veto it, under some complex voting rules.

Under the 1989 Local Government and Housing Act local councils lost their right to subsidize council rents out of local revenue.

Housing outcomes?

This was a comprehensive package of housing measures driven by a clear philosophy and the intention of giving more market power to tenants. The difficulty was that really no market for poor tenants' custom existed. There were no private landlords who could get sufficient return to make the political risk worthwhile. Very few housing associations wanted to get into the business of taking on large estates of very poor tenants. The danger to their reputations of owning such problem areas made that an unattractive prospect. Tenants themselves feared that new landlords would put up rents and might want to move them out of their houses. When proposals to buy were made, few gained tenants' support. Assured tenancies began to expand but did not serve the needs of poor tenants.

Markets work well when people with money face many sellers. That was not the case with social housing. Few Housing Action Trusts had been created by 1994 for very much the same reason. The Department of the Environment, even at one remove, did not want to be lumbered with managing the most deprived and crime-ridden areas in the country. That promised to be a civil servant's and a minister's graveyard.

Much of the 1988 Act, for all its radicalism, remained a dead letter. That is not to say that social housing was not changing. Little by little housing associations of varied kinds and sizes came to be the new main providers of social housing. The range of landlords for poor and vulnerable people was far more varied than it had been and the new housing associations were managing their property effectively. The monopoly of social housing had been broken and the quality of management had been improved by action taken by both Labour and Conservative governments from 1974 onwards.

As against that the social problems that were accumulating on the most deprived estates were worsening by the year. This was the reverse side of the very success Conservative housing policy had had in extending owner occupation to the great bulk of the population.

It is not until the major parties really come to terms with this problem that it has any hope of solution. Yet it only affects a small minority of the population, most of whom do not vote. As the Welfare State comes to be concerned increasingly with the poor and only the poor, will the ordinary voter have any interest in what happens to them? Housing is the first test case. The issues are remarkably similar in whatever European country we look (Power, 1993).

The prospects are not all bad. Governments of both main political parties in the UK have supported concentrating efforts on the worst estates, improving the quality of management and decentralizing it. The Priority Estates Project was an initiative begun by the Labour government in 1979 and continued, after some initial doubts, by the Conservative government, through the 1980s. Estate Action and a number of projects followed. All had some success (Glennerster and Turner, 1993; Power, 1988). Yet in the end they could do little on their own to reverse the tide of growing and extreme deprivation that was afflicting such areas.

Standards in Education

The ideas of a National Curriculum and some kind of national standard-setting had been around in the old Ministry of Education in the 1950s. The then Minister, Sir David Eccles, had bemoaned the fact that this was forbidden territory for politicians. A proposal to set up a Curriculum Study Group in the ministry had been seen off by an outraged National Union of Teachers and others in 1962. But the tide of opinion had turned in the early 1970s, for reasons touched on already, and this had been accelerated by the economic crisis of 1976. The prime ministerial initiative by Callaghan to take the standards issue seriously in 1977 (see p. 169) was the first public step. The DES could also see that it would be possible in this new climate to press for a new role.

In the 1950s and 1960s the old Ministry of Education had been brilliantly successful in expanding education through a series of reports that levered more money out of the Treasury. It was probably the lead promotional department and was an exciting place to work. It was admiral of a large fleet of smaller local authority vessels. It determined where local schools would be built, what organizational form they should take, what pace and form the expansion of higher education should take.

After 1976, for a period, there was a halt to educational expansion, only a tiny new building programme to allocate between local authorities, little opportunity to interfere with the design of local schools. What were these civil servants to do! What more natural than to see an enhanced role for the centre in curriculum design.

A series of discussion papers was produced exploring what might be in a national curriculum, though it was initially presented as a voluntary move to harmonization between schools. This had continued from 1977 to the mid-1980s.

By the time ministers were preparing for the 1987 election, in the midst of a long-running teachers' strike that was damaging teachers' credibility and support, it was possible for ministers to feel they could go the whole way, that is, to a statutory National Curriculum. There was broad agreement across the political spectrum on this. Teachers were in no position to resist, or so it seemed.

The proposals in the manifesto were to go well beyond a curriculum. There were to be assessment targets. Schools were to be judged on their performance in these tests. It was this step that lost the consensus that existed on a National Curriculum. Most teachers supported some core common syllabus for the key subjects. The government wanted to go several bridges further. It proposed a detailed curriculum for most subjects, regular testing of children at the ages of 7, 11, 14 and the last year of schooling, and the publication of the results for parents to make informed choices between competing schools. The result was a long-running battle between the teachers' unions and the government that was still unresolved in late 1994.

Choice and decentralization in education

The idea of giving vouchers to parents to buy education for their children had attracted Conservative intellectuals since Milton Friedman (1962) had advocated it in the early 1960s. We described in the previous chapter why it came to grief in the first Thatcher period. Greater rights of choice had already been given to parents using state schools. Perhaps there was mileage in extending this idea. Two strands of policy that were already well developed in a number of local authorities were added.

The first was decentralizing financial responsibility to the schools themselves. The extent to which state schools had devolved responsibilities had varied. Some had the power to spend their own small budget on books and small equipment as they wished. In other cases virtually everything the school used had to be purchased through the central local authority office miles away and with considerable delay. Local authorities paid the salaries of the teachers, allowing each school a quota of teachers of different ranks. This tended to mean that favoured schools in attractive areas kept their teachers, who progressed up their salary scales. As a consequence they did better in cash terms than schools in poor areas (Glennerster, 1972). A number of authorities tried to remedy this situation by giving more cash to schools in poor areas. This money could be spent on whatever the school wished. The Inner London Education Authority took this the furthest and gradually extended the principle. It was a Labour authority. Another more Conservative area, Cambridgeshire, took the experiment the whole way and gave each of its schools a total budget out of which they could employ what teachers and what other equipment or books they chose. It improved their capacity to react quickly and freely without LEA approval, and it was popular with these schools (Burgess, 1986). It was a new idea and it was not the voucher idea that the DES saw so many objections to. The government decided to extend the scheme to all schools. The 1987 manifesto contained a pledge to give all secondary and some primary schools their own budget. Governors and managers of schools had for a long time been pressing the government to give these bodies more freedom and to require the representation of parents on these bodies. A committee set up by the previous Labour government had proposed increasing community and parental representation on bodies that at one time had been entirely political appointees. Most authorities were going down this road. The government was proposing to go with the tide.

The second strand of policy was more controversial. Previous education Acts had increased parents' right to choose a school and gave powers of appeal if they were not given that choice. The 1987 manifesto went further, proposing to remove local authorities' right to limit the size of a popular school. Schools' budgets would be set according to the number of pupils they could attract on a formula basis: so much per pupil attracted to the school.

Taken together these elements amounted to a voucher scheme operating in the state system. Schools would compete for custom. When a pupil signed up, that would attract a sum of money, in exactly the same way as would happen under a voucher scheme.

More controversial still was the idea that some state schools should be able to become independent and supported by central government funds, recreating the direct grant schools in effect (Thatcher, 1993). In the event this proposal was modified to become the grant maintained or opted-out schools scheme. Parents dissatisfied with their local authority could exercise collective exit powers. This paralleled the similar powers given to tenants in the Housing Act of the same year.

The Education Reform Act 1988

This Act embodied these ideas and was the first really large structural change to the education system since the 1944 Act and the comprehensive school reforms of the sixties. Despite the Act's importance the process of consultation was minimal compared to the careful crafting and compromises reached in 1944. A few brief type-written consultation documents were circulated during the summer vacation of 1987 with replies required by the end of September or the middle of October. The debates that ensued were furious, again in contrast to the passage of the 1944 Act. There was little consensus in the education world especially on the setting of attainment exams from 7 on, the detail of the National Curriculum and the abolition of tenure for university teachers.

The key elements in the Act were:

- It laid a duty on the Secretary of State to establish a National Curriculum for all state schools setting out targets of knowledge children should have reached by 7, 11, 14 and 16: 'attainment targets'.
- Pupils would be tested on these at those ages in a uniform national way and the results would be published by each school. ·
- A standard number of pupils would be fixed for each school by central government.
- A formula would be set to allocate budgets to each school by each authority but it would be approved by the Secretary of State.
- Schools could opt out of local education authority control if the majority of parents voting approved. The schools would be funded directly from central government and would be called grant maintained schools.
- Polytechnics became independent, not run by local authorities. Later they were to become universities.
- A new University Funding Council was given powers 'to make grants (to universities) subject to such terms and conditions as they think fit' (Section 131(6)) and tenure was abolished. This was the most sweeping extension of state power over universities seen in the post-war period.

Student Loans

The 1987 manifesto had cautiously referred to the review of student finance that was under way. Burned once, the government was going to be very careful. The eventual scheme was caution itself. Fees were left untouched. There was to be no contribution to university fees paid by the ordinary home student. They would continue to be paid by the local authority on his or her behalf. Instead the student maintenance grant would be frozen but students could top it up with loans. The original idea had been to administer these loans through the banks but no one thought to ask the banks first, and the National Union of Students made it clear that it would call on students to boycott any bank that co-operated. None did.

The scheme was significant only in that it established the principle that students should repay part of the costs of the education that would benefit them financially. The scheme would cost the Exchequer *more* in the first instance because the loans were made out of public money. It would be into the next century before the revenue from the repayments would significantly outweigh the extra cost. (For a contemporary critique see Barnes and Barr, 1988. For a way forward see Barr *et al.*, 1994).

A Poll Tax

A third major element in the 1987 manifesto was the proposal to introduce a flat rate poll tax to finance local services. Ever since the Second World War local authorities had been given extensive new responsibilities to provide social services without anything but an unpopular property tax – the rates – as a way to finance them. Increasingly central government had to finance services that it willed through grants to local councils. In the 1980s, when central government tried to cut local grants, it found local councils willing to raise the rates to try and sustain services. Furious that its attempts to cut spending were being frustrated, central government tried increasingly interventionist ways of stopping the process. Rates were capped or limited by Parliament. Then, in desperation, councils were given a form of revenue – the poll tax – that was oppressive to administer and was not related to people's ability to pay (Butler *et al.*, 1994). This was meant to restrain high-spending councils but its evident unfairness rebounded on the government instead. Implemented in 1990, it proved so unpopular that it contributed to Mrs Thatcher's downfall and was replaced by the council tax in 1993. (For the story in more detail: Gibson, 1990; Glennerster *et al.*, 1991; King, 1990).

Though the council tax proved more acceptable it left the basic weakness in the finance of local services unresolved. Much of social policy is delivered locally by political bodies who only raise a small part of what they spend. This leaves accountability for service quality uneasily spread between central government, who pays, and local government who runs the services. The weakness of such a situation was lucidly argued in a report by the Layfield Committee in 1976.

Health Service Reform

There had been no mention in the 1987 election manifesto of any funda-mental changes to the NHS. In 1988, however, the consequences of the cash constraints on the service applied in the early and mid-eighties began to have their effect. Between 1983 and 1987 the real purchasing power available to the NHS had barely increased. Yet the demands on it from an ageing population, let alone other factors, were increasing by about 1 per cent a year. The result was that the resources available per head of population, weighted for age, had declined in each of those years (Kings Fund Institute, 1988). The consequence of this fierce control on spending was that waiting lists grew and well publicized consequences on services followed. Districts were running out of money well before the end of their financial year. A child was unable to gain access to intensive care for lack of staff and the case became a national story. The Prime Minister was put on the defensive regularly in the House of Commons, an unusual phenomenon, and she reacted in characteristic style.

Instead of relaxing the spending constraints she called for the whole future of the NHS and its finance to be rethought from scratch. A committee was given a year to come up with an answer. It was no ordinary committee but a 'ministerial group' that Mrs Thatcher herself was to chair. It seemed to her that 'the NHS had become a bottomless financial pit' (Thatcher, 1993: 608). Given the success of containing spending in the previous four years that was a revealing remark. It is clear from her account that she began with no particular view about what should be done. It was only two years since the ground had been gone over before. This time the Prime Minister was determined that some-thing should result.

Change the basis of funding?

Two main approaches to funding the service, according to Mrs Thatcher (1993) dominated the early discussions. One was to move the NHS to a system of health insurance with a specific health insurance contribution alongside the social security contribution. The NHS would then have been self-financing and outside the public spending round. This would have been fine for the Health Service but not for the Treasury and would have produced more, not less, health expenditure. The other idea was to expand the contribution private finance could make and ways to boost private health insurance were explored. It is at this point that Lawson's memoirs become very interesting (Lawson, 1993, Ch. 49).

He claims that at a private dinner with Mrs Thatcher in January 1988 to discuss the forthcoming Budget he suggested the time had come to review the NHS. He also suggests that reform plans had been deliberately left out of the manifesto. Even more interestingly he claims, subsequently, to have been convinced that the basic way the Health Service was financed was correct and that here was one area where the private market simply did not work. Indeed, the NHS was performing remarkably well compared to other countries. 'What we had to do was to concentrate on making it even better.' He also claims to have fought the proposal to give tax relief to private insurance and only compromised on the extension of relief to the over-65s to limit its impact. 'I duly introduced it, trying to conceal my embarrassment, in my 1989 budget' (p. 617).

Lawson, and as far as we can tell the Treasury, proved staunch defenders of the basic idea of the NHS not because it was popular but because it made economic sense. This is largely supported by Mrs Thatcher's account. She was clearly furious at the Treasury's line!

The purchaser–provider split

Ways of introducing private finance to solve the problems of the NHS largely dropped out of the discussions. How could the system be made to produce more for the same money? An early idea, later watered down, was to float off all the hospitals as independent or privatized units. In its watered-down version this became the proposal to give hospitals the right to trust status rather like the old voluntary hospitals. Here the Conservative Party was proposing to return to a pattern it had supported in 1945. A more original idea was to give the public the right to choose to belong to different local Health Maintenance Organizations, or funds, who would buy care for their patients.

As time went on this idea got narrowed down to making district health authorities the bodies that would buy care from the semi-independent hospitals. This would introduce a 'purchaser–provider split'. Hospitals would compete for the right to win contracts from the districts. If a hospital went on performing badly it would lose its contract. The district would get 'exit' power on behalf of its population. The principles, applied in the case of education and housing, were to be applied to the NHS too.

Mrs Thatcher was getting worried that the review was not being radical enough. Her own policy unit at Number 10 were critical of the way the discussions were going. They were unhappy that the idea of *patients* having choice had been lost. Hospitals would have to compete for districts' contracts but districts would not have to compete for patients' custom. They returned to an idea that had been canvassed before: making GPs the purchasers of hospital care for their patients. Patients would have choice of GP and therefore who would purchase on their behalf.

Later on in the proceedings John Moore, whom Thatcher thought was performing poorly, was replaced by Kenneth Clarke. He had been a junior minister in the department when this idea had been discussed before. It was revived and introduced almost as a late appendix to the main part of the reforms, as the GP fundholding scheme. (For an account of its origins and progress see Glennerster *et al.*, 1994. For an account of the whole process of reform see Butler, 1992.)

The White Paper

At one point it seemed as if the discussions were getting nowhere but Mrs Thatcher insisted that the original timetable be kept. A White Paper would be published one year from the date the review was announced. The result was a paper that was typical of this period and very different from the Fowler reviews of the previous era. Bold radical changes were proposed in outline with little or no detail. The civil servants and the local managers would make up the rules and the details of the scheme as they went along. The White Paper, *Working for Patients* (Department of Health, 1989b), provoked the most furious public and professional reaction. The Labour Party portrayed it as proposing the privatization of the Health Service and the internal market as introducing commercial principles into health care. The British Medical Association, ironically in view of its opposition in 1946–8, threw its weight against the reforms and in favour of the NHS as it was. It financed a nation-wide poster campaign to this end. Clarke, who liked a good fight, stuck to the government's guns as Bevan had done, and passed the legislation largely unchanged.

The government, however, shaken by the Opposition and the public support it was getting, did slow down the pace at which the reforms were implemented. It told its local managers to change as little as possible before the coming election and it increased spending on the service substantially. Emphasis in ministerial guidance moves from promoting competition to collaboration and maintaining 'a steady state'. As Butler (1994) points out,

> In retrospect, however, it is clear that as Mrs Thatcher's grip on office began to weaken, so ministers and their officials began to distance themselves from the stance they had been taking . . . 'Buyers' become . . . 'purchasers' and then 'commissioners'. 'Sellers' become 'providers'. General practice 'budgets' become 'funds' . . . 'Marketing' becomes 'needs assessment'. (p. 22)

All this shows how far the public and the profession had absorbed the non-commercial ethic and philosophy of the founders of the service. Despite the service's failings any suggestion that it was to be 'privatized' touched a raw nerve. So, too, did the idea that some patients would get preferential treatment.

The National Health Service and Community Care Act 1990

The Health Service sections of this Act amounted to the biggest change in the structure and logic of the service since the 1946 Act.

- Hospitals and community services could opt out of direct control by their district health authorities. They would become autonomous trusts run by trustees who own the assets with a debt owed to the Treasury. They would manage the hospital directly. If it could not attract the custom to survive, in theory, it would contract or close. The trusts were to be directly accountable to the Secretary of State. By 1995 almost all hospitals had become trusts, and so had most community services.

- District health authorities would cease to be responsible for managing trust hospitals and would assume the primary task of determining the health needs of their area. Having done so they would purchase or make contracts with hospitals and community services, inside or outside their area, to provide the services the district thought it could afford. The district would be financed by central government, via regions, on the basis of the population size, age structure and relative health status.
- General Practitioners with more than 9,000, later 7,000, patients could choose to hold their own budgets to purchase non-emergency treatment from hospitals (later to be community services too). These GPs would also be given a budget to meet the costs of the drugs they dispensed. If they saved on that they could use the savings to spend on hospital treatment or vice versa.

Outcome of the health reforms

In the event the outcomes were neither as terrible or as positive as the protagonists forecast. The government sharply increased its spending on the NHS in the years before and after the reforms. Target spending announced in the 1993 Budget put the NHS back under tight controls, which were similar to those in force when the reforms were initiated.

No final judgement on the reforms can be made until it is clear how they survive such pressure. Nor, as we saw, were the full rigours of competition enforced in the early years. One of the elements in the reforms that had most impact, in the narrow but important field to which it applied, was GP fundholding. It redressed the balance of power to some extent towards GPs, giving them some sanction over hospital consultants whom they felt were doing less than a good job. (For an evaluation of the reforms as a whole see Robinson and Le Grand, 1994.)

To a large extent those in the NHS have continued to do what they always did. Doctors and NHS managers have been resistant to thinking in competitive terms. There seems much wider agreement than expected that the separation of the planning and contracting function of districts from the running of hospitals was a sensible move. Indeed, to a large extent it merely took forward changes that were already evolving.

Districts now look far too small as purchasers alone. They were created, after all, to run district hospitals. Several districts are merging in many places with the bodies that look after GPs to form 'health commissions'. Regions are disappearing into regional offices of the NHS Management Executive. As we remarked earlier, the result has a strong likeness to the Green Paper of Richard Crossman!

Community Care

The community care reforms had little to do with community care as such and a lot to do with saving public expenditure, and provide an interesting counterpoint to the other reforms.

Under the old Supplementary Benefit rules it was possible, in very exceptional circumstances, for an old person to have his or her fees in a private old people's home paid out of the Social Security budget. An old person might run out of savings but it then might not be in his or her best interests to be moved to a local authority home. Such cases were very rare. In 1979 the total cost of such payments amounted to £10 million. In the early 1980s, as the Supplementary Benefit scheme was put into the form of explicit regulations, this facility became better known. The old person's fees could be paid by the local social security office at the going local price for homes.

Several things began to happen. People began to rid their elderly relatives of their assets and claim Supplementary Benefit to cover the costs of their being in the home. Local authorities, under pressure to cut spending, began to see that if they closed homes or privatized them the old people could still be looked after in residential care and the central government would have to pay for them through the social security scheme. Private home owners began to realize that if they increased fees locally in line with other homes the social security scheme would have to pay up. There could be no better example of the way individuals will change their behaviour in fairly ruthless ways to avail themselves of public money.

The paradox was that this was an almost perfect voucher scheme that had grown up by accident. Families could choose a home for their elderly relative and the state would pay. This maximized choice and consumer power. Unfortunately, it also maximized the growth of public expenditure on this group. It exposed the latent demand for the care of elderly people that local authorities and families could not manage. Faced with what seemed like an open cheque-book, many people used it. In the period between 1979 and 1991 the level of social security spending on residential care rose from £10 million to £2,072 million.

Not surprisingly the government was desperate to limit this spending. It also ran counter to declared public policy, which was that of enabling old people to stay in their own homes. A series of official reports struggled with solutions and analysis (Audit Commission, 1986; Griffiths Report, 1988; House of Commons, 1984/5). It was Roy Griffiths who probably finally convinced Mrs Thatcher that, to stop the outflow powers to give public money, the care of the elderly should be taken from the social security system and given wholly to local authorities. A way had to be found to sugar the pill for Mrs Thatcher, who was so opposed to giving local authorities any more money. The answer lay in insisting that local social services departments become largely purchasing agencies – 'enabling authorities'. The extra money they were to get would not necessarily or mainly be spent on local authority services. The government would insist that the great bulk be spent on the private sector. Since there was no real private sector except for the residential homes, much of the money was to find its way back to the same private homes, in the early stages of the reform.

The community care element in the NHS and Community Care Act 1990

Legislation included the following main changes:

- From April 1993 the social security system would cease to provide support for new residents in private or voluntary homes.
- Local authorities had a duty to assess the needs of any person they believed required community care. They must provide services either themselves or by buying them from a private or voluntary agency.
- They must prepare a community care plan.
- They must set up an arm's-length agency to inspect premises in which care is being provided.

Outcomes of community care

Since the main provisions only came into force in April 1993 there has been little time to evaluate the long-term effects. As with the health reforms the government was anxious to smooth the changes, both by urging authorities not to act too radically too soon and by making a transitional special community care grant available, with tight rules on its spending. As with health the language from the centre has been softened from 'purchasing' to 'commissioning'. Just as in the case of the NHS reforms those working in the services have been very uncomfortable with the whole idea of introducing markets and competition and with local authorities becoming mere enabling authorities (Wistow *et al.*, 1994). The result is that the pace of real change has been slow. Bureaucracies and values that evolve within them over forty years do not change that quickly.

Another 'Fundamental' Review

Even before Mrs Thatcher was defeated in the leadership election of November 1990 the tight strings on public spending were being loosened a little to find money to ease the NHS and the poll tax reforms. Major's election as leader and the run-up to the general election of 1992 produced a temporary increase in public spending. The share of the GDP going to social policy purposes rose from 22 per cent in 1990 to 26.7 per cent in 1993. This was higher than in 1979, when it was 23 per cent. So much for the reforms' capacity to get more out of less.

The Treasury was not amused. The scale of borrowing was getting out of hand. That autumn, Clarke, the new Chancellor, in the newly combined spending and tax Budget, was going to have to raise taxes substantially. The time had come for another attempt to get public spending down. In February 1993 Mr Portillo announced a fundamental review of the long-term prospects for public spending and a no-holds-barred look at the spending of the social ministries of social security, health and education.

Here we were, again, back in the same exercise as R. A. Butler in the early 1950s, Thorneycroft in the late 1950s, Callaghan in the mid-1960s, Healey in the mid-1970s, Howe and Lawson in the early 1980s.

The outcome, by late 1994, was unclear but seemed to be less than earth shattering. The options for change were summarized at the time by Hills (1993). None were easy political nettles to grasp.

Taxation

Taxes and the poor

Through the 1980s the Conservative government had reduced the headline marginal rates of income tax. When they came to power the standard rate of income tax was 33 per cent. By 1994 the main rate covering most people was 25 per cent with the first band of earnings taxed at 20 per cent. The overall burden of taxation was not very different, however. As we saw earlier, higher Value Added Tax and social security contributions together had filled the revenue gap. They had fallen disproportionately on poorer households.

In the run-up to the 1992 election, though public expenditure had been increased, taxes had not and this meant rapidly increasing levels of public borrowing to cover the shortfall. Two budgets in 1993, the first introduced by Norman Lamont and the second by Kenneth Clarke, very substantially increased the level of overall taxation. Once again many of these increases took the form of more indirect taxation. The most unpopular of these was the attempt to extend VAT to domestic fuel. Though it was defeated in 1994, the result was other increases in indirect taxation. Looking at the changes in tax and social security between 1985 and 1994 Giles and Johnson's (1994) analysis, however, suggested that,

> Worst hit were unemployed couples with children, followed by lone parent families, with over three-quarters of the former, and nearly two-thirds of the latter losing from the changes over the decade . . . Two earner couples gained much more frequently than single earner couples, reflecting higher total incomes and twice the opportunity to gain from direct tax cuts. (p. 14)

More precise figures show that 78 per cent of unemployed couples with children were worse off as a result of the tax changes of the period, on average losing 2.7 per cent in net income. Earning couples with children more often lost than those without children. Of couples with children and only one earner 62 per cent lost, and of two-earner couples with children 42 per cent lost. Here was a family policy of a kind expressed through tax changes.

Taxation, women and the family

From the 1970s the new Equal Opportunities Commission began to bring pressure on government to think about the gendered nature of the tax system. A married woman was treated merely as a part of her husband's income and property for tax purposes. Incomes of both were aggregated and married men received an additional allowance for being married. This applied whether the wife was wholly dependent or not on the husband's income. The husband therefore received more *net* pay per pound earned than a woman, making a nonsense of the equal pay provisions. Critics asked, why should a husband receive extra money for supporting his wife (through paid work) instead of the wife receiving money for supporting her husband (through currently unpaid work)? The government did move to begin a public discussion on some of these issues in 1980 by publishing a Green Paper, *The Taxation of Husband and Wife*.

This floated a number of proposals. It suggested replacing the married man's allowance with a system that enabled a non-earning spouse to transfer her personal tax allowance to her husband. This would have encouraged more women to stay at home or at least increased the incomes of single-earner households.

It suggested the replacement of the lone parent allowance, which was equivalent to the married man's allowance, by a higher lone parent payment. The payment of benefits is generally seen as less desirable than giving tax allowances. The reason given is that benefits appear as public expenditure and allowances do not (i.e. a book-keeping strategy). So it was uncharacteristic to support higher benefits to lone parents. Land suggests (1983) that this would have given government more control over who got these payments. This proposal was not in fact taken up.

It took many years for these proposals to bear fruit but in 1989 two changes were introduced. The married man's allowance became the 'married couple's allowance'. Either partner could claim it. Also they could opt for separate assessment. This later became automatic. Husbands and wives are now treated as separate individuals for tax purposes.

The 1993 Budget began to reduce the importance of the married couples' allowance. It reduced its value by only permitting it to be offset against the 20 per cent tax rate.

Majorism

What if, anything, did Mr Major's government contribute to social policy? (For a detailed assessment see Kavanagh and Seldon, 1994.) To a large extent it was concerned with implementing the reforms of the late Thatcher period. Major did seem genuinely to want to improve the standards of social provision like the NHS. His contribution was to insist, in 1991, that all public services produce a charter of rights and standards for consumers of those services. Few people seem to have heard of these or to use them for redress. As a means to an end, it was a step back to the world of performance indicators and indirect sanctions rather than the vigorous competitive market between public and private providers that was Mrs Thatcher's preferred model.

Yet, half-way through his period in office, and worried by the power of the right in his party over Europe, he appeared to give the right its head at the Conservative Party Conference in 1993. A revival of an old theme tune began: renewed stress on a return to traditional family values, complaints about the abuse of the social security system and public housing by single parents. If there was something new about this period, it was the flavour of these speeches and the policy initiatives that began to follow. Government had already become concerned with the consequences of broken marriages and the cost to the Exchequer.

Divorce and the Family

Divorce law had changed in various respects during the 1980s.

In 1984, after several Law Commission reports, the previous three-year ban on divorce except in cases of exceptional hardship or depravity, was replaced by an absolute ban on divorce in under one year. This was taken as a symbolic gesture of the state's support for the institution of marriage. It was an attempt to stop couples rushing into divorce. In 1994 the government was still considering proposals by Lord Mackay on obligatory pre-divorce mediation.

It was the financial consequences of divorce that began to concern the courts, families and politicians in the 1980s and 1990s. The result of higher levels of divorce, doubling in the 1970s, was to create many more second families, as those who had divorced remarried. (The number of divorces flattened off in the 1980s.)

The Campaign for Justice on Divorce pressed for an overhaul of the system of maintenance. Was it fair for the second family to have to pay for the first wife, especially if it meant the second family living in poverty? On the other hand, opponents argued, was it right for there to be no penalties for breaking a marriage? First responsibility was to the children of any previous marriage and to repaying the wife, who had, perhaps, invested her life opportunities in that marriage.

In fact, most maintenance went to support the children of the previous marriage and was set at very low levels by the courts just because the income of the new marriage was not sufficient to support two families.

Under the 1984 Matrimonial and Family Proceedings Act first consideration had to go to the children. Maintenance for the spouse was linked to conduct and so, too, was custody of children and property if the court thought it inequitable to ignore it.

The State and the Family

Conservatives under Mrs Thatcher were encouraged to be unashamed economic liberals. Yet they also remained defenders of the traditional family and favoured strong government action and incentives to sustain this institution. This was not as contradictory as it seemed. If the state was to withdraw from its major role the family had to take on more responsibilities. Yet, if the 1970s and 1980s were any guide, the family seemed less and less capable of fulfilling that role. Commonly, debates on the issue of government intervention in the family tend to polarize between the argument that state intervention *supports* the family by lightening its burden, and the argument that state intervention *weakens* the family by stripping it of some of its functions. Post-war policies upheld the general notion of the privacy of the family, but provided greater welfare services both for individuals, and more directly, for families (free school meals, preventive family casework, family allowances, etc.) in order to help families survive greater pressures.

The post-1979 Conservative government has taken the opposite tack.

The New Right attack on a 'dependency culture' is fought on economic and moral grounds. Moral decline is seen as the cause of economic decline. The argument is that the Welfare State has displaced the role of the family as the main provider of welfare; children no longer look after their elderly parents, parents cannot control their children, fathers abandon their families; without a role model of a nuclear family teenage boys become 'yobs' and teenage girls become unmarried mothers; when the state, and not the family, becomes the first port of call in times of trouble the result is increased public expenditure and a growing tax burden which is a disincentive to industry. Increased expenditure is directly affected by 'the breakdown of the family' because of numbers on benefits, and indirectly is the result of the perceived link between lone parenthood and crime. Single parenthood was damaging, moreover, and should be discouraged anyway (Dennis and Erdos, 1994). American influence on Conservative thought here became particularly important, though the policy regimes and incentives were very different (Murray, 1984). These arguments were contested by other social scientists (Burghes, 1994).

The logical solution according to New Right thought is to replace state props to the family and individuals with intra-family props. Intra-family relationships cannot be managed by government, but the hope is that a withdrawal of outside support will push families to look after their own. There have been several policy examples of this, some dating from the Thatcher administration and accelerated under Major. From 1980 local authorities were no longer required to provide school meals. In 1988, Income Support was made unavailable for 16–18-year-olds at the same time as child benefit was no longer available for those of them who were no longer in full-time education. In 1986 benefits were reduced for 18–25-year-olds. In 1996, when the Jobseeker's Allowance replaces Unemployment Benefit, 18–25-year-olds will face a 20 per cent drop in benefit. This was announced in the 1993 Budget. The justification given was that younger people have lower earnings expectations, and are less likely to be living independently. The Child Support Act reasserts parental responsibility. The introduction of student loans, and the withdrawal of benefits from students increased their dependence on their families. The Criminal Justice Bill introduces the idea of parental responsibility for a child's crimes. A parent can be required to pay a 'bind over', which is forfeited if the child commits another offence. Care in the community actually implies care *by* the community, which means care by families.

While all these measures were designed to put more responsibility on the family, the government was forced to respond to pressures from the EEC and the labour market which were demanding more female labour market participation. In order to achieve this, concessions were made to working mothers. In 1990, employers could offset the costs of providing workplace child-care against tax. In 1993, in response to an EC Directive (though not implemented until October 1994, the latest possible date), maternity provision was made as soon as a woman started work, and was extended for part-time workers. Although these measures were funded by government, it could be said that the government was more concerned with helping women to enter and to stay in the labour market, than with improving conditions within it. This is apparent in the light of the abolition of Wages Councils in 1993, which was presented as necessary in order to maintain the number of jobs. This attitude was also clear in 1994 when Michael Portillo, Employment Secretary, resisted the European changes regarding parental and paternity leave. Any such arrangements, he said, should be made privately between employer and employee; government legislation would be inappropriate and would restrict competition.

Lone Mothers

The problem of the single mother exploded into one of the nastiest of social family policy issues of the 1990s. It also went to the roots of one of the apparent contradictions in modern Conservative thought.

By 1993 there were well over a million lone parents, making up 14 per cent of all families with dependent children. Sixty-six per cent of these were dependent on Income Support. This figure had increased from 330,000 in 1980 to 770,000 in 1989. Sixty per cent were divorced, 33 per cent never married and 7 per cent widowed.

At the end of the 1980s a degree of agreement had emerged between those acting as advocates of single parents and government that something should be done to ensure that natural fathers be required to support their children. For the government this would have two advantages. First, it would reduce the burden on the Exchequer. Second, it would bring home to a man who left his wife the financial consequences of his actions and hence act as a deterrent. For the single parent left behind it would mean that the state was taking on the responsibility of getting maintenance out of the father. As the 1990s unfolded the government's attitudes hardened.

> They [lone parents] were no longer seen as victims with special needs for financial support and, in the case of young unmarried mothers, for case work, but rather as irresponsible and probably, again in the case of unmarried mothers, manipulative people willing for example to have a baby in order to jump the queue for social housing. (Lewis, 1994)

Unmarried mothers became the prime targets partly because they made up the group that was growing fastest and putting more pressure on the public purse. They were also the group that might be most responsive to a harsher benefit climate. There was a strong belief that higher benefit rates encouraged young women to have babies and that cutting off benefit would reduce the scale of single parenthood. This policy was urged by Charles Murray, who had become a kind of guru for the Conservative think tanks.

A paper apparently prepared for Cabinet and leaked to the *Guardian* (9 November 1993) evidently reviewed the academic research and concluded that there was no evidence that higher benefit rates had encouraged women to have children on their own. Indeed the fastest rise had taken place during a period when benefits fell relative to earnings. The research does not show any link between unmarried motherhood and criminality or that unmarried mothers have had children to jump the housing queue. Despite evidence from Europe that better child care and maternity provisions do encourage earlier return to work no major steps in these directions have been taken. Lone mothers will not have a long-term right to local authority housing, the housing Minister announced in 1994.

Privatizing maintenance

Not only were there more lone mothers but, through the 1980s, fewer were employed. More became dependent on social security. The number in receipt of Income Support grew from 320,000 in 1979 to a million in 1991 (DSS, 1993b).

The government began to underline the father's responsibility for maintenance. First, it imposed limits on the process of 'diversion' which had guaranteed the value of maintenance payments to women on Income Support. This now was only made available to women whose husbands had defaulted in the last six months or who had suffered violence. Under the liable relative formula, where the DSS administered the maintenance, the father had to pay something towards the parent with care. These measures were taken further in a really important shift in the boundary line between private and public maintenance law, The Child Support Act 1990. This extended the boundary of the state significantly.

Child Support Act 1990

Under the Act all lone mothers on either Income Support, Family Credit or Disabled Worker's Allowance must authorize the Secretary of State to take action to recover maintenance from an absent father. A formula is used to decide how 'spare' income is divided between the father and the ex-wife, between first and second families. The formula includes an element of maintenance for the caring parent at Income Support levels to ensure that, if the ex-husband can afford it, he, not the state, takes on responsibility for the previous wife. The body set up to administer the system was the Child Support Agency. It will eventually take over from the courts all aspects of the assessment, collection and enforcement of child maintenance for children whose parents live apart. Public law has effectively replaced private law in this area. As Lewis (1994) points out, the Act also realigns parental responsibility on biological lines.

> It rejects rather than tries to reconcile the historical accepted idea in public law [visible in the cohabitation rule] that men support the families they live with, and in private law that they should pay something towards the families they have left; it seeks instead to make them pay for both in so far as there are biological children in both.

The logic runs counter to that in the Children Act 1989, which lays emphasis on the family group that is actually doing the caring. The logic is one of deterrence. The Act was also retrospective. It ignored whatever 'clean break' arrangements had been entered into and it produced bitter opposition from fathers, in particular. In January 1995 the Secretary of State, Mr Lilley, was forced to announce major changes in the way the agency was to operate, new legislation would enable the agency to take account of clean break settlements made before the agency was created.

The whole sequence of policy illustrated how confused the boundary line between the public and private worlds of the family had become. If the family works it can be left alone. If it fails and leaves women and children vulnerable the state must step in. To do so, however, raises what economists would call a moral hazard problem. Make it easier and less painful and family breakdown will increase. The government in 1994 was still in the midst of sorting out this moral tangle, as indeed was society more generally.

Children

There was one piece of social legislation that had cross-party support as well as opponents in this period – that on children. The Children Act 1989 marked a watershed in legislation on children and the state's treatment of intra-family relationships.

In the 1980s there had been parliamentary and Law Commission reports on children's issues following three deaths of children as a result of abuse and the Cleveland affair (Butler-Sloss, 1988). Here social workers had been criticized for interference while other reports called for more state intervention to prevent abuse.

Families, rather than the wider society, were usually treated as the objects of blame in these discussions. The Act tries to balance two sets of contradictory pressures: greater child protection with greater parental rights, and greater state power to intervene in family autonomy. As the 'Introduction to the Children Act' notes,

> The Act seeks to protect children both from the harm which can arise from failures or abuse within the family and from the harm that can be caused by unwarranted intervention in their family life. There is a tension between those objectives which the Act seeks to regulate so as to optimise the overall protection provided for children in general. (para. 1.31)

The Act marks a shift of emphasis from parental rights to parental responsibilities. Never-married mothers and married parents of a child automatically have parental responsibility. Others, non-married fathers or those who have been looking after a child as if it were a child of the family (grandparents, say) can *apply* for parental responsibility. The welfare of the child is 'paramount' in all court proceedings. Where parents are living apart neither party has sole power and authority. There are instead residence orders, contact orders, specific issue orders and prohibited steps orders to settle disputed claims.

Through various provisions of the Act it stresses that wherever possible children should remain with their families, provided this is consistent with their welfare. Where a local authority does have to care for a child,

> This should preferably be under voluntary arrangements with the parents who will retain their responsibility, acting so far as possible as partners of the local authority and the substitute carers. (para. 1.9)

There can be no better illustration of the dilemmas that face modern social policy legislators. They would like to leave individuals and families to cope without interference and taxpayer responsibility. Yet modern life is becoming more complex and families more vulnerable. Society (voters) is not prepared to let government simply walk away. Unwilling as they may be, governments will continue to be deeply involved in families.

10 Where Now?

The Welfare State of the mid-1990s was a much larger edifice than its 1948 prototype. Even correcting for the rise in prices in the interval, expenditure on the Welfare State in 1993 was well over five times that of 1951 in 1993 prices. Health and education were taking about the same share of the total but social security was taking a lot more (see Figure 10.1).

What had all this extra spending achieved? How far had the objectives of the founders been realized?

A basic minimum

We have seen that there never was a classic Welfare State of perfect proportions. The Beveridge design for social security was flawed from the outset. Its minimalist flat rate nature meant that it never won the support of the middle classes, yet neither was it means tested and targeted on the poor. It fell horribly between two stools. Other countries went either one way or the other. What Britain in the end came to develop, by incremental stages, was an extremely complex system of means-tested support. It went a long way towards achieving Beveridge's national minimum safety net but by quite a different route from the one that he envisaged.

When, in the 1980s, it was called upon to catch millions who became unemployed in a manner neither they, nor the politicians responsible, ever expected, it held. It did put a modest floor under many families.

As can be seen from Figure 10.2 the combined effect of taxes and social policy benefits put an income floor of about £6–8,000 a year under the poorest third of the households in the population in 1991. This was made

Figure 10.1   The size of the Welfare State, 1951 and 1993

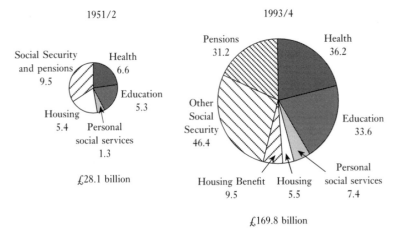

1951/2

Social Security and pensions 9.5

Health 6.6

Education 5.3

Housing 5.4

Personal social services 1.3

£28.1 billion

1993/4

Pensions 31.2

Health 36.2

Other Social Security 46.4

Education 33.6

Housing Benefit 9.5

Housing 5.5

Personal social services 7.4

£169.8 billion

The sums are in billions of pounds expressed in 1993/4 prices on a UK basis.

Source: National Income and Expenditure Blue Books

up of a mixture of cash benefits and income in kind, such as the education of their children.

Those in the middle (the fifth decile) neither gained nor lost. They got as much back from the Welfare State as they put in. The top half of the income range paid to keep a floor under the poorest third.

Full employment, work and benefits

In the 1980s, as benefits for young people were withdrawn, this basic safety net began to be eroded. Both political parties began to toy with the idea that benefits should be given to people of working age, who were able to work, only in return for participation in some training or work programme.

The reason for this change of approach lay essentially in the collapse of the second pillar of the post-war settlement, the promise of full employment. In the 1950s and early 1960s it was feasible for local employment

Figure 10.2 Combined effects of taxes and benefits in the United Kingdom, 1991

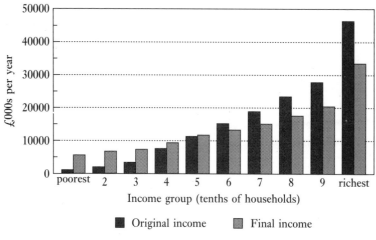

Source: Hills 1993

and National Assistance officers to implement the rule that receipt of benefit was conditional on the claimant 'actively seeking work'. There were so many jobs on offer that repeated refusal to accept one stood out and the numbers of 'work-shy' or dubiously unemployed were tiny. When large-scale unemployment became the norm this policing function broke down. At the same time those in work came to resent the numbers on benefit. Abuses both grew and were more resented. To administer a system of enforced work would, however, be an enormous task and involve the potential for abuse. The difficulties were exactly the same as those that had made the previous rules break down: the genuine shortage of jobs in many areas of the country.

There were, even so, good reasons to try some kind of arrangement of this kind. Those who remain out of the labour market for long periods lose contact with work altogether. They stop looking for work and cease even to be effective in performing their one economic role which is to exert a downward pressure on wages by swelling the demand for jobs. Both for their sake and for the sake of the wider economy they should be helped to reintegrate into the labour force in a positive way. Such a policy was unlikely to be feasible with continuing high levels of unemployment.

The importance of Beveridge's original assumption of full employment for social policy was as evident in 1995 as it had been in 1945. Achieving it, though, had become far more difficult than a simple matter of budget deficit spending. It was seen to involve measures to make the labour market more competitive, workers better trained, benefit structures that encouraged work rather than the opposite as well as macro–economic policy. The integration of economic and social policy was essential. Some glimmer of political common ground was just becoming discernable by 1995.

From cradle to grave

Another key idea in the Beveridge Report had been the notion that social security was not primarily about redistribution to the poor but was a means of enabling people to move their incomes from periods in their lives when they were in great need to periods when they were better off. Most families went through periods of relative deprivation when they were bringing up children and in old age. The Welfare State could be thought of as a kind of universal savings bank. To a remarkable degree that is what it has turned out to be. As Figure 10.3 shows the state adds to individuals' average income early in life, slices a large part of income off in their lives up to about the age of 55 but from then on the average individual is drawing heavily on his and her accumulated credit. To work, of course, this requires that the present voters will honour this implicit contract between the generations.

Mr Portillo, in 1994, suggested that this contract should be broken and that people should increasingly finance their own old age. Regardless of the more technical issues involved this raises the central political problem of what to do about the implicit contract with existing or upcoming pensioners. Assuming that it is honoured the present generation of younger people would have to bear a dual burden: honouring yesterday's contract with today's old *and* financing their own old age. That is not an easy political message to sell. What was in practice happening through the 1980s was a gradual reneging on the contract. The level of basic pensions relative to the earnings of those in work was allowed to fall steadily and

Figure 10.3 Incomes by age as affected by 1991 tax and social security systems in Great Britain

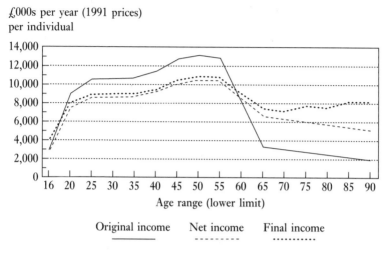

£000s per year (1991 prices) per individual

Age range (lower limit)

Original income   Net income   Final income

Note: This figure shows how the combination of taxes and welfare benefits in cash and kind (e.g. health and education) affected individuals over their lifetimes at the relative levels of generosity in 1991. Original incomes are those before tax or benefits. Net income is after tax and cash benefits. Final income includes the value of services in kind.

Source: Hills 1993

was to go on falling. A draft circular in 1994 suggested that the NHS might no longer accept long-term responsibility for old people who had no alternative means of care. Local authorities and families will have to take on increasing burdens here, too. Some families are in a position to do so, very many are not. The long-term care of the frail elderly is set to become a major focus of social policy in the next century.

Universality

The only service to fit the common myth of universality, a service freely available to all from the cradle to the grave, was, up to this point, the National Health Service. Despite the conflict surrounding its birth and the accusations of profligacy that went with it, the service turned out to be one of the cheapest and most effective health-care systems in the world. It did, however, suffer from the creeping decline that is likely to affect any monopoly run by its professional staff – the arrogance of power and the neglect of its consumers. Token measures of consumer participation in the 1970s were followed by the introduction of quasi-market reforms in the 1990s. It is too early to judge their final impact but some have challenged the power of consultants and hospitals and forced a more consumer-based approach on the service. The reforms did not cut costs. On the contrary they increased them. There was some danger that the reforms might have let a costly genie out of the bottle, just as the Guillebaud Committee had in the 1950s.

Selectivity or targeting turned out to be less easy a way forward just because so many of the changes in social policy in the past fifty years have made the British system of social security one of the most selective in the western world. The extent of this targeting and its disincentive consequences caused the last major review of social security in the mid-1980s to go round in very complex and elegant circles.

Altruism and communality?

The notion that the Welfare State reflects some notion of caring altruism is also called into question by a cool historical look. Welfare states, on one view, arise because they meet the interests of classes in society who are seeking to spread their burden of insecurities more widely (Baldwin, 1990). In 1945 the state, during and after a total war effort, took responsibility for securing adequate food, shelter, health and education for the population at low but sustainable levels through some kind of national regulation or provision. So long as such national collective action continued to be necessary to secure these ends it retained political support. Even a party in power for long periods that was fundamentally opposed to the basic concept of collective provision was unable to make much headway in dismantling these structures. The strong support that the National Health Service has retained throughout the period derives not so much from any feelings of communality or altruism but from the fact that it is perceived to be a good buy. The long hard look the Treasury gave the subject in the 1980s convinced it and a radical Tory Chancellor of the day of this fact. Ordinary people may not have done cost benefit analyses or international comparisons but in their gut they know that any private health care that they tried to take out to deliver the same cover as the NHS would be simply beyond their reach.

The same used to be true of housing. But the economics of housing are different from health. It has become possible for most families to purchase a house. If families and individuals can spread their own costs and risks over time and retain choice and control they prefer to do so. When that happens support for a public system erodes. Those who are left unable to join this new independence evoke little public sympathy, at least in any sustained way that wins elections. Social security is moving in the same direction.

Private schooling is still beyond most families and will remain so for some time; the economics of schools are more like health than housing.

Social policy as a savings bank

If we examine how the great social policy budget is spent we find (Falkingham and Hills, 1995) that three-quarters of all the taxes that people pay come back to them individually but at different times in their lives. Only a quarter of the total goes to others, i.e. the lifetime poor. In many ways the personal insecurities of the 1990s and 2000s are going to be far greater than they were in the 1940s. The 1940s were a period of job security. Not only was there full employment and the prospect of a new job if you did lose the one you had but work with the same employer or in the same industry for a lifetime was common. Employment-based pension schemes and health insurance based on the workplace made more sense then than they do now.

Growing inequality

For most of the previous century earnings relationships had been fairly stable between higher- and lower-paid people. Incomes overall had been gradually equalizing. This has been especially true comparing pre-war and post-war incomes. This trend to greater equality continued from 1945 to the mid-1970s. Then a change of great significance happened. Incomes for those in work began to grow more unequal (Gosling *et al.*,

1994; Rowntree, 1995). The great middle England of the skilled industrial worker went. Low-paid, temporary and part-time work took its
place. Much of the change took place within occupations and industries
and could not be blamed on the new industrial structure alone. The effect
seems likely to be long term.

> After 1977 . . . increases in wages across generations were limited to the
> top of the distribution . . . recent cohorts . . . seem to have entered the
> labour market at lower real wages than their earlier counterparts or . . . have
> not been able to enter the labour market at all. (Gosling *et al.*, 1994: 17)

The impact of growing inequality

As a result of this growing inequality more of the activity of the Welfare
State has been taken up in sustaining the safety net under the increasing
numbers of very poor people. There has been less available for the mainstream services like health and education that most people used. The
Welfare State was having to work much harder simply to stand still.

Economists measure inequality in a number of ways but one the most
common is the Gini coefficient, as it is called (see Table 10.1). A figure
of 100 is equal to the maximum amount of inequality, one person earns
everything and the rest nothing; 0 is the measure of complete equality.
From 1975 to 1987, before and after the coming of mass unemployment
and more unequal earnings, the measure of inequality, before the intervention of the state, rose from 43 per cent to 52 per cent, a very large rise
in historical terms. In 1975 the Welfare State managed to reduce that
inequality by 12 points. In 1987 it reduced it by 16 points, it was working
a third harder, but it had still not managed to wipe out the original
increasing inequality. Worse, large sums were being spent on this activity
and the ordinary taxpayers could not see as much gain from their taxes in
improved health and education services as they had in the past. Education actually suffered a sharp fall in expenditure relative to the GNP in
this period.

Nor did these trends show any sign of slowing down. A series of
research reports published in 1994 and 1995 were doing what the Abel-
Smith and Townsend work of the 1960s had done; they were showing the
extent of the growing divide in society. An official report in 1993 first
caused a lot of interest and debate (DSS, 1993a). Before housing costs are

Table 10.1   The impact of welfare spending on equality, 1975 to 1987

	1975	*1979*	*1987*
Gini coefficients			
Original income	43	45	52
Final income	31	32	36
Reduction in inequality	12	13	16
Percentages			
Share of original income taken by:			
Bottom fifth	0.8	0.5	0.3
Top fifth	44	45	51
Share of final income after the Welfare State:			
Bottom fifth	7.1	7.1	6.2
Top fifth	38	38	42

Note: The first three rows of the table show changes in the measure of inequality called a 'Gini coefficient'. A figure of 100 represents the maximum extent of inequality. A figure of 0 represents complete equality. The increase in the index from 1975 to 1987 was substantial in historical terms.

The final four rows show the percentage of all incomes received by the richest and the poorest households. Original income is before taxes or benefits, i.e. before social policy has come into play. Final incomes are after tax is taken off and benefits have been received.

Source: *Economic Trends*, HMSO, May 1990

taken into account the poorest 10 per cent of families in 1990 were 1 per cent worse off than in 1979 despite the rapid rise in earnings of many above-average families. If these families' housing costs are taken into account they were 14 per cent worse off in real terms.

Frustration of voters was not surprising, but the reasons were to be found more in the altering economic structure of the country than in any changes in these basic services. The cost of the Welfare State was rising but it was not benefiting the median voter much. The Inquiry by the Rowntree Foundation into Income and Wealth (1995) confirmed and extended the conclusions:

• The increase in inequality during the 1980s dwarfed the fluctuations seen in inequality in previous decades.

- The income share of the poorest tenth of society has fallen back from 4.2 per cent in 1961 to 3.0 per cent in 1991 with most of the fall occurring during the 1980s. The share of the richest tenth rose from 22 per cent to 25 per cent over the three decades.
- The real incomes of the poorest tenth ranked after housing costs actually fell sharply from a peak in 1979 of £73 a week to just over £61 a week in 1991 (both in 1994 prices).
- Families with children make up more than half of the poorest decile group compared with only about a third three decades ago.

(Goodman and Webb, 1994: 66)

The incomes of families had owed a great deal to the increasing participation of women in the labour market. By 1993, 75 per cent of women with children were working *full*-time. Mothers' employment often begins with part-time work when their children are 3–4 years old. That is the point at which child care or school begins to be available for some. Even so, in the early 1980s many women with children under 5 depended on their partners to provide care while they were at work and nearly half worked in the evening or at night. Pressures on the family to keep up its living standards during difficult times are clear from these figures. It is worth remembering that the Welfare State is itself a very large employer of women, overall the biggest, and nearly half of these jobs are part time.

In 1993 all female workers became entitled to maternity pay and leave as soon as they started work. In 1983 the government had opposed a draft European directive on parental leave rights and leave for family reasons. Because most women with children under 5 work part time most employers so far see no reason to provide child-care facilities. There are thus pressures for mothers to work and counter-pressures that prevent child-care facilities being extended. Women and families have been caught in the middle.

Though the greater labour participation of women clearly raises the purchasing power of families with children its overall effect on inequality depends on which wives work. If it is the wives of high earners their working only adds to inequality in household income. If it is the wives of the low paid who are working the effect is to even out household incomes. One study suggests that the early impact of greater women's participation in the work-force in the UK was to increase inequality, especially in the early 1970s, when it was the most educated households that began the process. In Germany, by contrast, the opposite has been true (Gardiner, 1993).

The growing inequalities in the labour market were added to in the 1980s by tax policies that were designed to reward the higher earners. The main gainers from the tax measures of the 1980s were those in the top decile (Hills, 1988).

Is there anything social policy can do about this growing gap? Tax policy would be one means. The Labour Party has been committed to some kind of minimum income. If set too high that could exclude some on the margins of the labour market from employment altogether and make matters worse.

Dennis Snower (1993) has argued that governments should redirect their attention away from middle-class recipients of mainstream social services, like health and education, and focus instead on the really poor. They should do so partly by giving loan guarantees to the poor to buy their own education and for other purposes. They should also tackle poverty in work and the poverty trap by giving wage subsidies to those in work. What kind of political constituency there would be for such a programme is far from clear. One way or the other the growing inequalities in income are likely to be a key political issue in the late 1990s.

Higher standards and more equal outcomes

Despite the growing inequalities that came to the labour market and to after-tax incomes in the 1980s, it should not hide the fact that in education, health and housing basic standards rose and inequalities were reduced in the years from 1945 to 1985. After that trends to greater inequality began to set in and some absolute standards began to fall too.

Of those born in the 1920s nearly two-thirds left education without gaining any qualifications. Of those born in the 1960s the percentage had fallen to less than 20 per cent (see Figure 10.4). While class differences in the educational achievements of children remained, they had narrowed significantly since 1945 (Glennerster and Low, 1990). However, what Halsey calls the 'service classes' continued to have an advantage in gaining access to higher education (Egerton and Halsey, 1993).

As we saw, in 1953 nearly 60 per cent of primary school children were being taught in classes of over forty. By 1991 hardly any were; only 19 per

Figure 10.4   Highest educational qualifications by year of birth, Great Britain, 1990

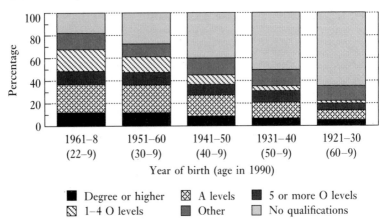

Source: Hills 1993

cent were in classes of over thirty and the average size of class in England in 1992 was twenty-seven. The average size of secondary classes was twenty-one while in the 1950s the majority of classes were over thirty.

Individuals on average enjoyed longer lives in the 1980s and 1990s than they had in the 1940s. This was a process that pre-dated the NHS but it is clear that overall inequalities in expectation of life went on narrowing until about the mid-1980s. The same is true of regional inequalities (Illsley *et al.*, 1991).

Housing standards have also improved enormously since the 1940s. In 1951, 70 per cent of all households were living in overcrowded or insanitary conditions or lacked a basic amenity like a lavatory or bathroom. This must seem barely credible to today's young people. By 1991 the number of people living without basic amenities had fallen to 1 per cent.

Paying for welfare

As standards have risen so have expectations and benefit levels. It was becoming increasingly costly to perform the safety net function for the reasons outlined already. Other factors, too, were pushing up costs and potential future costs. Families have become less secure and when marriages break up there has been an incentive for couples to rely on the state to support one of the partners and the children. Should the state underwrite the risks of marriage?

The number of the very old was rising, putting growing pressure on families and on the local authority and health services that served them. In the early part of the next century more people will reach retirement age. Pension costs will then begin to rise. There have been some exaggerated claims about the extent and timing of this 'burden'. One less alarmist study concluded that to retain the same standards of services and pensions that applied in the early 1990s would mean a slow but steady increase in taxation as a percentage of the GDP. The rise was not astronomic − 0.5 per cent a decade (Hills, 1993) − but voters seemed to be saying they did not want *any* increase and the Conservative Party, at least, was committed to reducing taxation in the long term. International trends were making high taxes difficult to sustain anyway. International capital and well-educated labour was footloose as never before. Governments in the 1990s had to think much more carefully about the impact of their tax policy on international competitiveness than the governments of the 1940s. A Dutch auction in tax rates and social security costs between countries was under way in the 1990s. The political constraints that every government since 1945 had struggled with are now more complex and international (See Page and Deakin, 1993).

The result was that all the main political parties began to search to find more acceptable ways of paying for the benefits that the electorate still seemed to want. These might include requiring more pension provision from individuals, introducing an addition to the social security contribution to pay for the long-term care of the elderly or introducing tax incentives to encourage individuals to take out private insurance to cover such care. Before long students will find that they are going to have to pay back the cost of their higher education. None of these measures would, of course, reduce the cost of care or education or old age. If the state is not to pay, individuals will have to, directly and now.

David Green (1993), from the Institute of Economic Affairs, argues that the whole history of social policy since 1945 has been characterized by the 'crowding out' of small-scale mutual help organizations (like the one my father took me to in 1948) by the state. The time has come to recreate these mutual benefit organizations and take the state out of welfare.

The political choices have become particularly uncomfortable. The fact that other countries face even worse ones is probably no comfort to British politicians. Most other European, Japanese and North American populations will soon undergo the same rapid change in the age balance that the UK did between 1940 and 1980. They will learn the problems of adjustment too. Many of these countries base their finance of social security on high employer contributions. As international competition grows employers are keen to lessen this burden. Most other countries have yet to reduce their obligations and generosity to the old in the way the British government did in the 1980s. Most have far more expensive systems of health care than the UK.

The insecurities of the coming decade may make some kind of Welfare State even more necessary than it was in the 1940s. The UK's Welfare State may be better adapted to survive than that of many other countries, not because of its profligacy but because of its very meanness, and because most people realize that it is in their selfish best interests to keep it.

Delivering social policy

Not only has the scale of social spending grown substantially since 1945 it has also become much more centralized.

The Labour government between 1945 and 1951 took away local authority powers to run hospitals and its social legislation gave central government much more powerful strategic policy and resource allocation functions. All this was done in the name of equality of access. The trend continued through the years of expansion. More surprisingly it gathered pace alarmingly during the period of Mrs Thatcher's government despite its initial avowed intention to localize power.

Two very different trends were evident in the 1980s. One was the delegation of budgetary control to smaller units: schools, hospitals, housing estates. The other was the stripping of local government of independent powers to tax and run services with a degree of autonomy. Universities were tightly controlled and potentially unlimited powers were taken over them (Glennerster *et al.*, 1991).

The reasons for this trend were several. One was the frustration with the resistance of Labour councils to Mrs Thatcher, but there were deeper forces at work. The first was long term. Britain has never managed to get itself a decent system of local government taxation. In its stead central government has had to come in to meet the growing costs of social services that local government has been asked to run. The reason Britain has never been able to devise a decent local tax system is the jealousy the Treasury feels towards any taxing powers other than its own.

The second reason for the growth in central power in the 1980s was that central government departments felt they had lost a role in directing an expansionary system, that of captaining a ship in full sail. As we saw in the case of education they soon found another role for themselves, running the National Curriculum, running opted-out schools.

The third reason was political. Mrs Thatcher's aim was to divest the state of power. However, much day-to-day power lay with local councils, who were keen to keep it, were they Labour or Conservative. To divest the state of power then, power had to be centralized first. The danger of this strategy, and the outcome, has been that the state has centralized but not divested its power. Much of that central power has come to be exercised by remotely accountable quasi-governmental agencies (quangos).

Part of the new agenda for social policy has to be to find a more acceptable form of local finance and democracy while keeping the devolved responsibilities for schools and other agencies that the 1980s brought.

There is plenty here to keep politicians busy. Social politics is not dead yet.

Appendix 1 and 2

Appendix 1   Main Social Policy Legislation

Date	Ch.	Name
1944	31	Education Act
1945	17	Wages Councils Act
1945	41	Family Allowances Act
1946	34	The Furnished House (Rent Control) Act
1946	48	Housing (Financial and Miscellaneous Provisions) Act
1946	50	Education Act
1946	62	National Insurance (Industrial Injuries) Act
1946	67	National Insurance Act
1946	81	National Health Act
1948	29	National Assistance Act
1948	43	Children Act
1949	51	Legal Aid and Advice Act
1949	60	Housing Act
1950	25	Matrimonial Causes Act
1956	69	Sexual Offences Act
1957	25	Rent Act
1957	56	Housing Act
1958	35	Matrimonial Causes (Property and Maintenance) Act
1958	40	Matrimonial Proceedings (Children) Act
1960	44	Matrimonial Proceedings (Magistrates' Courts) Act
1963	45	Matrimonial Causes Act
1964	10	Family Allowances and National Insurance Act
1964	19	Married Women's Property Act
1964	56	Housing Act
1964	96	National Insurance etc. Act
1965	71	Murder (Abolition of Death Penalty) Act
1965	72	Matrimonial Causes Act
1965	75	Rent Act
1967	39	National Health Service (Family Planning) Act
1967	60	Sexual Offences Act
1967	75	Matrimonial Homes Act
1967	87	Abortion Act
1969	46	Family Law Reform Act
1969	55	Divorce Reform Act

1970	41	Equal Pay Act
1970	45	Matrimonial Proceedings and Property Act
1970	51	National Insurance (Old Person's and Widow's Pensions and Attendance Allowance) Act
1970	55	Family Income Supplements Act
1971	72	Industrial Relations Act
1973	18	Matrimonial Causes Act
1973	38	Social Security Act
1974	44	Housing Act
1975	11	Social Security Benefits Act
1975	60	Social Security Pensions Act
1975	61	Child Benefit Act
1975	65	Sex Discrimination Act
1975	71	Employment Protection Act
1976	50	Domestic Violence and Matrimonial Proceedings Act
1976	81	Education Act
1976	82	Sexual Offences (Amendment) Act
1977	48	Housing (Homeless Persons) Act
1978	22	Domestic Proceedings and Magistrates' Courts Act
1984	42	Matrimonial and Family Proceedings Act
1986	50	Social Security Act
1988	9	Local Government Act
1988	40	Education Reform Act
1988	41	Local Government Finance Act
1988	50	Housing Act
1989	41	Children Act
1989	42	Local Government and Housing Act
1990	6	Education (Student Loans) Act
1990	19	National Health Service and Community Care Act
1990	37	Human Fertilization and Embryology Act
1991	48	Child Support Act
1993	19	Trade Union Reform and Employment Rights Act

(Chapter numbers are those in the *Public General Acts* volumes)

Appendix 2   Social Policy Ministries and Ministers 1940–94

Ministry	Prime Minister	Chancellor of Exchequer	Home Secretary (1)	Minister of Health (2)	Minister of Education (3)	Minister of Housing and Local Government (4)	Minister of Social Security (5)
May 1940–May 1945 Coalition govt	Churchill	Wood Anderson	Anderson Morrison	MacDonald Brown Willink	Ramsbotham Butler	–	Womersley (6) Jowitt (7)
May 1945–July 1945 Caretaker govt	Churchill	Anderson	Somervell	Willink	Law	–	Womersley (6) Hore-Belisha (7)
July 1945–Oct. 1951 Labour govt	Attlee	Dalton Cripps Gaitskell	Chuter Ede	Bevan Marquand	Wilkinson Tomlinson	–	Griffiths Summerskill
Oct. 1951–April 1955 Conservative govt	Churchill	Butler	Maxwell Fyfe Lloyd George	Crookshank Macleod	Horsburgh Eccles	Macmillan Sandys	Peake
April 1955–Jan. 1957 Conservative govt	Eden	Butler Macmillan	Lloyd George	Macleod Turton	Eccles	Sandys	Peake Boyd-Carpenter
Jan. 1957–Oct. 1963	Macmillan	Thorneycroft Amory Lloyd Maudling	Butler Brooke	Vosper Walker-Smith Powell	Hailsham Lloyd Eccles Boyle	Brooke Hill Joseph	Boyd-Carpenter MacPherson
Oct. 1963–Oct. 1964 Conservative govt	Douglas-Home	Maudling	Brook	Barber	Boyle	Joseph	Wood

Government				Dept of Health and Social Security	Dept of Education and Science (9)	Department of the Environment (9)	
Oct. 1964–June 1970 Labour govt	Wilson	Callaghan Jenkins	Soskice Jenkins Callaghan	Robinson Crossman (8)	Stewart Crosland Walker Short	Crossman Greenwood	Herbison Hart Crossman (8)
June 1970–Feb. 1974 Conservative govt	Heath	Barber	Maudling	Joseph	Thatcher	Walker	
Feb. 1974–Mar. 1976 Labour govt	Wilson	Healey	Jenkins	Castle	Prentice Mulley	Crosland	
Mar. 1976–July 1979 Labour govt	Callaghan	Healey	Jenkins Rees	Ennals	Mulley Williams	Shore	
July 1979 Conservative govt	Thatcher	Howe	Whitelaw	Jenkin	Carlisle	Heseltine	
Oct. 1981	Thatcher	Howe	Whitelaw	Fowler	Joseph	Heseltine	
July 1983	Thatcher	Lawson	Brittan	Fowler	Joseph	Jenkin	
Jan. 1984	Thatcher	Lawson	Brittan	Clarke	Joseph	Jenkin	
March 1986	Thatcher	Lawson	Hurd	Clarke	Joseph	Baker	
Oct. 1986	Thatcher	Lawson	Hurd	Clarke	Baker	Ridley	
July 1987	Thatcher	Lawson	Hurd	Moore	Baker	Ridley	
July 1989	Thatcher	Lawson	Hurd	Dept of Health: Clarke — Dept of Social Security: Newton	MacGregor	C. Patten	

Ministry	Prime Minister	Chancellor of Exchequer	Home Secretary	Secretary of State for Health		Secretary of State for Education	Secretary of State for the Environment	Secretary of State for Social Security
Feb. 1990	Thatcher	Major	Waddington	Clarke	Newton	MacGregor	C. Patten	
Nov. 1990	Major	Lamont	Baker	Waldegrave	Newton	Clarke	Heseltine	
May 1992	Major	Lamont	Clarke	Bottomley	Lilley	J. Patten	Howard	
August 1993	Major	Clarke	Howard	Bottomley	Lilley	Dept for Education / J. Patten	Gummer	
July 1994	Major	Clarke	Howard	Bottomley	Lilley	Shepherd	Gummer	

Notes:

1 Lost responsibility for children's services in 1971 to the Department of Health and Social Security under the Seebohm reorganization.
2 Amalgamated with Social Security in 1968 to form Department of Health and Social Security.
3 Became Department of Education and Science, 1964.
4 Functions performed by Health and a separate Ministry of Town Planning until 1951; combined with Ministry of Transport and other functions to form Department of the Environment, 1971.
5 Separate Pensions and Social Insurance until 1945; then Ministry of Pensions and National Insurance until 1966; then Ministry of Social Security; then amalgamated with Health to form Department of Health and Social Security, 1968; split again in 1989.
6 Pensions.
7 Insurance.
8 Secretary of State for Social Services; combined Health and Social Security, 1968.
9 Departments are of higher status than ministries, having wider responsibilities ('super-ministries'). The politician in charge is a Secretary of State.

Bibliography

Abel-Smith, B. (1958) 'Whose Welfare State?', in N. Mackenzie (ed.) *Conviction*, London: MacGibbon and Kee

Abel-Smith, B. (1964) *The Hospitals 1800 to 1948*, London: Heinemann

Abel-Smith, B. and Townsend, P. (1955) *New Pensions for Old*, London: Fabian Society

Abel-Smith, B. and Townsend, P. (1965) *The Poor and the Poorest*, London: Bell and Sons

Addison, P. (1975) *The Road to 1945: British Politics and the Second World War*, London: Cape

Adonis, A. and Hames, T. (1994) *A Conservative Revolution? The Thatcher–Reagan Decade in Perspective*, Manchester: Manchester University Press

Alcock, P. (1984) 'Remuneration or remarriage?', *Journal of Law and Society*, 11(3), pp. 357–65

Ashford, D. E. (1986) *The Emergence of the Welfare States*, Oxford: Blackwell

Atkinson, A. B. (1972) 'Inequality and social security', in P. Townsend and N. Bosanquet (eds) *Labour and Inequality*, London: Fabian Society

Atkinson, A. B. (1993) 'What is happening to the distribution of income in the UK?', STICERD Welfare State Discussion Paper WSP/87, London: London School of Economics

Audit Commission (1986) *Making a Reality of Community Care*, London: HMSO

Bacon, R. and Eltis, W. (1976) *Britain's Economic Problem: Too Few Producers*, London: Macmillan

Baldwin, P. (1990) *The Politics of Social Solidarity*, Cambridge: Cambridge University Press

Baldwin, P. (1994) 'Beveridge in the *Longue Durée*', in J. Hills, J. Ditch and H. Glennerster, (eds) *Beveridge and Social Security: an International Retrospective*, Oxford: Clarendon Press

Banks, T. (1979) 'Programme budgeting in the DHSS', in T. Booth (ed.) *Planning for Welfare*, Oxford: Blackwell

Banting, K. G. (1979) *Poverty, Politics and Policy: Britain in the 1960s*, London: Macmillan

Barker, R. (1972) *Education and Politics 1900–1951: a Study of the Labour Party*, Oxford: Oxford University Press

Barnes, J. and Barr, N. (1988) *Strategies for Higher Education: the Alternative White Paper*, David Hume Paper No. 10, Aberdeen: Aberdeen University Press

Barnett, C. (1986) *The Audit of War: the Illusion and Reality of Britain as a Great Nation*, London: Macmillan

Barnett, M. J. (1969) *The Politics of Legislation*, London: Weidenfeld and Nicolson

Barr, N. (1993) *The Economics of the Welfare State*, London: Weidenfeld

Barr, N. and Coulter, F. (1990) 'Social Security: solution or a problem?', in J. Hills (ed.) *The State of Welfare: the Welfare State in Britain since 1974*, Oxford: Clarendon Press

Barr, N., Falkingham, J. and Glennerster, H. (1994) *Funding Higher Education*, Poole: BP Educational

Beveridge, W. H. (1924) *Insurance for All and Everything*, London: Daily News

Beveridge Report (1942) *Social Insurance and Allied Services*, Cmd 6404, London: HMSO

Beveridge, W. H. (1944) *Full Employment in a Free Society*, London: Allen and Unwin

Beveridge, W. H. (1953) *Power and Influence*, London: Hodder and Stoughton

Bindman, G. and Carrier, J. (1983) 'A multi-racial society', in H. Glennerster (ed.) *The Future of the Welfare State: Remaking Social Policy*, London: Heinemann

Blackaby, F. (ed.) (1979) *De-Industrialisation*, London: Heinemann and the National Institute of Economic and Social Research

Blaug, M. (1984) 'Education vouchers: it all depends on what you mean', in J. Le Grand and R. Robinson (eds) *Privatisation and the Welfare State*, London: Allen and Unwin

Bruegel, I. (1983) 'Women's employment, legislation and the labour market', in J. Lewis (ed.) *Women's Welfare: Women's Rights*, Beckenham: Croom Helm

Burgess, T. (1986) 'Cambridgeshire's financial management initiative for schools', *Public Money*, 6(1), pp. 21–4

Burghes, L. (1994) *Lone Parenthood and Family Disruption*, Occasional Paper no. 18, London: Family Policy Studies Centre

Burk, K. and Cairncross, A. (1992) *'Goodbye, Great Britain', the 1976 IMF Crisis*, New York: Yale University Press

Butler, D., Adonis, A. and Travers, T. (1994) *Failure in British Government: the Politics of the Poll Tax*, Oxford: Oxford University Press

Butler, J. (1992) *Patients, Policies and Politics*, Milton Keynes: Open University Press

Butler, J. (1994) 'Origins and early development', in R. Robinson and J. Le Grand (eds) *Evaluating the NHS Reforms*, London: Kings Fund Institute

Butler, R. A. (1971) *The Art of the Possible*, London: Hamish Hamilton

Butler-Sloss, Lord Justice (1988) *Report of the Inquiry into Child Abuse in Cleveland 1987*, Department of Health and Social Security, Cm. 412, London: HMSO

Cairncross, A. (1992) *The British Economy since 1945*, Oxford: Blackwell

Castle, B. (1980) *The Castle Diaries 1974–76*, London: Weidenfeld and Nicholson

Centre for Contemporary Cultural Studies (1981) *Unpopular Education: Schooling and Social Democracy in England since 1944*, London: Hutchinson

Cmd 6404 (1942) *Social Insurance and Allied Services* (Beveridge Report), London: HMSO

Cmd 6502 (1944) *A National Health Service*, London: HMSO

Cmd 6527 (1944) *Employment Policy*, London: HMSO

Cmd 6636 (1945) *Report on the Circumstances that Led to the Boarding Out of Denis and Terence O'Neill at Bank Farm, Minsterley and the Steps taken to Supervise their Welfare* (Monckton Enquiry), London: HMSO

Cmd 6922 (1946) *Report on the Care of Children* (Curtis Report), London: HMSO

Cmd 8996 (1953) *Houses: the Next Step*, Ministry of Housing and Local Government, London: HMSO

Cmd 9333 (1954) *Report of the Committee on the Economic and Financial Problems of Old Age* (Phillips Committee), London: HMSO

Cmd 9663 (1956) *Committee of Enquiry into the Cost of the National Health Service* (Guillebaud Committee), London: HMSO

Cmd 9703 (1956) *Technical Education*, Ministry of Education, London: HMSO

Cmd 9725 (1956) *The Economic Implications of Full Employment*, London: HMSO

Cmnd 247 (1957) *Report of the Departmental Committee on Homosexual Offences and Prostitution* (Wolfenden Report), London: HMSO

Cmnd 1191 (1960) *Report of the Committee on Children and Young Persons* (Ingleby Committee), London: HMSO

Cmnd 1246 (1960) *Rent Act Enquiry*, London: HMSO

Cmnd 1432 (1961) *Control of Public Expenditure* (Plowden Committee), London: HMSO

Cmnd 2154 (1963) *Higher Education* (Robbins Report), London: HMSO

Cmnd 3006 (1966) *A Plan for Polytechnics and other Colleges: Higher Education in the Further Education System*, London: HMSO

Cmnd 3163 (1966) *Help Towards Home Ownership*, London: HMSO

Cmnd 3602 (1968) *Old Houses Into New Homes*, Ministry of Housing and Local Government, London: HMSO

Cmnd 3703 (1968) *Report of the Committee on Local Authority and Allied Personal Social Services* (Seebohm Committee), London: HMSO

Cmnd 4683 (1971) *Better Services for the Mentally Handicapped*, London: HMSO

Cmnd 5174 (1972) *Education: a Framework for Expansion*, Department of Education and Science, London: HMSO

Cmnd 5579 (1974) *Report of the Committee on the Working of the Abortion Act* (Lane Committee), London: HMSO

Cmnd 5629 (1974) *Report of the Committee on One Parent Families* (Finer Report), London: HMSO

Cmnd 5720 (1974) *Educational Disadvantage and the Educational Needs of Immigrants*, Department of Education and Science, London: HMSO

Cmnd 6453 (1976) *Report of the Enquiry into Local Government Finance* (Layfield Committee), London: HMSO

Cmnd 6845 (1977) *Policy for the Inner Cities?*, London: HMSO

Cmnd 6869 (1977) *Education in Schools*, Department of Education and Science, London: HMSO

Cmnd 7746 (1979) *The Government's Expenditure Plans 1980–81*, London: HMSO

Cmnd 8093 (1980) *The Taxation of Husband and Wife*, HM Treasury, London: HMSO

Cmnd 8427 (1981) *Brixton Disorders 10–12 April 1981*, Report of an Enquiry by the Rt. Hon. Lord Scarman OBE, London: HMSO

Cmnd 9184 (1984) *The Next Ten Years: Public Expenditure and Taxation into the 1990s*, London: HMSO

Cmnd 9469 (1985) *Better Schools*, Department of Education and Science, London: HMSO

Cmnd 9517 (1985) *Reform of Social Security* Department of Health and Social Security, London: HMSO

Cmnd 9691 (1985) *Reform of Social Security: Programme for Action*, Department of Health and Social Security, London: HMSO

Cm. 412 (1988) *Report of the Inquiry into Child Abuse in Cleveland 1987* (Butler-Sloss Report), Department of Health and Social Security, London: HMSO

Cm. 555 (1989) *Working for Patients*, Department of Health, London: HMSO

Cm. 1264 (1990) *Children Come First*, Department of Social Security, London: HMSO

Cm. 1541 (1991) *Higher Education: a New Framework*, London: HMSO

Cole, G. D. H. (1957) *The Case for Industrial Partnership*, London: Macmillan

Conservative Party (1951) *Britain Strong and Free*, London: Conservative Central Office

Conservative Party (1987) *The Next Moves Forward*, London: Conservative Central Office

Cox, C. B. and Dyson, A. E. (eds) (1969) *Fight for Education: a Black Paper*, London: Critical Quarterly Society

Crosland, C. A. R. (1956) *The Future of Socialism*, London: Jonathan Cape

Crossman, R. H. S. (1952) *The New Fabian Essays*, London: Fabian Society

Crossman, R. H. S. (1975) *The Diaries of a Cabinet Minister, vol. 1: Minister of Housing 1964–66*, London: Hamish Hamilton, Jonathan Cape

Crossman, R. H. S. (1977) *The Diaries of a Cabinet Minister, vol. 3: Secretary of State for Social Services 1968–70*, London: Hamish Hamilton, Jonathan Cape

Crossman, R. H. S. (1981) *The Backbench Richard Crossman*, London: Hamish Hamilton, Jonathan Cape

Curtis Committee (1946) *Report on the Care of Children*, Cmd 6922, London: HMSO

Cutler, T., Williams, K. and Williams, J. (1986) *Keynes, Beveridge and Beyond*, London: Routledge and Kegan Paul

David, M. and Land, H. (1983) 'Sex and social policy', in H. Glennerster (ed.) *The Future of the Welfare State: Remaking Social Policy*, London: Heinemann

Davies, G. and Piachaud, D. (1983) 'Social policy and the economy', in H. Glennerster (ed.) *The Future of the Welfare State: Remaking Social Policy*, London: Heinemann

Deakin, N. (1994) *The Politics of Welfare: Continuities and Change*, London: Harvester

Dennis, N. and Erdos, G. (1994) *Families Without Fatherhood*, London: Institute of Economic Affairs

Department of Education and Science (1967) *Children and their Primary Schools* (Plowden Committee), London: HMSO

Department of Education and Science (1968) *First Report of the Public Schools Commission*, London: HMSO

Department of Education and Science (1970) *Second Report of the Public Schools Commission*, London: HMSO

Department of Education and Science (1972) *Education: a Framework for Expansion*, Cmnd 5174, London: HMSO

Department of Education and Science (1974) *Educational Disadvantage and the Educational Needs of Immigrants*, Cmnd 5720, London: HMSO

Department of Education and Science (1977) *Education in Schools*, Cmnd 6069, London: HMSO

Department of Education and Science (1985) *Better Schools*, Cmnd 9469, London: HMSO

Department of Health (1989a) *An Introduction to the Children Act 1989*, London: HMSO

Department of Health (1989b) *Working for Patients*, Cm. 555, London: HMSO

Department of Health and Social Security (DHSS) (1970) *The Future Structure of the National Health Service* (2nd Green Paper), London: HMSO

Department of Health and Social Security (DHSS) (1978) *Social*

Assistance: a Review of the Supplementary Benefits Scheme in Great Britain, London: HMSO

Department of Health and Social Security (DHSS) (1985a) *Reform of Social Security*, Cmnd 9517, London: HMSO

Department of Health and Social Security (DHSS) (1985b) *Reform of Social Security: Programme for Action*, Cmnd 9691, London: HMSO

Department of Social Security (1990) *Children Come First*, Cm. 1264, London: HMSO

Department of Social Security (1993a) *Households Below Average Income: a Statistical Analysis 1979–1990/91*, London: HMSO

Department of Social Security (1993b) *The Growth of Social Security*, London: HMSO

Dilnot, A. and Webb, S. (1988) 'The 1988 Social Security reforms', *Fiscal Studies*, 9(3), pp. 26–53

Dobash, R. and Dobash, R. (1979) *Violence Against Wives*, New York: The Free Press

Dobash, R. and Dobash, R. (1992) *Women, Violence and Social Change*, London: Routledge

Donnison, D. V. (1960) *Housing Policy since the Second World War*, Occasional Papers in Social Administration, Welwyn: Codicote Press

Dunleavy, P. (1981) *The Politics of Mass Housing in Britain 1945–75: a Study of Corporate Power, and Professional Influence in the Welfare State*, Oxford: Clarendon Press

Dunleavy, P. (1991) *Democracy, Bureaucracy and Public Choice*, Hemel Hempstead: Harvester

Durbin, E. F. M. (1949) *Problems of Economic Planning*, London: Routledge and Kegan Paul

Durbin, E. (1985) *New Jerusalems: the Labour Party and the Economics of Democratic Socialism*, London: Routledge and Kegan Paul

Eckstein, H. (1958) *The English Health Service*, Cambridge, Mass.: Harvard University Press

Edwards, J. and Batley, R. (1978) *The Politics of Positive Discrimination: an Evaluation of the Urban Programme 1967–77*, London: Tavistock

Egerton, M. and Halsey, A. H. (1993) 'Trends by social class and gender in access to higher education', *Oxford Review of Higher Education*, 19(2)

Ellison, N. (1988) 'The idea of equality in the British Labour Party 1931–64, unpublished Ph.D. thesis, University of London

Evans, M. and Glennerster, H. (1993) 'Squaring the circle? The inconsistances and constraints of Beveridge's plan', STICERD Welfare State Programme Discussion Paper WSP/86, London: London School of Economics

Evans, M., Piachaud, D. and Sutherland, H. (1994) 'Designed for the poor – poorer by design? The effects of the 1986 Social Security Act on family incomes', STICERD Welfare State Programme Discussion Paper WSP/105, London: London School of Economics

Falkingham, J. and Hills, J. (1995) *The Dynamics of Welfare*, Hemel Hempstead: Harvester

Field, F. (1982) *Poverty and Politics: the Inside Story of the Child Poverty Action Group's Campaigns in the 1970s*, London: Heinemann

Field, F. and Piachaud, D. (1971) 'The poverty trap', *New Statesman*, 3 December 1971

Finer Committee (1974) *Report of the Committee on One Parent Families*, Cmnd 5629, London: HMSO

Fleming Committee (1944) *The Public Schools and the General Education System*, London: HMSO

Flora, P. and Heidenheimer, A. (eds) (1981) *The Developments of Welfare States in Europe and America*, London and New Brunswick, NJ.: Transaction Books

Floud, J. and Halsey, A. H. (1957) 'Intelligence tests, social class, and selection for secondary schools', *British Journal of Sociology*, 8, pp. 33–9

Foot, M. (1975) *Aneurin Bevin 1945–1960*, St Alban's: Paladin

Friedman, M. (1962) *Capitalism and Freedom*, Chicago: University of Chicago Press

Frost, N. and Stein, M. (1990) 'The politics of the Children Act', *Childright*, 68

Galbraith, J. K. (1958) *The Affluent Society*, London: Hamish Hamilton

Gamble, A. and Walton, P. (1976) *Capitalism in Crisis Inflation and the State*, London: Macmillan

Gardiner, K. (1993) 'A survey of income inequality over the last twenty years – How does the UK compare?', STICERD Welfare State Programme Discussion Paper WSP/100, London: London School of Economics

Gibson, J. (1990) *The Politics and Economics of the Poll Tax: Mrs Thatcher's Downfall*, Warley: EMAS

Giles, C. and Johnson, P. (1994) *Taxes Down, Taxes Up*, London: Institute of Fiscal Studies Commentary no. 41

Glennerster, H. (1962) *National Assistance: Service or Charity*, London: Fabian Society

Glennerster, H. (1972) 'Education and inequality', in P. Townsend and N. Bosanquet (eds) *Labour and Inequality*, London: Fabian Society

Glennerster, H. (1975) *Social Service Budgets and Social Policy: British and American Experience*, London: Allen and Unwin

Glennerster, H. (1976) 'In praise of public expenditure', *New Statesman*, 91(2345), pp. 252–4

Glennerster, H. (1992) *Paying for Welfare: the 1990s*, Hemel Hempstead: Harvester

Glennerster, H. and Korman, N. (1983) *Planning for Priority Groups*, Oxford: Blackwell

Glennerster, H. and Low, W. (1990) 'Education and the Welfare State: Does it add up?', in J. Hills (ed.) *The State of Welfare: the Welfare State in Britain from 1974*, Oxford: Clarendon Press

Glennerster, H. and Pryke, R. (1964) *The Public Schools*, London: Fabian Society

Glennerster, H. and Turner, T. (1993) *Estate Based Housing Management: an Evaluation*, London: HMSO

Glennerster, H. and Wilson, G. (1970) *Paying for Private Schools*, London: Allen Lane

Glennerster, H., Matsaganis, M. and Owens, P. (1994) *Implementing Fundholding*, Milton Keynes: Open University Press

Glennerster, H., Power, A. and Travers, T. (1991) 'A new era for social policy: a new Enlightenment or a new Leviathan?', *Journal of Social Policy*, 20(3), pp. 389–414

Goodin, R. and Le Grand, J. (1987) *Not Only the Poor: the Middle Classes and the Welfare State*, London: Allen and Unwin

Goodman, A. and Webb, S. (1994) *For Richer for Poorer: the Changing Distribution of Income in the United Kingdom 1961–91*, London: Institute of Fiscal Studies

Gosden, P. H. J. H. (1976) *Education in the Second World War*, London: Methuen

Gosling, A., Machin, S. and Meghir, C. (1994) *What Has Happened to Wages?*, London: Institute of Fiscal Studies

Gough, I. (1979) *The Political Economy of the Welfare State*, London: Macmillan

Green, D. G. (1993) *Reinventing Civil Society: the Rediscovery of Welfare without Politics*, London: Institute of Economic Affairs

Green, A. and Steedman, H. (1993) *Education Provision, Educational Attainment and the Needs of Industry: a Review of Research for Germany, France, Japan, the USA and Britain*, London: National Institute for Economic and Social Research

Gretton, J. and Jackson, M. (1976) *William Tyndale: Collapse of a School or a System?*, London: Allen and Unwin

Griffiths Report (1983) *Recommendations on the Effective Use of Manpower and Related Resources*, London: DHSS

Griffiths Report (1988) *Community Care Agenda for Action*, London: HMSO

Hall, P. (1976) *Reforming the Welfare: the Politics of Change in the Personal Social Services*, London: Heinemann

Hall, P., Land, H., Parker, R. and Webb, A. (1975) *Change, Choice and Conflict in Social Policy*, London: Heinemann

Halsey, A. H. (1991) 'Failing education?', in *British Social Attitudes: the 8th Report*, Aldershot: Dartmouth Publishing

Halsey, A. H., Heath, A. F. and Ridge, J. (1980) *Origins and Destinations*, Oxford: Clarendon Press

Harris, J. (1975) 'Social planning in war-time: some aspects of the Beveridge Report', in J. M. Winter (ed.) *War and Economic Development*, Cambridge: Cambridge University Press

Harris, J. (1977) *William Beveridge: a Biography*, Oxford: Oxford University Press

Harris, J. (1986) 'Political ideas and the debate on state welfare, 1940–5', in H. L. S. Smith, *British Society in the Second World War*, Manchester: Manchester University Press

Harris J. (1990) 'Enterprise and Welfare States: a comparative perspective', *Transactions of the Royal Historical Society*, 40

Harris, J. (1992) 'Political thought and the Welfare State 1870–1940: an intellectual framework for British social policy', *Past and Present*, 135, pp. 116–41

Harris, J. (1993) *Private Lives, Public Spirit: a Social History of Britain 1870–1914*, Oxford: Oxford University Press

Harris, J. (1994) 'Contract and citizenship in social welfare 1934–48', paper given at the conference, Comparing Social Welfare Systems in Europe, Oxford, May 1994

Harrison, A. J. (1989) *The Control of Public Expenditure*, Oxford: Transaction Books, Policy Journals

Hayek, F. A. (1944) *The Road to Serfdom*, London: Routledge and Kegan Paul

Heclo, H. and Wildavsky, A. (1981) *The Private Government of Public Money*, London: Macmillan

Hennessy, P. (1992) *Never Again: Britain 1945–51*, London: Cape

Higgins, J. (1978) *The Poverty Business*, Oxford: Blackwell

Hill, M. (1990) *Social Security Policy in Britain*, Aldershot: Edward Elgar

Hills, J. (1988) *Changing Tax*, London: Child Poverty Action Group

Hills, J. (ed.) (1990) *The State of Welfare: the Welfare State in Britain from 1974*, Oxford: Clarendon Press

Hills, J. (1993) *The Future of Welfare: a Guide to the Debate*, York: Joseph Rowntree Foundation

Hills, J. and Mullings, B. (1990) 'Housing: a decent home for all at a price within their means?', in J. Hills (ed.) *The State of Welfare: the Welfare State in Britain from 1974*, Oxford: Clarendon Press

Hills, J., Ditch, J. and Glennerster, H. (eds) (1994) *Beveridge and Social Security: an International Retrospective*, Oxford: Oxford University Press

Hinchliffe Committee (1959) *Report of a Committee on the Costs of Prescribing*, London: HMSO

Hirschman, A. O. (1970) *Exit, Voice and Loyalty: Responses to Decline in Firms, Organisations and States*, Cambridge, Mass.: Harvard University Press

HM Treasury (1980) *The Taxation of Husband and Wife*, Cmnd 8093, London: HMSO

HM Treasury (1984) *The Next Ten Years: Public Expenditure and Taxation into the 1990s*, Cmnd 9184, London: HMSO

Holmans, A. E. (1987) *Housing Policy in Britain*, Beckenham: Croom Helm

Honnigsbaum, F. (1979) *The Division of Medicine in British Medicine: a History of the Separation of General Practice from Hospital Care 1911–68*, London: Kegan Page

Honnigsbaum, F. (1989) *Health, Happiness and Security: the Creation of the National Health Service*, London: Kegan Page

House of Commons (1980/1) *Fifth Report from the Home Affairs Committee: Racial Disadvantage*, HC 424-I Session 1980/1, London: HMSO

House of Commons (1984/5), *Second Report from the Social Services Committee, Community Care with Special Reference to Adult Mentally Ill and Mentally Handicapped People*, HC 13-I Session 1984–5, London: HMSO

Husband, C. (1982) *Race in Britain, Continuity and Change*, London: Hutchinson

Illsley, R., Le Grand, J. and Mullings, C. (1991) 'Regional inequalities in mortality', STICERD Welfare State Programme Discussion Paper WSP/57, London: London School of Economics

Johnson, N. (1987) *The Welfare State in Transition: the Theory and Practice of Welfare Pluralism*, Brighton: Wheatsheaf Books

Johnson, N. (1990) *Reconstructing the Welfare State: a Decade of Change*, Hemel Hempstead: Harvester Wheatsheaf

Jones, H. O. W. (1992) 'The Conservative Party and the Welfare State 1942–1955', unpublished Ph.D. thesis, University of London

Jones, K. (1994) *An Economist among Mandarins: a Biography of Robert Hall (1901–1988)*, Cambridge: Cambridge University Press

Kavanagh, D. and Morris, P. (1989) *Consensus Politics from Attlee to Thatcher*, Oxford: Blackwell

Kavanagh, D. and Seldon, A. (1994) *The Major Effect*, London: Macmillan

Kennedy, H. (1992) *Eve Was Framed: Women and British Justice*, London: Chatto and Windus

Keynes, J. M. (1936) *The General Theory of Employment, Interest and Money*, London: Macmillan

Kiernan, K. and Wicks, M. (1990) *Family Change and Future Policy*, York: Joseph Rowntree Memorial Trust

King, D. (1990) 'Accountability and equity in British local finance: the poll tax', in R. J. Bennett (ed.) *Decentralisation, Local Governments and Markets: Towards a Post-Welfare Agenda*, Oxford: Clarendon Press

Kings Fund Institute (1988) *Health Finance: Assessing the Options*, London: Kings Fund

Klein, R. (1989) *The Politics of the National Health Service*, 2nd edn, London: Longmans

Kullmann, M. (1960) 'Notting Hill hustings', *New Left Review*, 1, pp. 19–21

Labour Party (1957) *National Superannuation*, London: Labour Party

Labour Party (1959) *The Tory Pensions Swindle*, London: Labour Party

Labour Party (1961) *Signposts for the Sixties*, London: Labour Party

Labour Party (1963a) *Thirteen Wasted Years*, London: Labour Party

Labour Party (1963b) *Years of Crisis*, London: Labour Party

Labour Research Department (1994) *Maternity Rights: a Guide to the New Law*, London: Labour Research Department

Lambert, R. (1964) *Nutrition in Britain, 1950–60*, Welwyn: Codicote Press

Land, H. (1983) 'Who still cares for the family? Recent developments in income maintenance, taxation and family law', in J. Lewis (ed.) *Women's Welfare/Women's Rights*, Beckenham: Croom Helm

Land, H. (1994) 'The demise of the male breadwinner – in practice but not in theory: a challenge for social security systems', in S. Baldwin and J. Falkingham (eds) *Social Security and Social Change: New Challenges to the Beveridge Model*, Hemel Hempstead: Harvester Wheatsheaf

Lane Committee (1974) *Report of the Committee on the Working of the Abortion Act*, Cmnd 5579, London: HMSO

Law Commission (1966) *Report on the Reform of the Grounds of Divorce: the Field of Choice*, no. 6, London: HMSO

Lawson, N. (1993) *The View from No. 11: Memoirs of a Tory Radical*, London: Corgi

Le Grand, J. and Estrin, S. (eds) (1989) *Market Socialism*, Oxford: Oxford University Press

Lewis, J. (1980) *The Politics of Motherhood: Child and Maternal Welfare in England 1900–1939*, London: Croom Helm

Lewis, J. (1984) *Women in England 1870–1950: Sexual Divisions and Social Change*, Brighton: Wheatsheaf

Lewis, J. (1992) *Women in Britain since 1945*, Oxford: Blackwell

Lewis, J. (1994) 'The problem of lone mother families in 20th century Britain', paper given at the Social Policy Association conference, Families in Question, Liverpool, July 1994

Lewis, J. and Piachaud, D. (1987) 'Women and poverty in the twentieth century', in C. Glendinning and J. Millar (eds) *Women and Poverty in Britain*, Brighton: Wheatsheaf

Lipsey, D. and Leonard, D. (1981) *The Socialist Agenda: Crosland's Legacy*, London: Jonathan Cape

Lowe, R. (1989) 'Resignation at the Treasury: the Social Services Committee and the failure to reform the Welfare State 1955–57', *Journal of Social Policy*, 18(4), pp. 505–26

Lowe, R. (1990) 'The Second World War, consensus and the foundations of the Welfare State', *Twentieth Century British History*, 1(2), pp. 152–82

Lowe, R. (1993) *The Welfare State in Britain since 1945*, London: Macmillan

Lowe, R. (1994) 'The rejection of Beveridge in Britain', in J. Hills, J. Ditch and H. Glennerster, *Beveridge and Social Security: an International Retrospective*, Oxford: Oxford University Press.

McCann, K. (1985) 'Battered women and the law: the limits of the legislation', in J. Brophy and C. Smart (eds) *Women In Law*, London: Routledge and Kegan Paul

McCarthy, M. (1986) *Campaigning for the Poor: CPAG and the Politics of Welfare*, Beckenham: Croom Helm

Machin, S. and Waldfogel, J. (1994) 'The decline of the male breadwinner', STICERD Welfare State Programme Discussion Paper WSP/ 103, London: London School of Economics

McKeown, T. (1979) *The Role of Medicine*, Oxford: Blackwell

Macleod, I. and Powell, E. (1952) *The Social Services Needs and Means*, London: Conservative Political Centre

Macnicol, J. (1980) *The Movement for Family Allowances 1918–45*, London: Heinemann

Marshall, T. (1950) *Citizenship and Social Class*, Cambridge: Cambridge University Press

Marshall, T. (1963) *Sociology at the Crossroads*, London: Heinemann

Martin, J. P. and Evans, D. (1984) *Hospitals in Trouble*, Oxford: Blackwell

Marwick, A. (1990) *British Society since 1945*, Harmondsworth Penguin Books

Miliband, R. (1961) *Parliamentary Socialism*, London: Allen and Unwin

Miliband, R. (1969) *The State in Capitalist Society*, London: Weidenfeld and Nicolson

Millar, J. (1989) *Poverty and the Lone Parent Family: the Challenge to Social Policy*, Aldershot: Avebury

Ministry of Education (1945) *The Nation's Schools: their Plan and Purpose*, London: HMSO

Ministry of Education (1954) *Early Leaving*, Report of the Central Advisory Council for Education, London: HMSO

Ministry of Education (1956) *Technical Education*, Cmd 9703, London: HMSO

Ministry of Education (1959) *15–18*, Report of the Central Advisory Council for Education (Crowther Report), London: HMSO

Ministry of Education (1963) *Half Our Future*, Report of the Central Advisory Council for Education (Newsom Report), London: HMSO

Ministry of Housing and Local Government (1953) *Houses: the Next Step*, Cmd 8996, London: HMSO

Ministry of Housing and Local Government (1968) *Old Houses into New Homes*, Cmnd 3602, London: HMSO

Monckton Enquiry (1945) *Report on the Circumstances that Led to the Boarding Out of Denis and Terence O'Neill at Bank Farm, Minsterley and the Steps taken to Supervise their Welfare*, London: HMSO

Morgan, K. O. (1990) *The People's Peace British History 1945–1990*, Oxford: Oxford University Press

Murray, C. (1984) *Losing Ground: American Social Policy 1950–1980*, New York: Basic Books

Narendranathan, W., Nickell, S. and Stern, J. (1983) 'Unemployment benefits revisited', Centre for Labour Economics Discussion Paper no. 153, London: London School of Economics

National Commission on Education (1993) *Learning to Succeed: a Radical Look at Education Today and a Strategy for the Future*, London: Heinemann

Nevitt, A. A. (1966) *Housing Taxation and Subsidies*, London: Nelson

Newsom Report (1963) *Half our Future*, London: HMSO

O'Connor, J. (1973) *The Fiscal Crisis of the State*, New York: St Martin's Press

O'Higgins, M. (1983) 'Rolling back the Welfare State: the rhetoric and the reality of public expenditure and social policy under the Conservative government', in C. Jones and J. Stevenson (eds) *The Year Book of Social Policy in Britain 1982*, London: Routledge and Kegan Paul

Page, R. and Deakin, N. (1993) *The Costs of Welfare*, Aldershot: Avebury

Peacock, A. T. and Wiseman, J. (1961) *The Growth of Public Expenditure in the United Kingdom*, London: Allen and Unwin

Phillips Committee (1954) *Report of the Committee on the Economic and Financial Problems of Old Age*, Cmd 9333, London: HMSO

Pimlott, B. (1989) 'Is post war consensus a myth?', *Contemporary Record*, 2(6), pp. 12–14

Pimlott, B. (1992) *Harold Wilson*, London: HarperCollins

Pinder, J. (1981) *Fifty Years of Political and Economic Planning*, London: Heinemann

Plowden Committee (1967) *Children and their Primary Schools*, London: HMSO

Potts, M., Diggory, P. and Peel, J. (1977) *Abortion*, Cambridge: Cambridge University Press

Power, A. (1988) *Property Before People: the Management of Twentieth-Century Council Housing*, London: Allen and Unwin

Power, A. (1993) *Hovels to High Rise: State Housing in Europe since 1850*, London: Routledge

Robb, B. (1967) *Sans Everything: a Case to Answer*, London: Nelson

Robbins Committee (1963) *Higher Education*, Cmnd 2154, London: HMSO

Robinson, E. E. (1968) *The New Polytechnics*, London: Cornmarket Press

Robinson, R. and Le Grand, J. (1994) *Evaluating the NHS Reforms*, London: Kings Fund

Rose E. J. B. (ed.) (1969) *Colour and Citizenship*, Oxford: Oxford University Press

Rose, H. (1981) 'Rereading Titmuss: the Sexual Division of Welfare', *Journal of Social Policy*, 10(4), pp. 477–502

Rose, H. (1985) 'Women's refuges: creating new forms of welfare?', in C. Ungerson (ed.) *Women and Social Policy: a Reader*, London: Macmillan

Rowntree, B. S. (1941) *Poverty and Progress: a Second Social Survey*, London: Longman Green

Rowntree, B. S. and Lavers, R. G. (1951) *Poverty and the Welfare State*, London: Longman Green

Rowntree Foundation (1995) *Inquiry into Income and Wealth*, York: Joseph Rowntree Foundation

Scarman, Rt. Hon. Lord (1981) *Brixton Disorders 10–12 April 1981* (Scarman Report), Cmnd 8427, London: HMSO

Seldon, A. (1981) *Churchill's Indian Summer*, London: Hodder and Stoughton

Seldon, A. (1986) *The Riddle of the Voucher*, London: Institute of Economic Affairs

Simms, M. (1985) 'Legal abortion in Great Britain', in H. Homans (ed.) *The Sexual Politics of Reproduction*, Aldershot: Gower

Smart, C. (1984) *The Ties that Bind: Law, Marriage and the Reproduction of Patriarchal Relations*, London: Routledge and Kegan Paul

Snower, D. J. (1993) 'The future of the Welfare State', *The Economic Journal*, 103, pp. 700–17

Tawney, R. H. (1924) *Secondary Education for All: a Policy for Labour*, London: Labour Party

Tawney, R. H. (1964) [1931] *Equality*, with an introduction by R. M. T. Titmuss, London: Allen and Unwin

Thain, C. and Wright, M. (1990) 'Coping with difficulty: the Treasury and public expenditure 1976–89', *Policy and Politics*, 18(1), pp. 1–15

Thatcher, M. (1993) *The Downing Street Years*, London: HarperCollins

Thompson, F. M. L. (1990) *The Cambridge Social History of Britain*

1750–1950, vol. 3, Cambridge: Cambridge University Press

Titmuss, R. M. T. (1950) *The Problems of Social Policy*, London: HMSO

Titmuss, R. M. T. (1958) *Essays on the Welfare State*, London: Allen and Unwin

Titmuss, R. M. T. (1963) *The Irresponsible Society*, London: Fabian Society (also published in his *Essays on the Welfare State*, 2nd edn).

Titmuss, R. M. T. (1972) *The Gift Relationship*, London: Allen and Unwin

Townsend, P. (1954a) 'Measuring poverty', *British Journal of Sociology*, 5, pp. 130–7

Townsend, P. (1954b) 'Poverty ten years after Beveridge', *Planning*, 19

Townsend, P. (1957) *The Family Life of Old People*, Harmondsworth: Penguin Books

Townsend, P. (1970) *The Concept of Poverty*, London: Heinemann

Viet-Wilson, J. (1994) 'Condemned to deprivation', in J. Hills, J. Ditch and H. Glennerster (eds), *Beveridge and Social Security: an International Retrospective*, Oxford: Oxford Univerity Press

Walker, A. (1982) *The Poverty of Taxation*, London: Child Poverty Action Group

Weale, A., Bradshaw, J., Maynard, A. and Piachaud, D. (1984) *Lone Mothers, Paid Work and Social Security*, Occasional Papers on Social Administration no. 77, London: Bedford Square Press

Webb, S. and B. (1920) [1897] *Industrial Democracy*, 2nd edn, London: Longmans

Webster, C. (1988) *The Health Services since the War*, vol. 1, London: HMSO

Webster, C. (1990) 'Conflict and consensus: explaining the British Health Service' *Twentieth Century British History*, 1(2), pp. 115–51

Weeks, J. (1990) *Coming Out*, London: Quartet

Whiteley, P. (1981) 'Public opinion and the demand for social welfare in Britain', *Journal of Social Policy*, 10(4), pp. 435–75

Wistow, G., Knapp, M., Hardy, B. and Allen, C. (1994) *Social Care in a Mixed Economy*, Milton Keynes: Open University Press

Wolfenden Report (1957) *Report of the Departmental Committee on Homosexual Offences and Prostitution*, Cmd 247, London: HMSO

Wootton, B. (1943) 'Before and after Beveridge', *Political Quarterly*, 14(4), pp. 357–63

Wright, M. (ed.) (1980) *Public Spending Decisions: Growth and Restraint in the 1970s*, London: Allen and Unwin

Index